EDUCATION, SOCIAL STRUCTURE AND DEVELOPMENT

EDUCATION, SOCIAL STRUCTURE AND DEVELOPMENT

A COMPARATIVE ANALYSIS

Bill Williamson

Foreword by A. H. Halsey

First published 1979 by
THE MACMILLAN PRESS LTD
London and Basingstoke
Associated companies in Delhi
Dublin Hong Kong Johannesburg Lagos
Melbourne New York Singapore Tokyo

Printed in Great Britain by
Billing & Sons Limited, Guildford, London and Worcester

British Library Cataloguing in Publication Data

Williamson, Bill, b. 1944
    Education, social structure and development
    1. Educational sociology
    I. Title
    370.19′3   LC191

    ISBN 0–333–24136–3
    ISBN 0–333–24137–1 Pbk

Contents

Foreword

Comparative sociology is fiendishly difficult. It has always strained to the uttermost the resources of theory and method available to what is, after all, an infant and underdeveloped intellectual discipline. Even the fact that one of its founding fathers, Max Weber, bequeathed us standards of stupendous achievement is also daunting: for he has few successors. All the more then must we admire Mr Williamson's attempt at an ambitious comparative sociology of education. It is a brave effort and promises much for the development of the subject.

Mr Williamson is modest on behalf of his own achievement. He fully appreciates Professor Anderson's remark that comparison between complex societies is at once logically impossible and scientifically imperative. It is logically impossible for the absurd reason that you cannot compare complexities which are very different. It is scientifically imperative if sociology is to claim possession of general propositions. Williamson himself points out that powerful comparison presupposes articulated theory and standardised data. He also appreciates that education has to be studied historically as well as comparatively. The notorious problems of 'counter-factuals' have necessarily to be overcome in such work.

In my view Williamson has been wise to present his work, in effect, as a series of self-contained case studies within a broad framework of interpretation. Existing theory is not strong enough to support a heavier weight of comparison. As they stand, Williamson's analyses of Britain, Germany, USSR, China, Cuba, Ghana and Tanzania are illuminating of these countries as individual examples in the First, Second and Third Worlds and at the same time they are tentative exploration of the general theory of education and development. His ideas in this form may be tested by the overlapping writings of, for example, Margaret Archer (who also adds a study of France) in her *Social Origins of Educational Systems*.

The reader will surely be impressed by Williamson's unpretentious but wide-ranging use of sociological theory. To say this is not necessarily to agree with his theoretical stance. I am myself struck by how little he has been able to extract either from Marxism or phenomenology for his purposes, even though he is much influenced by both of these intellectual traditions. No matter. The result is a challenging contribution to our knowledge of how education changes in relation to economies, polities and cultures. All students of these questions are now in Williamson's debt.

A. H. Halsey

Preface

This book grew out of a course of lectures on the sociology of education. The lectures themselves were given actually at the request of my students. I mentioned to them one day that I had been invited by a local branch of the United Nations Schools Association to give a talk to sixth-formers on the role of education in social and economic development in the Third World. We discussed my lecture and several students insisted that the sixth-formers should be told about Tanzania; others felt that China should be examined; still others argued for Cuba, Brazil, Turkey and so on. What they were all agreed on was that the focus of their education course on the advanced capitalist societies and on Britain in particular, was too narrow. By this point it was impossible to begin my prepared lecture for the students united in a spontaneous demand that their course be changed to include discussions of, as they put it, 'more interesting societies'. I told them about angels fearing to tread where fools rush in but they were undeterred. We planned a new syllabus (this was in January, half-way through the academic year) and I agreed, with their help, to put together a new course.

This book grew out of those discussions. It represents however, my own attempt to grapple with some of the issues involved in looking at education comparatively. I would like to thank my students collectively for the help they have given me but I myself take full responsibility for the book's defects.

Parts of this book first appeared as papers to the staff—postgraduate seminar in sociology in the Department of Sociology and Social Administration in the University of Durham. I would like to thank my colleagues for their comments. I want particularly to thank Dr Michael Syer who helped me a great deal to clarify my thoughts and who fed more questions to me than I could possibly cope with.

The manuscript of this book was typed by two people, Gail Price and Trudy Harrison. Gail is a secretary in the Department of Sociology and Social Administration. Trudy is my mother-in-law. I would like to thank them both for being so efficient and so good-humoured that the preparation of the typescript produced, for me, at least, no worries.

Trudy typed the bulk of the manuscript and I am especially indebted to her. She says herself that her machine nearly broke down at some of the things she had to type (our politics vary somewhat); however, we still remain friends.

My own family, I now realise, have helped me far more than I could have legitimately expected. They have put up with short-temperedness, grumbles, absences and manic enthusiasm about issues in which they themselves had little interest. I apologise to to my wife Diane, to my children Johnny and Joanna and I promise that if I ever write another book I will do it strictly in working hours.

Bill Williamson
Durham
February 1978

Introduction
Education, Sociology and Development

The recurrent theme of this book is the role which education plays in social and economic development. The book itself is intended, however, as a contribution to the sociology of education although I hope it reaches a much wider audience. I would like it to be read by students and teachers, politicians and planners, laymen and specialists alike. I hope it provokes argument, disagreement and further research. Aware that there are no specific recommendations for educational policy in this book I hope, nonetheless, that those who read it might be prompted to think about policy and that my account of educational systems in different kinds of societies might lead to fresh evaluations of more familiar contexts. This, after all, is the hope of all comparative studies of education.

My aim is to relate the concern of the sociology of education with processes of social reproduction through education to the broader problems of development and underdevelopment in different types of society. I seek to show that the sociology of education can profit theoretically from a widening of its scope into comparative studies and that the economic and political problems of underdevelopment can be illuminated by studies of education.

This latter point is surely no longer contentious. In the past few years there has been a growing realisation that in many societies education not only does not contribute to economic growth but can actually hold it back. Some of the principal defects of many education systems—their elitism, their failure to measure the kinds of people they produce to the needs of the society in which they function and, perhaps most fundamentally, their great resistance to change—combine to produce this effect. Such defects, too, reflect the broader social structures in which education systems function. There is no inevitability, however,

1

that education systems should produce such outcomes; under appropriate conditions the function of education can change. Several attempts
to do this are examined in the course of this book.

Devising plans for the modernisation of educational systems is not
simply, however, a technical matter of finding the optimum mix of
scarce resources, even less is it a matter of deschooling society as
suggested by Ivan Illich (1971). It involves choices not only among
competing priorities but among different social values and models of
development. To pretend otherwise is to obfuscate seriously its political
character. In the course of this book I return time and again to the
problems of relating educational systems to the broader aims of
development. And each time the question of which interests are best
served by educational change raises itself. The problems of planning in
education are then seen to involve less the technical question of what
changes need to be brought about than the political one of who shall
benefit most from changes which are implemented.

Given that this is the case, questions of the broader ends of social
development and of social justice cannot be separated off from questions
of change in education. The point is hardly new but we do well to
remember it, for change in education is Janus-headed. Whatever the
direction of change there is always a complex equation to be solved—
who benefits? Who bears the cost?

The contribution of the sociology of education to these questions has
been, in recent years at least, small. It has been the economists who have
asked questions about how education contributes to economic growth.
Within the sociology of education itself there has been a move from the
macro question of education and social change to a greater concern with
problems closer to the coalface of classrooms. Such problems as
curriculum change, teacher–pupil relationships, the formation of pupil
identities or, more generally, the whole complex question of how culture
is transmitted through schools have become much more central to the
subject (W. Williamson, 1974; J. Karabel and A. H. Halsey, 1977).

This shift can be precisely dated and simply explained. It dates from
the publication of *Knowledge and Control* (1971), the collection of readings edited by M. F. D. Young. This book radically altered the agenda
of British research in the sociology of education. It restored the importance of knowledge itself as a subject for sociological research sug-
gesting, as one of the authors, Basil Bernstein put it: 'How a society sel-
ects, classifies, distributes, transmits and evaluates the educational knowledge it considers to be public, reflects both the distribution of power
and the principles of social control' (in M. F. D. Young, 1971: 47).

From this point on it was no longer possible to take for granted the problems which politicians or educators themselves set about education as representing the kinds of problems sociologists should be concerned with.

This shift in focus is explained, largely, I think by three factors. The first is a growth of an interest among sociologists in various types of interpretive sociological theories and with the sociology of knowledge itself, both being reactions to the positivistic character of much conventional social research. The second is a dissatisfaction among a younger generation of sociologists with the achievements, both theoretically and politically of the kind of research which dominated the subject in the late 1950s and the early 1960s, research which was firmly rooted in a British tradition of political arithmetic. Finally, the massive incorporation of the sociology of education into teacher training courses resulted in more attention being given to questions of educational practice as such, rather than to politics or social policy.

The second major theme of this book is that the time has now come for the sociology of education to break away from its institutional anchorage and explore new territories. It is time to put some of the analytical categories of the subject to work and to build, not only on the original suggestion that cultural transmission was the most productive point of focus, but that to understand this phenomenon properly it must be studied comparatively. This was, in fact, the suggestion made by I. Davies in his contribution to *Knowledge and Control* in an explicit way (1971). And Michael Young himself stressed the importance of comparative studies of the selection of knowledge and of 'thought systems' in the introduction to the book. As a strategy to develop further the theoretical framework of the subject these suggestions have not, however, been taken seriously. This book is intended as a very tentative step to rectify this and to effect some sort of reconciliation within the sociology of education, between those who are concerned with cultural transmission, social interaction and social reproduction, and those whose interests lie in the macro question of education and social change.

EDUCATION AND SOCIAL REPRODUCTION

My argument is this: the sociology of education will profit by becoming explicitly comparative in its approach; theories of development and underdevelopment will profit from studies of education. The profit for the latter begins with the realisation that education is not a commodity but a programme of action.

The French sociologist, Emile Durkheim defined education in the following way (1972: 204):

> Education is the influence exercised by adult generations on those that are not yet ready for social life. Its object is to stimulate and develop in the child a certain number of physical, intellectual and moral states which are demanded of him by both the political society as a whole, and by the particular milieu for which he is specifically destined.

On this definition education is the organised intelligence of a society functioning to consolidate in each successive generation the values, norms and habits of thought which are embedded in its culture. Organised education in the form of schooling is only the mechanism through which the more general purpose is realised; all societies have systems of education but in Durkheim's view the form of education will vary according to evolutionary complexity of the society in question.

Durkheim's view was that the school represented the moral order of a society and, tracing our modern conception of the school to the Christian tradition, he compared the process of becoming educated to the process of being converted. The aim of conversion is not, he claimed, simply to inculcate people with particular beliefs; it is to create 'a general attitude of the mind', 'a certain habitus' so that the world can become known in a new all-pervasive and distinctive light. This can happen quickly in the case of religious conversion. 'But', as Durkheim explains, 'this same transformation can take place more slowly, under a gradual and barely perceptible pressure; and this is what is achieved by education' (1972: 207). As he put it:

> For us . . . the principal object of education is not to provide the child with a greater or lesser degree of items of knowledge, but to create within him a deep-lying disposition, a kind of perspective of the soul which orients him in a definite direction, not only during childhood, but for life . . . Our conception of the goal has become secularised; consequently the means themselves must change. But the abstract scheme of the educational process has not altered (1972: 208).

A major limitation to Durkheim's work is seen, however, just at the point where his theoretical insight seems most profound. His work in sociology as a whole lacks any sense of different groups in society, (except in the limiting case of societies in normative disarray) seeking power to realise their interests and to shape the form of social institutions to suit their own purpose. His work, as many writers have pointed out, rests on an undifferentiated view of society. For this reason Durkheim himself is not led to enquire about *whose* values form the central core of an education system, yet this is a most important question to be asked in societies with a complex and hierarchical division of labour. In such societies custom and tradition no longer constitute a common framework of meaning and authority against which educational values can be measured. Education in such societies is often, in fact, a major focal point of social and political conflict, an ideological battleground.

Berger and Luckmann have pointed out a further weakness in Durkheim's sociological perspective, namely that it is insufficiently attentive to the phenomena of intersubjectivity and identity as aspects of social interaction and to processes of world building which they themselves call 'the social construction of reality' (1966).

Both of these problems need to be clarified since they relate to the way in which the distribution of power in society affect education and to the nature of the educational experience itself. These are not unrelated issues. The way in which education lends *structure* and *meaning* to the world thereby determining how the world is *perceived* and *known* is the mechanism through which structures of power relations are either consolidated or transformed. Such relations are consolidated in their form to the degree that they are seen to be *legitimate* and therefore understood as natural and appropriate forms of interpersonal influence. They will change, however, when their legitimacy is no longer perceived or understood or accepted. Under these conditions structures of power will either be overturned or they will be coercive. Whatever form the relationship takes will depend upon how people understand and perceive the world in which they live and education is the organised process in which such understandings evolve.

The link between the two problems is the phenomenon of knowledge in society and the role of knowledge in achieving, or, as the case may be, not achieving, what Berger and Luckmann called 'the integration of an institutional order' (1966: 82). Berger and Luckmann have argued that the orderly nature of social routines in most societies and the commonly held beliefs that social routines are in some way inevitable, natural and right, are the product of a 'reflective consciousness' which, through the use of language, is able to relate the behaviour of individuals to a larger framework of meaning belonging to a society as a whole. In this way social institutions come to acquire the interrelatedness and coherence which is the basis of social order. On this view, social institutions are socially constructed constellations of meaning and action and what can be understood by such notions as, say, the family or the political system, is therefore determined by the knowledge which a society's members have of such institutions; it depends, therefore on a socially available, taken-for-granted stock of knowledge. And, as Berger and Luckmann (1966: 82) say: 'If the integration of an institutional order can be understood only in terms of the "knowledge" that its members have of it, it follows that the analysis of such "knowledge" will be essential for an analysis of the institutional order in question'.

They make a very important point, additionally, when they say that the knowledge in question is not complex theoretical knowledge or the codes of an official ideology. Rather it is 'primary knowledge' or knowledge at the 'pre-theoretical level'.

It is the sum total of 'what everybody knows' about a social world, an assemblage of maxims, morals, proverbial nuggets of wisdom, values and beliefs, myths and so forth, the theoretical integration of which requires considerable intellectual fortitude in itself, as the long line of heroic integrators from Homer to the latest sociological system-builders testifies (1966: 83).

Such knowledge, they say, defines roles and conduct and, as a consequence of this, generally accepted truths about reality and the way in which reality can be known. It is learned in the course of socialisation and in this respect it fixes in the consciousness of the individual the objective structures of the world in which the individual lives. It accords a high 'cognitive status' to particular ways of acting, thinking and feeling in particular circumstances and denies 'cognitive status' to other ways of perceiving the world.

If we follow this line of thought through it is clear that the sociologically significant outcome of schooling is not that schools somehow pass on knowledge or specific skills; it is that schools consolidate habits of thought and attitudes which make clear to people what are the basic values of society and the place which different types of people and therefore they themselves have in society. It says something, therefore about the order behind social relationships and the relationship of the individual, or his group, to that order.

It is important to note, too, that learning is not something confined to the classroom and to books and lessons. In fact, the classroom and the lessons are perhaps the least significant aspects of school learning; of far greater importance are the great public routines of the school, the ceremonies, symbols and rituals of the school's corporate life. As Bernstein and Peters have pointed out ritual in schools functions to relate the individual to a social order and to heighten his respect for it (1971). The rituals of differentiation and consensus help people to recognise the way in which they are different from each other, for example in terms of age or sex but also to recognise how similar they are, particularly in the sense of belonging to the same moral community. School rituals, therefore, which include such practices as morning assembly, speech day, sports day, punishment, together with the appropriate insignia, totems, uniforms with which they are associated, bind the individual through a rigid pattern of action to what Bernstein and Peters call a 'distinct collectivity' which is, of course, society itself.

Pierre Bourdieu has underlined this point and, indeed, added to it, when he points out that individuals owe to their schooling a 'frame of problematic reasoning' made up of 'areas of encounter and agreement, common problems and common methods of approaching those common problems' (1967). Within such broad agreements there are dominant patterns which become 'deeply interiorised' by the individual and provide the basic categories with which the individual can improvise a wide range of thoughts and perceptions. The individual is therefore trapped into particular ways of thinking which are dominant in his culture and such ways of thinking are woven into the fabric of the language he speaks.

For those theorists who claim to offer a Marxist analysis of education—Althusser (1972) and Bowles and Gintis (1976)—the main function of education is to prepare people for their economic fate in capitalist production, either to be exploiters or to be exploited. Education has therefore to be studied in its relationship to forms of production and to processes of occupational placement and, in Marxist theory, it is conceived of as being subordinate to the economic order of society.

For Bowles and Gintis the educational system 'tailors the self-concepts, aspirations, and social class identifications of individuals to the requirements of the social division of labour' (1976: 129). This is what they call 'the correspondence principle'. The principles of school organisation governing pupil–teacher relations reflect the hierarchy of authority in work. The fact that the pupil has no control over his work in school reflects the lack of the workers control over his work, in other words, it reflects alienated labour. The fragmentation of the labour force through skill levels and competition has its counterpart in the fragmentation of pupils through competition for scarce academic rewards. Bowles and Gintis are thus much more concerned with the way education relates to the economic organisation of society. Berger and Luckmann (1966) and Bourdieu and Passeron (1977) are, in contrast although not in opposition, far more concerned with education and the broader realm of culture. They all, however, have a common preoccupation with education and social reproduction. The main outlines of this way of thinking about education can be set out schematically as shown in Figure 1.1.

Figure 1.1 is intended as a simple synopsis of the perspective already discussed. It does no more than underline the fact that private experience and social structure interpenetrate one another and that a society's system of education plays a central role in reproducing a given institutional order.

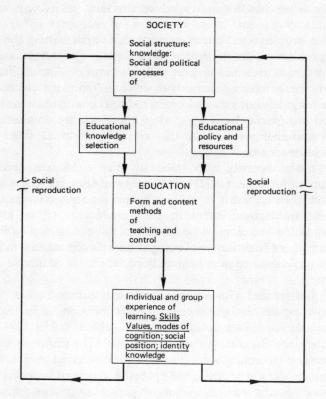

Figure 1.1 A Schema for the Analysis of Education

As it stands, however, the diagram is static. It indicates that what is available as education in a given society is the outcome of political processes which determine the pattern of educational facilities and the content of what is to be learned. It indicates also that the daily practice of schools is geared to transmitting, reinforcing and legitimating a given taken-for-granted view of the world and that learning is a process of acquiring as personal property the concepts and values of a culture—the formulae or master symbols of legitimation which give the world a particular meaning.

But the discussion so far has been framed entirely in the present tense and has paid little attention to the ongoing processes of challenge, change and resistance which typify intergroup relationships in society and which result in distinctive yet changing politics of education. Because of this, the discussion conceals the wide range of different meanings which are managed in the schools of different societies and the way in which schools even within the same society change over time.

The discussion has therefore, neglected both the political and ideological dimensions of education as well as the factors which, in different societies, explain differences in its form and content. It is only when the circumstances in which reproduction takes place are varied that we can gain some view of why the consequences of education are so different in different contexts, or why the intended results of education are not realised in practice; and this last problem is vital in the field of studies of development and underdevelopment.

The strategy of comparative sociological analysis can help here; the circumstances of reproduction can be varied systematically and the effects measured. One of my principal aims in this book is to try and demonstrate this argument rather than simply assert it.

There are, however, great difficulties in doing comparative work of this kind. There is no common source of data for all societies; there may be none of the data needed for some kinds of studies. It is hardly likely therefore, that comparative research can be based on fully standardised data. This, though, is the least of the difficulties; the more pressing problems are of a theoretical kind. It is clear from a long tradition of sociological research that comparative study requires the use of classifications of different societies and that the act of classification is not in some way theoretically neutral. Indeed all classifications of society presuppose a theory of social change and a theory of social structure, however implicitly. For this reason it might be thought that comparative studies can only begin when these theoretical issues have been solved or, at least, when theories of social structure and change have been made in some way explicit.

Both issues together, the data problem and the theory question, render comparative studies, to say the least, difficult; some would say impossible. I share this view but find myself simultaneously in agreement with C. A. Anderson, who, in a much neglected paper on the importance of typologies in comparative research once said: 'Comparison between complex societies is, so to speak, logically impossible yet scientifically imperative' (1959: 20). This is precisely the spirit in which I have written this book although I am aware that from a strictly scientific view its achievements, such as they are, are limited. What I have done, however, is to examine several modern societies using the same analytical language for each case and approaching each one in a similar way. It is hardly a systematic comparison—that, I feel, is too far away from us yet—but I hope it points the way forward to such comparisons in the future.

In the next chapter I shall discuss some aspects of how education and socioeconomic development are related. In Chapter 2 I have set out the basic framework of comparison that guides my later discussion of specific societies.

Each case study is preceded by a short introduction setting out the reason for the undertaking of that particular case study. But each case study represents a coherent thing in itself so that it is possible, in fact, to concentrate attention on selected chapters without losing some of the sense of the overall analytical purpose of the book.

1 Education
and Development

The role which education plays in bringing about economic growth or in hindering it is not clearly understood. At best the role is a paradoxical one. Eric Hobsbawm, the historian, has noted (1968) that the technology behind the Industrial Revolution in England was not so complicated that an ordinary skilled artisan could not have designed it. It was certainly not a technology which presupposed high levels of investment in research or training to develop the skills necessary for its design and implementation. The factors, therefore, which, at least initially, lay behind the industrial development of Britain had little to do with education. Education for the masses came to play a very important role in the formation of an industrial labour force in the course of the nineteenth century, reinforcing factory discipline and teaching respect for authority, but that was much later when the scaffold of the new society had already been erected.

Hobsbawm's remarks deserve to be quoted a little more fully since they bear directly on the problem of working out strategies of educational change for the poor societies of the modern world. He points out that the technology of the industrial revolution was simple because simple ideas could often produce striking results in a situation of expanding markets, low costs and falling prices. This was the situation which gave the Industrial Revolution such a push forward. This situation put business and industry

. . . within the reach of an enterprising, not particularly well-educated or subtle, not particularly wealthy body of businessmen and skilled artisans, operating in a flourishing and expanding economy whose opportunities they could seize. In other words, it minimised the basic requirements of skills, of capital, of large scale business or government organisation and planning, without which no industrialisation can succeed (1968: 68).

On the other hand it is a *sine qua non* of future economic growth in Britain, given its present economic system, that there should be very high levels of investment in human capital formation, in research and development and in industrial training to preserve and extend the bodies of knowledge and skill which are integral to the work of industry and commerce. It was the existence of such knowledge which, despite the destruction of war, more than anything else made it possible for the German economy to be rebuilt after 1945. It is further investment in the discovery and application of knowledge which will allow the industrial societies of the developed world to retain their world economic power and the fine competitive edges upon which their fragile prosperity rests.

For societies of the Third World the argument is somewhat more complex. Few would deny that Third World societies require massive changes in patterns of education, research and training if they are to generate the expertise to exploit new technologies and man the services to which development ought to lead them—such as health, education and transport.

For as Hobsbawm notes (1968: 61), the situation in the 'emerging nation' of today is one in which

The most elementary step forward—say, the construction of an adequate transport system—assume a command of science and technology which is centuries removed from the skills familiar to more than a tiny fraction of the population until yesterday . . . Even the minor skills and habits whose existence we take for granted in developed societies, but whose absence would totally disrupt them, are scarce as rubies: literacy, a sense of punctuality and regularity, the conduct of routines.

Such skills are fundamental to the growth and continuation of an industrial society. As Hobsbawm explains (1968: 62):

It is a great deal easier to find the capital for the construction of a modern industry than to run it; much easier to staff a central planning commission with the handful of PhDs which most countries can supply, than to acquire the mass of persons with intermediate skills, technical and administrative competence and so on without whom any modern economy risks grinding in to inefficiency.

What is not clear at all, however, is what kind of changes in education ought to be brought about to better realise development or what effects education investment may have in different contexts. Adam Curle noted (1964: 97):

> Contemporary attention is so concentrated on the role of education in development that we are inclined to forget its capacity to stunt growth. Yet in most societies for most of recorded time, education has been a reactionary force rather than a progressive one.

And Ivan Illich, the iconoclast of development theory, who has worked furiously in the last few years to demythologise the education myth, at least in so far as education is equated with schooling, has argued (1973: 363) that: 'Schools rationalise the divine origin of social stratification with much more rigor than churches have ever done', for, as he explains earlier (1973: 362):

> The intense promotion of schooling leads to so close an identification of school attendance and education that in everyday language the two are interchangeable. Once the imagination of an entire population has been *schooled*, or, indoctrinated to believe that school has a monopoly of formal education, then the illiterate can be taxed to provide free high school education for the children of the rich.

Neither of these comments are critical of the idea of education as an instrument of development. They simply reflect a profound mistrust of formal western models of education implanted into poor societies to provide the appropriate skills and attitudes which poor societies desperately need in order to help break the bonds of their poverty and their continued exploitation.

It is not clear, although decisions are made daily in all world societies which affect the issue directly, what education ought now to mean in the context of development. Even such a worldly-wise body as the World Bank recently (1974: 11) stated that, given scarce resources, the question will be asked continually: 'Who shall be educated? How? For what? At whose expense? At what expense?' Such comments reflect deep convictions that investment in and growth in education, particularly in the poor societies of the world, has not brought with it the benefits which had been expected.

Before considering such beliefs in a more detailed way it is important to set out clearly why it was felt by economists and planners alike, particularly during the development decade of the 1960s, that educational investment was a necessary part of programmes of economic growth.

EDUCATION AND ECONOMIC DEVELOPMENT

Sam Bowles (1969) has pointed out that although the economics of education as a branch of economics has a long pedigree dating back to the classical economists, the idea of using education to accelerate economic growth has a much more recent history. He explains this by saying that in the context of *laissez-faire* economics which dominated the nineteenth century the need for collective educational planning was not felt or the concept understood. But in the period following the Second World War the economic concerns of governments, planners and economists themselves shifted from the longstanding preoccupation with cyclical fluctuations in the economy to the problems of sustained economic growth. The growing postwar interest in economic growth developed alongside a growing scepticism among many economists about the value of neoclassical theories of economic growth. The postwar economic miracles of Japan and Germany and the failure of poor economies to respond to massive injections of physical capital raised the question of just how far the ability of an economy to grow depended upon the availability of a human capital stock to exploit new technology and innovate economically.

It is against this backcloth that the work of the American economists T. W. Schultz (1961) and F. Denison (1964) needs to be read. As Bowles explains, research results in the 1950s cast some doubt on how far the rate of economic growth in America could be explained by the rate of increase in fixed capital formation. Bowles goes on (1969: 84):

It was suspected by many that the portion of growth unexplained by factor accumulation as conventionally measured (or the 'residual' as it was called) might in part be attributed to qualitative improvements in the labour force, particularly as affected by increasing levels of educational attainments. The independent work of Edward F. Denison and T. W. Schultz on United States growth in the twentieth century lent some credibility to this view; using different approaches, they estimated that about 20 % of the growth rate over this period was due to increases in the educational level of the labour force.

The work of Schultz and Denison has generated a major continuing debate in the economics of education. At one extreme the critics claim the concept of human capital to be valueless in economic analysis since it includes too much in one idea and cannot be specifically measured. This line of criticism has been developed by H. G. Shaffer (1968). Others have argued that the analytical procedures employed in calculating the importance of human capital investment and economic growth—the so-called Cobb–Douglas function—is inadequate and grossly misleading. The fact that the proportion of the rate of growth in an economy cannot be attributed to growth in fixed capital formation does not necessarily have to lead to the conclusion that the unexplained proportion is explicable as a result of education investment or any other form of investment in human capital such as health care. It could equally well lead to the conclusion that we simply do not know what explains the unexplained rate of growth. As Bowen has put it (1968: 76–7):

> The more general difficulty is, of course, the 'residual' nature of the residual. (The residual), as usually measured, no doubt embodies the results of some secular improvement in the quality of capital assets; it also encompasses changes in output attributable to economies of scale, to improvements in health of the labour force, to informal as well as formal education, to changes in produce mix, to re-organisation of the economic order and to who knows what else. Moses Abramovitz has called it a 'measure of our ignorance'.

Bowen goes on to recommend that because of the size of the ignorance factor in this area of economics there are no empirical grounds for spending more on particular social programmes such as research and development or free school lunches. There may, of course, be other grounds desirable in themselves, but economic analysis cannot, at this stage, provide the empirical proof that programmes of human capital formation will produce the measurable consequences which might be expected from them.

The argument about the methodological rigour of the residual approach to economic growth might, however, be a little disingenuous. Mary Jean Bowman has argued (1968: 111) that the real significance of Schultz's work stems from its 'sweeping vision' about the human investment revolution. And in a similar vein Mark Blaug has emphasised the importance of the human capital approach as a step in economic theory which opens up questions that have been virtually supressed since Adam Smith. He calls the human capital perspective 'a programme for research rather than a pronouncement of an indisputable insight' (1970: 6).

To the layman the debates among economists about the methodology of human capital research are bewildering and the actual results of the research Blaug refers to, disappointing. The simple argument that

better-educated people are likely to work more effectively and pro-
ductively, make better decisions and be more highly motivated to
improve on current technologies has no basis in fact. But nor is it
possible to support the opposite argument that investment in human
capital through education is either unproductive or counterproductive.
As with most complex questions the relationships that need to be
examined are far more subtle than simple formulas or political dogma
allow and in the case of human capital formation much more needs to be
known about the way in which social and political structures in society
respond to and mould patterns of educational investment and the results
of that investment.

The importance of this last point is nowhere more clearly demonstrated when the educational experience of some of the world's
poorer societies is considered. The overall argument that such societies
require education in order to grow economically comes quite unstuck
when the actual consequences of education investment and policies are
examined.

Three issues illustrate this point. They are all interconnected with one
another and are singled out here only for purposes of exposition. The
first concerns rural–urban imbalance in education provision; the
second, the relevance of particular types of curriculum to realise
development goals; and the third concerns patterns of inequality and of
opportunity among different groups in many world societies.

RURAL–URBAN IMBALANCE IN EDUCATION

Except in those countries which, through revolution, have tried to
modify the situation, the density of formal educational activity throughout the world is urban. Population migration to the cities of the world
increases urban demands for educational facilities in urban areas. Rural
areas typically remain underresourced educationally. They have fewer
schools and fewer teachers. They suffer population loss among those
whose value to the land, because of their energy and motivation, would
be great, but who seek opportunities in urban areas. In rural areas
illiteracy rates are higher; school dropout rates, too, are high. This can
be seen in Table 1.1 which compares rural and urban areas in Latin
America.

So far educational planning has had little effect in remedying this
situation. Peter Donaldson has noted, for instance (1971: 124), that:

TABLE 1.1
Comparison of education efficiencies in urban and rural areas in Latin America:
Successful completers and dropouts in primary education

	Total country Successful completers	Urban Successful completers	Rural Successful completers
		as per cent of entrances	
Colombia	27.3	47.3	3.7
Dominican Republic	30.4	48.1	13.9
Guatemala	25.4	49.6	3.5
Panama	62.3	80.7	45.3
Average percentage completers	39.0	51.0	22.0

Source: Based on the Unesco report, *The Statistical Measurement of Educational Wastage* and quoted in the World Bank Report on Education
(1974: 70)

If education is to act as an instrument of development policy it must
be purged of its present overwhelming urban bias and disdain for the
practical. All too frequently, the values which young people absorb at
school and at university lead them to regard work in the rural sector as
the hallmark of failure—and to seek, above all, employment which
involves no dirtying of the hands.

Such is the background to Julius Nyerere's plea in *Education For Self-
Reliance* (1967) for educational improvements which will prepare people
for work in the rural economy of Tanzania and not encourage urban-
based intellectual arrogance and disdain for the way in which the mass of
Tanzanians actually live. Some indication of the underdevelopment of
rural education can be seen in Table 1.2. The table indicates clearly that
the availability of complete schools varies directly with the wealth of the
country: the poorer the society, the poorer the system of rural education
and the greater the discrepancy between rural and urban areas. A real
challenge therefore faces programmes of education development in the
poor societies of the world—the challenge of devising ways of taking
education to rural areas and to overcome what Pearse (1973) has called
the problem of 'institutional appropriation', the tendency of educational institutions already established in urban areas to consume
additions to education resources and thereby deprive rural areas of any
real share in the growth of education. Meeting this challenge will

TABLE 1.2

Availability of complete primary schools in urban and rural areas: Percentage of
the total number of primary schools in each category (rural and urban) which
offer the complete number of grades

	Number of countries	*Complete urban schools as per cent of total urban schools*	*Complete rural schools as per cent of total rural schools*
(a) Countries by per capita GNP			
I—Up to $120			
(excluding India)	9	53	36
India		57	49
II—$121—250	7	72	32
III—$251—750	16	77	62
IV—$751—1500	2	89	56
V—Over $1500	6	100	99
(b) By major regions			
Africa	16	79	54
Asia (excluding India)	9	94	66
India		57	49
South and Central			
America	10	88	34
Europe	5	98	99

Source: Based on data in *Unesco Statistical Yearbook, 1972* and quoted in World
Bank report on Education (1974: 70)

involve, as I hope to show in this book, both overcoming inegalitarian
structures of resource distribution in poor societies as these govern who
shall get what from whatever growth is possible in education, and drastic
innovations in patterns of educational provision and in conceptions of
what it means to be educated.

RELEVANCE IN THE CURRICULUM

A second issue is that of what is taught in schools. Tibor Mende has
argued, for instance, that (1973: 101):

As a matter of fact, much of education now dispensed in poor countries is not only irrelevant to the solution of the problems they face but tends to be positively harmful. It perpetuates contempt for menial tasks, and widens the gulf between the privileged minorities and the under-educated or illiterate masses. Sometimes, with substantial foreign aid in the form of technical assistance, it stamps alien attitudes and values on minorities who, because of their foreign education, are destined to become members of the ruling groups.

The issue here, of course, is that of the relevance of particular kinds of education to particular contexts. In the field of the economics of educational planning, this issue has been very hotly debated. Professors Balogh (1974), Anderson (1973), and Foster (1965) have all argued that for Third World societies rural training is far more important than the kinds of training given in urban schools and universities if the primary aim is to achieve development. The problem is simply that many societies, including those which are not underdeveloped, produce educated personnel for whom the economy has no conceivable use. Tibor Mende notes (1973) that in India in 1960–61 there were over 1,192,000 professionals or above graduate level people in the labour force; 90 per cent of them held diplomas in law, arts and commerce. This was in a country in which of those employed, two-thirds are employed in agriculture. Graduate unemployment is endemic in India, Burma, Sri Lanka and Indonesia.

Unemployment among secondary schools leavers is similarly endemic in many societies of Africa and Latin America. The effect of misalignment between manpower needs and educational outputs can, in the short run, be to reinforce underdevelopment by slowing down the growth of poor economies through bottlenecks in the supply of appropriately qualified labour in key sectors and thereby increasing a society's reliance either on the import of foreign trained labour or the purchase of foreign training facilities. It is at the lower levels of the labour market which do not require highly trained manpower where this particular problem is likely to be most acute. Philip Foster has noted (1965) for instance that the attempt by the British colonial regime in Ghana to encourage the growth of technical education for Ghanaians failed completely. The pattern of African demand for education was for an education giving access to the urban-based jobs of government, commerce and administration—precisely those which afforded opportunities for social mobility during colonial days. Such demands, or expectations for academic education have thus become firmly rooted and threaten to subvert any attempt to restrict academic education in favour of technical studies aimed at rural change or low level technology.

The long-term consequences of such processes is, amongst other things, to lend encouragement to a philosophy of qualificationism in which a person's capacity to perform a job or to gain access to a job is measured by paper qualifications, irrespective of whether such qualifications are strictly necessary in a technical sense. Ronald Dore has recently described (1976: 5) this phenomenon as the 'qualification—escalation ratchet' and in so doing pointed to the paradox that: 'the worse the educated unemployment situation gets and the more useless educational certificates become, the *stronger* grows the pressure for an expansion of educational facilities'.

Nor is this problem confined to the underdeveloped world; qualification inflation is rampant in the developed economies and works to restrict the potential supply of labour to particular occupations, for some occupations are considered to be beneath what ought to be available to a school graduate and therefore to underutilise human resources. The World Bank report (1974: 20) summed up this particular problem in the following way:

> Serious imbalances are observed between the skills generated by education systems and actual needs of most developing countries. In some areas, the number of graduates surpasses the absorptive capacity of labor markets, while in others critical shortages of skills continue to create problems. These discrepancies between the supply of, and demand for, skills are caused by a complex set of social, cultural and political conditions and aspirations which condition the development to respond to countries' needs is accentuated by the fact that educational institutions have been borrowed from developed countries and have not acquired an indigenous character.

EQUALITY AND INEQUALITY

The third and final issue is that of inequality which is maintained and legitimated through education. The literature on this topic is so immense that to make only a few comments on the issue seems trite. Nonetheless, a few points do need to be underlined. The World Bank report (1974: 33–4) described the broad patterns in this way:

> The regressive character of educational systems and policies is a

prevailing feature in most cases, irrespective of the level of development of countries. Educational systems not only fail to ensure mass
participation, as discussed in the previous section; they also practice
discrimination in their process of selection, promotion and future
determination of careers. They show an elitist bias, favoring urban
upper- and middle-income groups at the expense of the rural and
urban poor. The appraisal of a recent sites and services project in
Zambia showed that half the population of the capital was living in
squatter areas, but all schools, with one exception, were located
elsewhere. Consequently, the primary school enrollment was
only 36 % in the squatter areas, against 90 % in the rest of the
capital. Dropout and repetition rates were also higher among the
squatters.

Students of higher-income origin have a greater chance not only of
access to education, but also of promotion within the system. This is
seen in the socioeconomic profile of the dropouts, repeaters and
successful students, and in the fact that middle- and upper-income
groups are particularly over-represented in higher education. In some
countries, other factors, such as sex, ethnic origin or religion, play a
role which is frequently combined with the effect of income levels.
These inequalities are aggravated by differences in the quality of
teachers, educational facilities and other inputs between schools
serving different geographic areas and income groups.

For underdeveloped societies, patterns of rural–urban imbalance in
educational resources are inextricably bound up with patterns of
inequality. Access to education gives further access to higher incomes,
authority and power. Gunnar Myrdal (1973: 199) has argued that:
'Monopoly in education is—together with monopoly of ownership of
land—the most fundamental basis of inequality, and it retains its hold
more strongly in the poorer countries'. In poor countries the educational
gap between rich and poor is much greater than in the richer more highly
developed societies. And the problem of inequality as an inhibitor of
economic change is probably far more serious in the poor countries than
it is in the rich ones. Gunnar Myrdal has argued that in South Asia the
pressure for secondary and tertiary education comes from families and
social groups who 'want to save their sons from the socially degrading
necessity of manual work'. Because of this association of ideas of
education as the way out of manual work many of the educated of South
Asia are actually unemployable. Myrdal speaks of the educated groups
of South Asia as being alienated (1973: 199):

The more successful among them are swallowed up by the Government bureaux and business firms; their detachment from the harsh realities of existence as they affect the mass of the population minimises their potential contribution to the task of development. Everyone who has visited the South Asian countries can testify to the strange make believe atmosphere that prevails in the higher echelons of the educated class. In the lower strata of the employed and unemployed educated there is even less sense of identification with national interests.

The capacity of such groups to secure education for their children has, therefore, the paradoxical effect that their children are denied the employment they expected.

For the poor, on the other hand, the situation of denial has far more serious consequences. The social processes which allow those with power to appropriate educational resources for themselves leave the poor not only poor but unable to *perceive* the structures which cause their poverty.

Paulo Friere (1972) has argued that there is a mode of consciousness appropriate to the closed, hierarchical societies of Latin America which he calls 'semi-intransitive consciousness' whose main feature is that it lacks 'structural perception'. Such perception does not allow the perceiver to see beyond the immediacy of his problems so that the perceiver cannot come to know the world about him in a critical way. Such is the origin, Friere claims, of the fatalism of peasants and their belief in supernatural forces. Friere speaks of the closed rural social structures of Latin America where large estates and large landowners are found (*latifundios*) as maintaining a 'culture of silence'.

Friere's arguments are not, of course, confined to Latin America. The culture of silence is a worldwide phenomenon found wherever the denial of education facilities or the existence of coercive educational structures inhibits the growth of critical 'structural perception' among the mass of the people. The culture of silence in this respect is just as likely to be found in the poor areas of modern cities in modern societies where the failure of education to develop is just as striking as in the rural areas of Latin America. The transmitted deprivation of the inner city has the same kind of consequences for the individual in modern society as the transmitted poverty of the rural areas in the underdeveloped society. In both cases people lack access to an important resource through which it would be possible to inject a greater degree of control into their lives and understand better the social forces which shape their current poverty.

In the short run, too, the lack of education inhibits the occupational opportunities of large numbers of people. Education level is an important determinant of income life chances. This is a general relationship which holds true in all societies and the correlation between education and earnings is greater in poor societies than in rich societies. Here lies the source of aspiration patterns geared to urban employment and the roots of such differentiation often have to be traced directly back to the structures of opportunity for employment laid down in colonial times. The effect, already noted, is that development through education or, at least, through the help of education amongst other programmes, is inhibited. Because of the growing inegalitarian and urban concentration of educational resources the skills required for development are not diffused and encouraged throughout society, and manpower of the type that can be mobilised is not formed to the extent required. All societies exemplify these problems but each in different ways.

It would be quite wrong, as subsequent chapters will make clear, to assume that the kinds of problems which have been discussed here are in some way unique to poor Third World societies. How best to relate the development of education to the goals of further economic and social development is a perplexing problem for all developed societies. Most modern industrial societies have achieved the provision of systems of mass education with higher levels of education to follow on for those selected for it. But such achievements bring their own problems. Selection procedures raise issues of social justice and equality which no modern industrial society has managed to resolve satisfactorily. And the complexity of provision places a huge burden on national economic resources; demands for education have become rapacious and far outstrip the capacity of the developed economies to meet them. In such circumstances difficult questions of the relevance of what is to be taught, and to whom it shall be taught, arise. Nor have developed societies solved the problem of regional disparities in educational provision. As I shall show in subsequent chapters this particular issue is just as intractable as that of inequality, which, of course, it partly reflects, although the ostensible means for solving it through programmes of resource distribution and positive discrimination are obvious. Qualification inflation, elitism, inequality and irrelevance while taking on a different character and having quantitatively different dimensions are thus problems of the developed world just as much as the underdeveloped world.

In the three examples given of the so-called world educational crisis it is clear that the way in which different social structures function is being felt in the field of education. Schools and universities are bound in to the structures of the society in which they function and to the patterns of expectations of different groups in society. Schools are directly affected by the mechanisms of income and resource distribution in different societies so that a complex chain of 'structural effects' serves to fashion and mould educational programmes inhibiting or promoting development goals as the case may be. An important aim of theorising in the field of comparative educational studies ought to be to try and recognise the precise form which such structural effects take in different contexts. Only when this is recognised can it be clear why during the 1960s development failed to develop and educational poverty remains a stubborn fact of underdevelopment.

The effect of such observations on the business of planning education and of devising economic theories concerning education and development is to make the problems to which theorising and planning are directed, even more complex. It is clear, however, that broad generalisation about education and economic growth are singularly unhelpful unless account is taken of the institutional factors in an economy and society which mould education.

In the next chapter an attempt is made to classify world structures in such a way that social, economic and political forces which operate in different national contexts can be more clearly identified.

2 Education and Social Structure in Comparative Perspective

The crisis in education which has been outlined in the last chapter shows itself in uniquely different ways in different societies. But such obvious uniqueness ought not to be a deterrent to making comparisons between, or generalisations across, a number of different societies and their educational systems. For it is through such comparison that we gain some broader understanding of the role which education plays in development and, perhaps more importantly, the role which it could play in the future.

The main theme of this book is that the patterns of educational underdevelopment described in the previous chapter have to be seen as the outcomes of particular *models of development* coming to terms with particular *structures of internal and external constraints* faced by different *types of society* in the grip of their own unique *historical experience*. I shall try to show that educational systems both shape and are shaped by the models of development which govern the way in which different societies change through time. Whether, therefore, education can play a role in promoting economic development or in hindering such development is something which cannot be assessed using the crude quantitative techniques of economics. In this respect I concur fully with Balogh's assessment (1974) of the economics of education as being too 'mechanistic' to grasp the subtleties of the education-development equation. The issue must be examined against a broader understanding of the interconnections which bind education into the fabric of different types of social structure. My aim is to clarify what these interconnections are.

My starting point follows from the theme of social reproduction discussed in the Introduction: education is a process of learning through which people come to understand the habits of thought and social values which are dominant in society; it is a heavily ritualised and highly

25

organised social process; its social function is to underwrite, explain and to transmit from one generation to the next a given pattern of social order which constitutes the backbone of everyday social behaviour. Education is not a uniform experience; what is experienced as education varies according to dominant principles of social classification—age, sex, religion, nationality and occupation—which operate in different societies at different points in time.

Because of this, the outcomes, measured in terms of the type of people schools produce, are very different in different kinds of society. This may seem to be trivially obvious but in fact it is a complex issue with an immediate practical relevance. It is complex because such variation does need to be explained. It is practical since, as I have shown in the previous chapter, the intended consequences of planning, investment and change in education, are very often not realised; instead of acting as a catalyst of social change, particularly in poor societies, education often stabilises the *status quo*. Instead of being an agent of development it can often be an agent of underdevelopment. It is a practical problem, therefore, to understand what the likely effects of change in education will be in specific societies.

To take this perspective further, involves a clarification of the factors which underlie variation in the social structures of different societies. Such factors, *chosen for their theoretical relevance to the problems under study*, can then be used to specify a number of distinct types of society within which controlled comparisons of educational processes can be made. In this way particular educational processes such as social selection or curriculum planning can then be inspected under varying conditions, a methodological procedure which, to the founding fathers of sociology, was the key to a scientific understanding of society. It is also, as I hope to be able to show, the essential first step in the development of a comparative sociology of education.

The difficulties with this argument and the pitfalls in the use of such an approach should not, however, be underestimated. Some of these, of data and the absence of agreed theory, have already been mentioned in the Introduction to this book. But there are others which raise some of the most basic and perplexing issues in the philosophy of social science. The logic of comparative sociology comes, it might be argued, dangerously close to the logic of the natural sciences in which explanatory statements always take a causal form in terms of general laws. Emile Durkheim, an ardent advocate of comparative analysis, set out the scientific agenda for sociology in precisely such terms.

The case against such an approach, most frequently associated with the work of Max Weber but developed later in several other traditions of theorising such as symbolic interactionism and social phenomenology, is that societies cannot be treated as natural systems and that explanation in the social sciences cannot take the hypothetical-deductive form of explanation in the natural sciences. At best, it has often been argued from this position, sociology can seek only, in a very special way to understand (*verstehen*) the actions of men in society drawing on the cultural resources of language, custom and empathy. The view I have taken is much closer to that of Max Weber and the method of sociological theorising using the ideal type.

Weber's view, at its simplest, was this: the social world is infinitely manifold and *meaningful* to its participants. Each society and culture is a unique configuration of different historical elements. To make possible the scientific study of social reality it is necessary to reduce it to 'intelligible typological proportions' (Bendix and Roth, 1971: 258). The formulation of abstract descriptions of societies, institutions or forms of political system—the ideal types themselves—is, on this view, the essential first step of comparative study. Such types sharpen the contrast always implicit in the comparison of different societies and heighten the similarities, both effects being an aid to more precise sociological description and analysis.

But type-formation, the essential first step of comparative study, is not an arbitrary process; it follows on from both the problems being studied—and from what Weber called 'rules of experience' (Bendix and Roth, 1971: 258). In Weber's case these took the form of what he understood as basic sociological truths which can be thought of as the basic starting assumptions of all research. Roth gives an example of such a rule of experience, drawn from Weber's political sociology but nonetheless very apposite to a main theme in this book.

The rule concerns the process of legitimation by which social arrangements are seen by those affected by them or involved in them to be both appropriate and fair. The rule, in Weber's words (quoted by Bendix and Roth, 1971: 259), is this:

> simple observation shows that . . . he who is more favoured feels the never-ceasing need to look upon his position as in some way 'legitimate', upon his advantage as 'deserved', and the other's disadvantage as being brought about by the latter's 'fault'.

From this point on Weber formulates different types of legitimate authority and is able in a wide range of historical and comparative studies, to deploy these types in empirical research. He can thus inspect the varied historical circumstances which can be combined with different forms of legitimate political domination.

The rationale for such an approach is that it leads to causal explanations of specific events or social processes, in particular societies without recourse to universal notions of historical laws or 'causal master keys' which would be true for all societies (see Bendix and Roth, 1971: 257). The understanding which it brings is, therefore, provisional and capable of being checked by others using the same concepts in different empirical circumstances.

In what follows I seek to build up a simple typology of societies upon which my account of education in particular societies will be based. My aim, in keeping with the logic of comparative study, is to vary the circumstances in which education, as defined in the Introduction, takes place. My approach like that of Weber is not designed to uncover the invariant relationships between education and development or the laws governing cultural transmission through schools. I seek only to give accounts of change in education in different societies which are adequate according to the 'rules of experience' from which I begin and which are captured in the idea of education as social reproduction and in keeping with the historical data I discuss. If my account retains the idea that it is real men who, according to their own lights, imagination and capabilities bring about change in society and not the unseen forces of natural laws, then I may not be following strictly the methods of Max Weber, but at least I shall come close in a modest way to the spirit of his approach.

The basic analytical elements of my approach are set out in Figure 2.1 below.

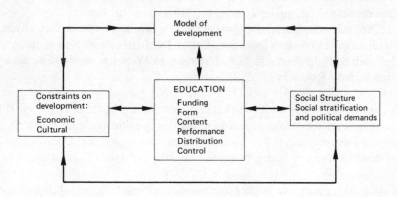

Figure 2.1   Social structure of development and education

When the elements of this scheme are explained and their relevance to education indicated, the basis of the classification of societies used in this book will be clear.

MODELS OF DEVELOPMENT

Social reproduction through education is a future-oriented process; it operates with some sense of what kind of people will be required for the future development of society so that the future of a society can be guaranteed. It therefore relates to the *model of development* of society which a ruling group uses to manage and to direct economic and social change and which embodies the dominant social values of a society. A model of development in the sense used in this book expresses the direction and manner of change in a society; it is the legitimating code of political practice formulating the sense of where a society or its dominant groups wants to be in the future. Such models are often expressed in crisp political formulae. '*Socialism and Self-Reliance*' '*Uhuru*', '*Laissez-Faire*' '*Freedom and Economic Growth*', '*Planned Socialist Industrialisation*', are all examples of such formulae; they are frequently repeated slogans which economically distil into a simple evocative image a whole programme of social and economic change towards valued ends; they penetrate everyday political behaviour giving it a meaning and significance which goes beyond its immediate object. The dull routines of practical politics can then be seen in a much more dignified and purposeful light; the daily work tasks of people can then be viewed as an integral part of an unfolding future. Often models of development are highly articulated programmes of change carrying an ideologically supercharged justification.

But it is still helpful to think in terms of models even when they are not made fully explicit or not obviously entrenched in an overtly ideological *weltanschauung*. In this case, the model of development defines what a society is, in the end, prepared to defend, if necessary by military force, and in this respect is defined by the boundaries of political consensus about what the future ought to be like, not in detail, but in terms of broad social values which only revolutionaries would oppose.

In western capitalist societies such values might include economic growth, political freedom, respect for the individual and safety from external interference in a nation's affairs. Agreement about them would then lend support to specific programmes such as maintaining an army at fighting readiness, developing schools to offer opportunities, managing the economy to achieve a steady growth of personal incomes and, fundamentally, maintaining the political conditions of a capitalistic mode of production. It is the model of development which, almost like a language code or system of musical notation, governs the detailed practice and content of daily decision-making in a whole range of social institutions from the State to the factory floor. It provides the ongoing rationale for society as it is and it lends support and succour to the emerging interests and motivation of individuals supplying them with the answer to the most basic existential question of them all, 'what should I aim at in my life? what kind of person ought I to become?' I do not wish to imply here that model and reality always correspond. In fact, they rarely do. This is why, as I shall show below, some notion of the degree to which a model is institutionalised in a particular society is vital.

Models of development are most often defined, however, in ideological terms, because of the specific historical circumstances of the modern world. Models of development do not exist in an historical vacuum; they respond to historical conditions. In the twentieth century these conditions include the basic fact of the Russian revolution in 1917 and the revolutionary ideology behind that revolution—Marxism. The conditions also include the massive imbalance in the world economy between the rich nations and the poor nations of the Third World. These two conditions are closely related. Geoffrey Barraclough has pointed out (1964) that the significance of Marxism goes well beyond the Soviet State. Its significance, he claims, lies in the fact that 'it provided an alternative for the emergent peoples, to whose condition this the liberal economic system of the west and the political and social institutions associated with it were not easily adaptable'. It was, added Barraclough, an alternative with a comprehensive emotional appeal. And finally, 'It has already shaped twentieth century society on lines different from anything known in the past; and its force is not yet spent' (1964: 232).

The significance of this is, of course, that, particularly for the people of the Third World, development is a process of seeking a direction to economic growth in conditions where it is not possible to conceive of non-ideological paths to development. Relationships of aid, trade and military alliance have trapped Third World societies into the global confrontation between the superpowers and their competing ideologies.

The analytical importance of this is that classification of models of development need to reflect the spectrum of ideological differentiation among world societies. A simple first step to make is to treat models of development as either broadly socialist in orientation or broadly capitalist. It is difficult to measure precisely such differences for within each category there are great differences; capitalist societies vary considerably in the degree to which the state intervenes in economic processes; socialist societies interpret their socialism in very different ways. Nonetheless, within such broad groupings the similarities which exist between societies with respect to political principles and forms of economic organisation are sufficiently strong to highlight the differences between the two broad groups and their different programmes for future development.

A further aspect of the fact that models of development do not exist in an historical vacuum is the likelihood that, at least for societies undergoing rapid social change, a particular model of development might be superseded by another. This is likely to occur in conditions of political instability where programmes of change derived from the model in question have not been fully implemented or are, in fact, unsuccessful. Numerous examples of such changes litter the recent history of many Third World societies. Analytically, therefore, we need to have some sense of how *institutionalised* a particular programme or model of development is.

The degree of institutionalisation, or the degree to which a given model is supported throughout a society and is therefore accepted as the legitimate backcloth to every day planning and political decision-making, will vary on a strong–weak dimension and will reflect the degree to which a dominant political group is in control and can effectively mobilise mass support for its programmes. The degree of institutionalisation of a model therefore, involves some notion of how far a significant number of people perceive the world in the terms of, or have acquired the general attitude of mind (the habitus) implied by, the dominant principles of development.

In characterising models of development as being either broadly socialist in orientation or broadly capitalist, I am, of course, simplifying and certainly the terms should not be taken as ideologically precise descriptions. What a capitalist or socialist society intrinsically *is* is something which can be left to the ideologists themselves to fight about. The terms are used here to typify the well-known political and philosophical principles which dominant groups call upon to legitimate what they claim to do. Within the socialist category there is a spectrum of ideas from Marxism to social democracy; within the capitalist category there is an equally wide spectrum from theories of the free market economy to those of state-regulated capitalism and the welfare state.

These dimensions of variation in models of development can be visualised in the following way (Figure 2.2).

Degree of Institutionalisation

		Strong	Weak
Model of development	Socialist orientation	USSR Eastern Europe China	All recently declared socialist states
	Capitalist orientation	USA West Germany	All rapidly modernising states

Figure 2.2   Degrees of institutionalisation in models of development

I shall show in subsequent chapters of this book, that particular models of development, among other things, help shape the pattern of growth of education, the distribution of educational life chances throughout a population, the form and content of schooling and, in particular, the standards of educational selection which operate to decide who shall be given access to different types of educational experience. Socialist models of development as exemplified in the Soviet Union and in modern Eastern Europe, for example, place a strong emphasis on education being *egalitarian* and *relevant* to the needs of society. Both themes are closely interwoven into the rhetoric, if not always the practice of their educational policies. In Western Europe, however, such values have much less strength; educational inequality is tolerated much more readily and the notion of relevance is felt by many to be inconsistent with the central purpose of education.

Earl Hopper has tried to capture these differences in his concept of 'ideologies of legitimisation' which are developed to bolster the position of dominant social groups and which 'define the types of people whom society values most highly and which justify why more power is given to them than to others' (1971: 99). 'These ideologies', he explains, and I think rightly, 'translate questions concerning the distribution of power into questions concerning the distribution of educational suitability' (1971: 99). My only quarrel with his argument is that it is too narrowly focused on the structural problem of social selection when it can be quite properly broadened to take account of not just which people will be selected for education but what values and forms of knowledge will be determined upon as the curriculum core of the schools themselves (see also Davies, 1971). The range of values with which I am concerned is from individualism and particularism at one extreme to universalism and collectivism at the other. What I hope to show is that such ideological differences suffuse educational politics penetrating directly into the daily practices of schools themselves and that such ideological differences must be treated historically since all schools, being essentially conservative institutions, carry the values of earlier periods while responding to new situations.

Thus the first set of factors which shape education systems are political and ideological.

CONSTRAINTS ON DEVELOPMENT

The second set of conditioning factors which shape education and models of development and which, in their turn, are shaped by development policy and education, are the specific constraints on development which a society faces. Development programmes in all societies must face up to the facts of limited resources and competing priorities but societies differ considerably in the kinds of choices they face and the kinds and levels of resources available to them. It is not sufficient, therefore, to know that a society is either rich or poor to gain some idea of its developmental potential. Crude measures of national income only tell half the story, for whether an economy can be made to grow, leaving aside for the moment the many different meanings of development, will depend upon the form of its economy and the goals of its political leadership.

Analytically we can conceive of the constraints imposed by economic factors as varying to the extent that a society is developed or underdeveloped. In an underdeveloped society resources for education are scarce, provision is poor and, as I have shown in the last chapter, the distribution of education is uneven.

The limited level of resources for education is not, however, the cause of the problem, rather it is itself a symptom of something else, the distortions which underdevelopment imposes on social and economic life. Precisely what these distortions are I shall examine below. But in developed societies there are in principle, and certainly by comparison, few resource constraints as such. Economies with a well-developed infrastructure of social provision and a firm economic base in modern manufacturing methods and mass markets, the product of historical successes in being the first societies to modernise industrially, can call upon vast economic resources to further improve their social facilities. I do not wish to imply, of course, that development is an option available only to those societies which are rich. A strong economy may be a necessary condition for development to take place but it is by no means a sufficient one.

SOCIAL STRATIFICATION AND POLITICAL DEMANDS

The third main element in my approach is the nature of the demands upon education resources which different groups in a society make. What is provided as education in a society is the outcome of different social groups either pressing on others what they think the others need— this particular theme is central to the provision of mass education in modern industrial societies—or demanding more of what kind of education they feel they are entitled to. The resulting compromise between provision and demand is always unstable. The world supply of primary education, for instance, far outstrips the world supply of schools and appropriately trained teachers to staff them. In the developed societies the demand for various forms of higher education is greater than the supply of places. In both cases, and often with very bitter political consequences, there are attempts to bring the supply and demand factors much more closely into line but the *level* and *form* of demand varies considerably even among those societies, for example, Britain and the Federal Republic of Germany which are similar to one another as advanced industrial societies. Such variation is a consequence of historical differences in social stratification and in the way different social classes have come to articulate their political interests. In some cases—Britain is a good example—a wider diffusion of educational opportunities has been a central political aim of the organised labour movement. In other societies—Germany before 1933 is a good example—education has not had such a high priority on the political agenda of the Social Democrats; little was demanded, little was gained; other problems were far more pressing so old-fashioned structures of education persisted without being threatened. This theme will be taken up throughout the case studies which follow this chapter.

When the two main dimensions of variation—level of development and political orientation—are combined they can be seen to affect education in the following way, as set out in Figure 2.3.

The diagram simply suggests connections, yet to be examined empirically in different contexts, between such aspects of *any* educational system as levels of resources, forms of schooling, the distribution of schooling, patterns of performance and levels of socioeconomic development and types of political orientation among different states. In addition it suggests, although in an admittedly crude way, the kinds of measures of such variation which might be employed in systematic comparative studies. That appropriate data for such comparison is not yet available is not something, at this stage, which need cause much concern. In the case studies which form the main part of this book these connections will be examined.

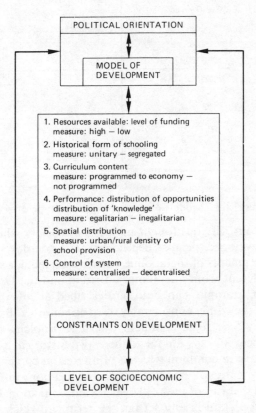

Figure 2.3 Models of development and education

The two dimensions of variation are themselves summary descriptions of complex relationships in different types of society whose special properties the dimensions reflect. Whether a model of development is socialist or capitalist in its orientation is not a matter of chance, rather it is the outcome of particular forms of social structure and politics, in which different dominant groups legitimate their domination in ways consistent with their own economic interests.

When they are combined in a cross-tabulation the following typology results (see Figure 2.4).

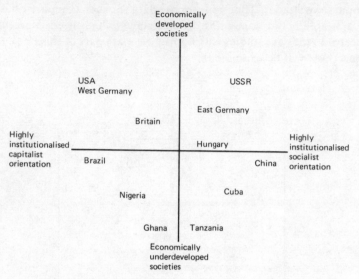

Figure 2.4   Models of development and type of economy

The typology sets out four main types of society which I shall call capitalist, developed socialist, dependent, and underdeveloped socialist. These four segments of sociopolitical space each include societies which are very different from one another. Britain and the United States of America for example, can both be described as advanced capitalist societies but they differ considerably from one another. But, as capitalist societies they face some common structural problems although they cope with them in ways unique to their own historical experience. It is what they have in common which is of interest in comparative studies. Since, as I have already explained, comparison among different societies presupposes theories of how different societies function and change, in what follows I shall briefly set out the terms in which the structural properties of each will be discussed.

ADVANCED CAPITALIST SOCIETIES

Edward Shils once pointed out that: 'One of the great difficulties [in making sense of modern society] is that we cannot imagine anything beyond variations on the theme set by the great figures of nineteenth and twentieth century sociology' (quoted by Bell, 1973: 55). The difficulties this perfectly valid observation presents for me are those of finding a way to talk about capitalist society which is faithful to the complexities of its *modern* form and which does not become hopelessly lost in the vast scholarship which the study of that form has generated (see Miliband, 1973; Bell, 1973; and Galbraith, 1971). In the classical theory of capitalist society and of capitalist development the main features of this form of society were conceived of in the following way:

1. Private ownership of the means of production.
2. A free market in labour.
3. The concentration of production into factories and the in-corporation of agriculture into the capitalist market.
4. Production geared to a market and aimed at realising profit.
5. The rationalisation of economic life to principles of clear capital accounting and the cash-nexus.
6. Production geared to a world market.

As developed by Marx and Lenin these features interacted with one another to produce a series of necessary outcomes. These included:

1. The overseas expansion of the capitalist mode of production—the development of imperialism and colonialism.
2. The concentration of capital into few hands.
3. The polarisation of society into social classes—bourgeoisie and proletariat—locked together in a death struggle.
4. The emergence of a revolutionary movement towards a socialist society.

Within the social sciences there is, however, a different analysis which stresses that capitalist society in its modern form is vastly different from the system described by Karl Marx. Several versions of this argument are available but they all involve at least one or more of the following assumptions.

1. Capitalist industry has given way through the spreading of share

ownership and technical change to corporate industry (see Galbraith, 1971).

2. The basis of social conflict is no longer the division of society into classes; rather it is the outcome of different social groups carrying different amounts of authority (see Dahrendorf, 1959).

3. The anarchy of the market mechanisms of capital formation have given way to planning in which the state plays a crucial role.

Such views do not go unchallenged (see Miliband, 1973; Westergaard and Resler, 1975). Modern capitalist society can still be portrayed, irrespective of its different appearances in different societies, as driven by the logic of the need for profits, necessarily inegalitarian and essentially exploitative.

There is no room in a book about education to engage in all of these debates. The position which I adopt, however, is this: capitalist society is an economic form rooted in the need to produce for profits. It is an international form of society whose earlier successes were based in part and continue to depend upon the economic subjugation of the poorer economies and societies of the world (see Frank, 1967). In modern capitalist societies with much higher standards of living for all sections of society, the state plays a regulative role in the economy transferring some of the major costs of running such a society to those peripheral social groups—the poor, the unorganised, the unemployed, the old— who are least likely to object (see Habermas, 1976).

Development in such societies has come to mean further economic growth, the exploitation of science and technology, the international regulation of the economy and higher standards of living. The *model of development* such ends reflect is one based on the assumption that private enterprise, left free to determine its own operating conditions and without undue interference from the state, is the most effective instrument for increasing wealth and productivity. In practice, however, the state in such societies does play an increasingly important role in regulating the economy but without threat to the basic institution of private ownership of the means of production (see Miliband, 1973).

The conditions most favourable to the realisation of such ends have, however, long passed. It is not at all clear whether high growth rates can be reconciled with full employment or a stable currency. In so far as economic growth and high productivity implies massive investment in labour-saving technology then such ends are inconsistent with the basic demand of the labour movement for full employment. Nor is it certain that the rapacious demands of multinational corporations (which control an increasing proportion of industrial output) for capital are consistent with the equally rapacious demands of the public sector for better health services, schools, roads and welfare.

Finally, it seems unlikely that modern conceptions of the quality of life can be reconciled with the needs of modern production. The problems of reproducing the social relationships of such a society are those of reconciling expectations for a high standard of living with the knowledge that for many such a standard will not be achieved. A full appreciation of the social divisions of such a society must go beyond the categories of crude Marxism but one should not lose sight of the essentially international profit-driven form of capitalist production. Securing the optimal conditions for profitability and growth is the essential *constraint* on the governments of capitalist societies; this aim has to be balanced against the *demands* of organised labour for higher wages, better services and more free time. Whether this balancing act can be achieved is not at all certain.

DEPENDENT SOCIETIES

The world is divided between a few very rich societies and a large number of very poor societies. Concepts like 'less-developed country' or 'underdeveloped society' only hint at the complex interdependence of poverty, low income, low productivity, high mortality rates, urban squalor, economic dependence, political corruption and illiteracy which to different degrees typify the life experience of nearly two-thirds of the world's population (see Myrdal, 1968; Dalton, 1974). This interdependence is shown in Figure 2.5.

The diagram is not intended to be empirical; it is intended to highlight three broad sets of *constraints* which, in societies of this type prevent particular *models of development* being realised. The constraints are, firstly, those imposed by the structure of the economy; secondly those which depend upon traditional patterns of economic behaviour; and finally, those which relate to the capacity of a political leadership to mobilise support for development. In some societies such factors interrelate in a growth-oriented way; in others they reinforce stagnation and dependency.

There is a vast contradictory literature dealing with these problems. Certainly there is little agreement about how such poverty can be explained or how such societies can escape it. One powerful form of theorising associated with the work among others, of Rostow (1960),

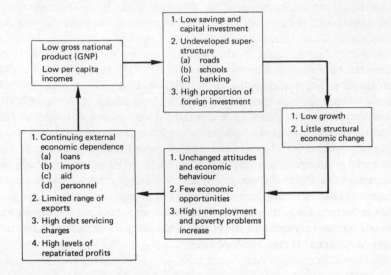

Figure 2.5 The vicious circle of poverty

Hoselitz (1960), McClelland (1961), and Parsons (1971) is modernisation theory. Its essential theme is that, with the correct economic policies, societies which are currently poor can, following a well-known trajectory, pass through the stages of development to become fully modern industrial societies.

The approach I have adopted, however, is closer to a different form of theory, dependency theory. Once again space only allows a rather bold assertion of the argument but it is this: economic backwardness is an historically based phenomenon, the outcome of poor societies having had their economies and social systems distorted and conditioned by the overseas expansion of capitalist enterprise (see Dos Santos, 1973). The dependent economy has evolved to meet the interests of expatriate economic interests with whom indigenous entrepreneurs cannot properly compete (see G. Williams, 1970).

In the absence of efficient mechanisms of capital formation the state in such a society itself becomes an important source of capital and a group emerges—Gavin Williams calls it (1970), the 'bureaucratic bourgeoisie'—which becomes the main beneficiary of foreign aid, state tax concessions and whatever economic growth takes place. A similar argument is offered by Tibor Mende (1973) and, in a savage attack on the 'national bourgeoisie' of former colonial societies, by Franz Fanon (1967).

What these accounts have in common is the view that economic backwardness is not a phenomenon intrinsic to pre-modern societies. Rather it is an historical, externally imposed condition which is reinforced internally by the willing compliance of political and commercial elites. As Dos Santos puts it (1973: 78): '"External" domination, in a pure sense, is in principle impracticable. Domination is practicable only when it finds support among those local groups who profit by it'. The implications of this view are, of course, that little fundamental economic change in the poor societies of the world can occur without major realignments in the international economy. A consequence of poverty is that poor societies are forced into debt dependency and aid dependency. Both facts coalesce to produce a great pressure for economic modernisation and for the development of a stronger sector to the economy. Only in this way can such a society hope to acquire the funds necessary for independent industrialisation. But in following such a policy such states incorporate themselves further into the international economy. Rural communities are brought into the money economy (Stavenhagen, 1973; Pearse, 1973) and new social classes begin to form—landless rural labourers, urban workers and landlords (see G. Williams, 1970; Lloyd, 1973).

Under such conditions and the additional tutelage of western aid the *model of development* most likely to be seized upon by dominant groups is a western-oriented, dependency model, for such a programme legitimates the further receipt of aid and forms of trade which, in the longer term, are most likely to be disadvantageous to the poorer sections of society. This line of argument has been developed in respect of aid policies by Teresa Hayter (1971) and, in relation to the export of technology from the rich countries to the poor ones, by Thomas Weisskopf (1972). And, as I shall argue later in the book, inequalities in education and western forms of education help to fashion the identity of dominant groups and convince them of the essential rightness of a dependency strategy of development. Such groups are often incapable of mobilising peasants and workers to work efficiently in the modern sector.

The historical constraints of dependency are thus reinforced by ideological convictions. Even when the ideology changes and different social groups press for dominance the historical and economic constraints on development nevertheless still remain sustaining attitudes and beliefs among peasants and workers which are extremely resistant to change. There is, therefore, often a gap between the legitimating rhetoric of politics and the extent to which political values are actually institutionalised. Perhaps here is the clue to a conundrum once posed by George Lichtheim (1974: 155): 'The real question is not whether capitalism exploits the undeveloped countries—of course it does, and always has, but why has it not done more to revolutionise them through the very mechanism of exploitation'.

DEVELOPED SOCIALIST SOCIETIES

Since the Bolshevik revolution of 1917 in Russia the option of a non-capitalist path of development has been on the agenda for all underdeveloped societies. The achievements of the Soviet Union in building an industrial society out of the chaos of a wartorn backward Russia represents a powerful model for other states to follow.

It is difficult to give a clear description of the *type of society* which has grown up in the Soviet Union, and since 1945 in Eastern Europe, since all such description is shot through with political evaluation. The Soviet Union has been described as a state capitalist society—for an account of such descriptions see Lane (1970)—Trotsky (1945) described it as a degenerate workers state.

My own position is this: the Soviet Union and other East European societies must be understood as developing socialist societies whose special features flow historically from the programme of industrial development followed by Lenin and Stalin—the command economy and the view, derived from Lenin (1920), that socialism is safe only in an industrial society. These features of the *Soviet model of development* had consequences for Soviet political values and social organisation which, given the backwardness of the society, produced a distinctive social system with special problems. The *constraints* of backwardness in a predominantly peasant society and the need, as seen by the Bolsheviks, to overcome them quickly through industrialisation, represents the backcloth against which the Soviet model of development was subsequently legitimated as a virture arising from necessity.

The need to industrialise rapidly has led some critics to see the Soviet Union as a 'dictatorship of development' (see Lowenthal, 1970; Nove, 1972). The implication is clear; socialism imposed from above can take a gruesome totalitarian form. Nor is this an argument confined to those critical of Marxism on political grounds. Corrigan, Ramsay and Sayer (1978) have argued a similar case from a very different perspective.

Others have detected a significant gap between the egalitarian values upon which the state bases its claims to legitimacy and the actual organisation of economic life. Z. Bauman, for instance, has argued (1971: 47) that there is a 'growing discrepancy between, on the one hand, the millenarian and egalitarian ideals embodied in the ideological complex . . . and the actual conditions which have developed in these socialist societies'.

A similar argument has been developed by Frank Parkin (1971). My account follows this line of argument. There does seem to be a dilemma in reconciling egalitarian values with the patterns of class formation which have emerged in Eastern Europe where the values of economic efficiency place a high symbolic premium on the growth of technical expertise and from which a strong sense of the desirability of a personal career is based. Peter Ludz, for example, typifies East Germany as a 'career society' (1970).

Secondly, there is, too, a basic dilemma involved in reconciling the ideologically legitimate expectation, derived from classical Marxism, that the worker ought to be in control of his work, with the actual forms of management which have evolved all over Eastern Europe. Several accounts of such management forms underline a great concern for scientific management and hierarchical industrial organisation (see Child, 1969; Meyer, 1972; Smith, 1967; Burks, 1973). This dilemma I shall call the involvement-control dilemma. It is a dilemma which is exacerbated by the introduction of various forms of 'new economic policy' where firms are expected to respond to market criteria rather than simply the output norms of centrally agreed plans. Such criteria threaten to open up conflicts of interest among managers and workers in such societies which are difficult to reconcile with the ideology of the classless society. Politics in such societies flows from the conflicts which arise in reconciling the interests of the state with those on the one hand of an emerging technical class and on the other with those of industrial workers, the group from which the Party derives its legitimacy and political strength (see Bauman, 1974).

I make two further assumptions, however. The first is that the form of social structure which has emerged in Eastern European societies is the outcome of a particular thrust in the politics of Soviet Marxism in which rapid, centralised industrialisation programmes are seen as the necessary conditions of the construction of socialism (see Corrigan, Ramsay and Sayer, 1978). From this flows the structural dilemmas I have mentioned. These are not in some inevitable way the essential features of socialism as such; rather they are the structural outcomes of one *form* of socialist construction. The second assumption is that the claims to legitimacy which such states make on the basis of further economic and material advance feed back on the political system creating expectations which only further economic change can hope to fulfil. But it is precisely such change which calls into question the ideological claims of the state to be egalitarian and which accelerates the formation of careerist, individualistic social attitudes. Whether the ideological organs of the state can reduce the salience of these pressures is not clear.

UNDERDEVELOPED SOCIALIST SOCIETIES

Different again are those societies which face the task of building socialist systems in predominantly peasant societies but in a world in which the experience of the Soviet Union is there for all to consider. Societies such as China, Cuba, North Vietnam, Mozambique and, if we apply our definitions retrospectively, the Soviet Union in the early 1920s, all face the problem of building socialism in conditions which, according to the precepts of classical Marxism, will not support them. Economies based on agricultural production, face the *constraints* of accumulating capital for independent industrialisation in conditions where such accumulation is difficult. Attitudes, production methods, income levels and manpower are not easily changed and socialist rhetoric is not in itself sufficient to persuade workers and peasants to behave in new ways. Nor, given the great ideological chasm which has opened up between the Soviet Union and China is there a clear modern blueprint for socialist construction under these conditions.

In Russia during the 1920s the problems of socialist accumulation of capital were discussed in relation to such issues as the level of state grain procurements from the countryside to feed the towns, the nature and form of agricultural collectivisation and the political role of the peasantry (see Lewin, 1968). Stalin's policies of forced collectivisation—policies which Bukharin sensed would meet with peasant resistance forcing Stalin to 'drown the uprising in blood' (Lewin, 1968: 260)—were one solution to the problem of rapid capital accumulation.

The Chinese since 1949 have tried a different strategy. In a very famous comment Mao once noted that: 'The agricultural policy of the Soviet Union has always been wrong in that it drains the pond to catch the fish and is divorced from the masses' (quoted by Gray, 1973a: 262)'. In contrast to the Soviets Chinese policies for the countryside have been aimed, at least so they claim, at changing the political consciousness of peasants and building up industry in step with the collective improvement of agriculture. The experience of the Chinese communists in the border regions of China between 1937 and 1949 convinced them that such a strategy was possible and right for China (see Snow, 1968; Belden, 1949; Hinton, 1972; Selden, 1971). The emphasis in their model of development is on collective entrepreneurship and changes in consciousness, both flowing from the full mobilisation of peasants in revolution (Gray, 1973a).

Once again the problems are too vast to attempt to discuss them here. My position, however, is this: underdeveloped socialist societies face the structural problem of involving peasants and rural workers in revolutionary change; they must strike a balance, therefore, between satisfying immediate demands for a better life and longer-term demands for capital accumulation which involves sacrifice and deferred consumption. In China, certainly, but also in Cuba, this problem has been tackled by the leadership placing a great emphasis on consciousness change and moral incentives to work (see Roca, 1977; Lehmann, 1971). The danger with such a strategy is that it requires herculean efforts from people who are poor and ignorant of ideology and it can quickly degenerate into the routine of central direction of the economy (see Gonzalez, 1976; Dumont, 1974).

The option of expanding industry quickly on the basis of modern industry and the most efficient technology must be a tempting one but it carries its dangers from a revolutionary point of view, of polarising society into the basic divisions of political and technical elites who solve problems and workers and peasants who take orders. I am not saying that this is the case in China or Cuba, the two societies I am concerned with in this book, rather that their commitment to a socialist model of development against the constraints of underdevelopment and the demands of the mass of the people for tangible evidence of improvement in their lives, creates structural problems which all such societies must solve. They will, of course, solve them in ways unique to their own history and revolutionary experience.

These, then, are the main types of society from which I have made my selection of case studies discussed in this book and the terms in which I believe their structural properties should be discussed. The assumption which I have made about how these different types of society function are clearly contentious. There is here no precise theory of social change nor any sense that societies must necessarily pass through distinctive stages of development. What is central to my approach, however, is that societies are connected with one another, historically, economically, culturally and ideologically; it is a major task of sociological theorising to grasp that interrelatedness.

This, I feel, speaks in its favour, for the possibility is then opened up of a whole series of case studies using the same basic analytical language thereby widening the range of *contexts* in which educational processes common to all societies can be inspected. What now remains is to illustrate how the structural properties and developmental forms of the different types of society have moulded and penetrated their educational practice.

3 Education in Capitalist Societies Britain and the Federal Republic of Germany

The aim of this chapter is to examine aspects of the social structure of education in two capitalist societies, Britain and the Federal Republic of Germany. Its aim is to relate the structure and functioning of education in the two societies to the historically evolving forms of their social systems. The point I seek to underline is that the social order which systems of education are required to reproduce is undergoing constant change and that the conditions of reproduction vary according to different types of capitalist development.

The comparison of Britain and West Germany is a useful one in that, while both societies have evolved educational systems which directly reflect their systems of social stratification, their social formations have been sufficiently different for their educational systems to show marked contrasts. The differences between the two societies can be attributed to a number of factors. These include differences in educational tradition, and differences in their rate and type of development towards industrial capitalist society. Industrialisation in Germany, unlike Britain, was state directed and, for reasons which I shall explain, did not act as a solvent to a traditional social structure to the same degree that it had done in Britain. In short, it did not destroy the hegemony of traditional ruling groups and their social values. The *models of capitalist development* which prevail in the two societies were, therefore, very different.

Similarly, the German labour movement developed political reflexes which were, in contrast to the labour movement in Britain, revolutionary. As I shall also explain, the differences between the two labour movements affected the degree to which they were prepared to accomodate themselves to the political procedures of the capitalist state and to accept the need for a politics of social reform. In Germany the

Social Democrats, in a sense, stood outside the political system. In Britain they sought to work within it. The political form of popular *demands* for education were therefore, very different in the two societies. These differences still exert themselves in the last quarter of the twentieth century for while the labour movement in Britain has experienced a continuous and successful involvement in social reform, and in so doing learned to adjust its demands to the contingencies of practical politics, the German labour movement was shattered by the Nazis and very badly disorganised after the Second World War. At the point, therefore, where British socialism was at its height, socialism in Germany was in the doldrums unable to oppose a postwar reconstruction of German society which retained many of the traditional values of Germany from the Weimar period and even of the period before the First World War. The importance of this is that the political *constraints* on education in Germany have been different to those in Britain.

Educational differences between the two societies are also related to the rate and form of technological change which they experienced. Britain evolved an industrial division of labour over a much longer period and in traditional industries. Germany developed rapidly on the basis of investment in modern technology. I shall describe something of the economic history of this noting for the moment that, while the Germans were driven to develop in this way simply to survive in an industrial world, the need to do so brought with it a much more positive attitude to science and technology and to scientific and technological education than the one which prevailed in Britain. The idea of the educated amateur, the gentleman and scholar who, with his trained mind could turn himself to the most serious business of either industry or state—a tradition bred in the exclusive atmosphere of the English public schools and the ancient universities of Oxford and Cambridge—did not take root in the German industrial bourgeoisie in the same way as it did in Britain. The two societies, therefore, provided for their needs for qualified scientific and technological manpower in very different ways, the Germans favouring the growth of technical schools and the growth of technology teaching in the universities. In Britain such developments were haphazard, hesitant and insufficient. The *educational values* to which significant social groups have aspired and which have been institutionalised in the educational system itself, have therefore, been different in the two societies.

There are many other differences. German schools and universities in the late twentieth century are different in many subtle ways from their sister institutions in Britain and these differences reflect the unique differences of two cultures. But there are, too, some striking similarities which stem from the fact that both societies have social systems which are basically capitalist but also state-regulated to a high degree. In the case studies which follow I shall relate the changing features of their capitalist economies to changes in education.

In all capitalist societies there has been a massive expansion in educational opportunities for the mass of the people; education has evolved to meet the manpower needs of the modern economy and expenditure on education is a lion's share of all public expenditure. Indeed, the level of expenditure on education goes well beyond what is functionally necessary either to meet the manpower requirements of the economy or, for that matter, the needs of society for an efficient system of social control.

Two factors stand out in explanation of this growth. The first is economic change generating a demand for trained expertise at all levels of production. The second is to meet a growth in popular demand for education at all levels. Such changes themselves are related to changing conditions in capitalist production. As the capitalist economy developed in the industrial period it became even more necessary to increase the productivity of the means of production to meet international competition. But at the same time, capitalist development brought into existence social groups which made new demands upon education and pressed for these demands to be met. Bowles and Gintis (1977) have referred to this process as a contradictory one, claiming that in this type of society there is a tension between growth and stability. They refer to it as the 'contradiction between the accumulation of capital and the reproduction of the capitalist relations of production' (1977: 202). The idea is that as capitalism becomes more successful the conditions for its further success are eroded since workers gradually demand more rewards thus forcing further innovation on capitalists. As they say: 'The capitalist economy and the bicycle have this in common: forward motion is essential to stability' (1977: 202). They, of course, assume that these demands in the end cannot be met.

This is a rather complex argument and to evaluate it fully would involve a step-by-step analysis of the Marxist theory which lies behind it. For the moment it is sufficient to point out that, even assuming their analysis to be incorrect, Bowles and Gintis have detected a serious problem. As general education levels have increased, the real value of educational qualifications has decreased. This is the process of qualification inflation which many modern capitalist economies suffer from (Dore, 1976; OECD, 1977). In addition, the capacity of such economies to supply educational demand by providing new resources is declining. This is not simply an artefact of the current world recession. Even during the 1950s it was clear that the rate of growth in education expenditure could not be maintained. Even high rates of increase in expenditure would not have been able to meet the level of demand for education; as it was, even moderate increases did not succeed in extending educational opportunities to those capable of benefiting from it (Halsey, 1972).

What then emerges is a disjunction between popular demands for education, the level of actual education provision and the needs of the economy; it is a disjunction which calls for a new alignment between educational systems and changing social structures.

The issue which best illustrates this disjunction is that of inequality in educational opportunity in such societies. In all capitalist societies the gradient of educational opportunities parallels that of social and economic inequality. Furthermore, there is little clear evidence that this is only a temporary problem which further progress will overcome. During the 1960s it was felt by many that the expansion of opportunities in education would result in significant changes towards a more equal society. Indeed, such a broad strategy of social reform was adopted by all West European societies during this period (Husen, 1972). The results are at first sight quite encouraging, as Table 3.1 shows. All over Western Europe the likelihood of working-class children gaining access to higher education has increased.

Such figures are, however, extremely crude and give only the barest glimpse of the patterns of inequality and of opportunity in these

TABLE 3.1

Estimate of ratio of chances of access to higher education for children from professional or managerial back-grounds relative to children from working-class background

	1960	1967–71
France	83:1	18:1
Germany	41:1	15:1
Italy	36:1	18:1
Sweden	26:1	—
UK	8:1	2:1
USA	8:1	3:1

Source: OECD, cited by Levin (1976)

societies. Levin (1976) suggests, for example, that these figures conceal the persistence of the class gradients which they might at first sight seem to contradict. And his argument is that the increase in educational opportunities has come from an expansion of the less prestigious forms of higher education.

Some sociologists have suggested that educational inequality is an inevitable consequence of a form of society which always generates economic inequalities, the former deriving in some necessary way from the latter. This is, in fact, the argument of Boudon (1974) and Jencks *et al.* (1972). Marxist scholars have, of course, as I have already outlined in the Introduction, been convinced of this for a long time. Bowles and Gintis (1976) see a direct 'correspondence' between the inequalities of the educational system.

Certainly, in the cases of Britain and West Germany there is a great deal of social and educational inequality but its form differs in the two societies. What I seek to show is that while market-generated inequalities, with their subsequent expression in social stratification, are refracted through the educational system of both societies, it is done so in different ways, reflecting earlier forms of social stratification and patterns of economic change. What this means, of course, is that systems of education have to be seen as being, to some extent at least, immune from immediate social and economic demands, to possess a great deal of institutional inertia. Education, therefore, does not serve the needs of one society; it serves the needs of three different societies simultaneously, the society of the past, the present and of the future.

The anticipated social form of the future is however, remarkably similar for all capitalist societies. As production is increasingly organised into high technology multinational companies the need to supply the economy with skilled manpower increases and the demand for unskilled labour decreases. The educational realignments presupposed by this are enormous and some of the social stresses it will bring are already evident. The likelihood is that those children who, through their limited education, can expect only manual employement, will have to face a future with the constant threat of unemployment hanging over them. Educational certificates are therefore, likely to have a much higher economic value than ever before and the difference between those who succeed in education and those who do not will widen. This, of course, need not happen, but it is significant that, in contrast to the 1960s, educational planners in western societies are much more concerned with the relationship of education to work, particularly for working-class youth and those without educational qualifications and with questions of recurrent education and of devising curricula which do not track people too early into a limited range of occupational specialisation (see, for example, OECD, 1977).

In Britain and in Germany three questions keep pressing through. Can greater equality of educational opportunity be achieved within the limits of existing resources and attitudes? Can the educational systems of the two societies serve the needs of a changing economy more efficiently? Finally, can education be made more relevant to the life experience and future prospects of the children who receive it? Overlying all three questions is the more fundamental one: can significant changes in education be brought about without a fundamental transformation in the social structure of modern society itself?

BRITAIN

The hereditary curse upon English education is its organisation upon lines of social class (Tawney, 1964: 142).

The combined impact in Britain on the 1970s of inflation, cutbacks in public expenditure, a drop in the birthrate and the failure of the social democratic left to accord education a high political priority, has exposed the problems of equality, efficiency and relevance in education in a particularly stark way. These issues in their British guise have their roots deep in the history of education and are part of the social organisation of British society itself. But these longstanding issues are now more starkly defined, because the scope for overcoming the many smaller problems which each of them signifies is now drastically reduced.

The broad strategies of growth in education and of the development of the common secondary school which were the solutions of the 1960s can be seen in retrospect as policies born of affluence. Further increases in educational expenditure and in the growth of opportunities—particularly in higher education—of the sort achieved in the 1960s would be inconsistent with economic stability even, perhaps, of political stability. It would be difficult to convince an electorate which has been encouraged to think of itself as overtaxed and which has suffered a decrease in real personal incomes that further taxation was necessary to finance the education service. The results of growth in education and of comprehensive reform are not so acceptable that further growth would be welcomed. In this respect the fragile consensus of the 1960s has now evaporated; the 'left' argue that educational reform in the 'liberal' mould has not been successful (Halsey, 1972). The 'right' argue it has gone too far and that its results have been damaging. Education in Britain, at least for the remainder of the 1970s and for the first half of the 1980s, faces a future of austerity.

In October 1976 Prime Minister James Callaghan speaking at Ruskin College, Oxford, initiated a 'great debate' about education and this was followed by a Government Green Paper illustrating ways in which the education service could be brought more closely into line with the needs of children and of industry (HMSO, 1977). In the late autumn of 1977 a departmental committee report, the so-called Taylor Report, was published setting out guidelines for the management of schools to broaden the base of community involvement in the running of the schools to ensure that they are accountable to a broader range of community interests (DES, 1977).

Another government agency, the Manpower Services Commission, is actively taking steps to manage the process of transferring children from school to work to improve the prospects of all young people in the labour market (Manpower Services Commission, 1977). The proposals of the MSC in such areas as work experience programmes, job creation programmes and careers advice are based on a recognition that high levels of youth unemployment are to be a feature of the British economy at least until the early 1980s and that the final years of schooling are currently not planned to take this fact into account. Finally, the increasingly powerful House of Commons Expenditure Committee reported in 1977 on the attainments of the school-leaver that:

> Rapid developments in our more complex technological society have produced the demand for educated and skilled manpower, and we do not yet appear to have mastered the art of adequately preparing sufficient numbers of school leavers to make a flying start in such a career (1977: XXIV).

Perhaps we are too close to these events to comprehend them fully but they do signal a growing awareness that the educational system of modern Britain requires yet further changes to bring it into line with both changing social expectations for education and changing industrial demands for different types of workers. This is quite apart from some of the traditional defects of education in Britain which cry out to be changed, such as its role in reproducing social inequalities and the attitudes of mistrust and incomprehension which accompany them.

Until such changes are effected the schools will have to cope, perhaps less successfully as resources decline, with a great deal of pupil indifference, low morale among teachers, dissatisfied parents, political ambiguity about education policy and increased demands from all quarters that in many mutually inconsistent ways, schools should simply be better.

What I seek to show is that these complex issues reflect different conceptions of what education ought to mean in a modern industrial society and that these conceptions have their roots in an historical evolving class system. It is only against that background that the present malaise in British education can be understood, and it is only when that system changes that many of the issues briefly touched on above will be resolved.

In what follows I shall give an account of the development of state education in Britain, relating it to changes in models of development, themselves the outcomes of struggles among social classes. The theme is inequality. What the account shows is that, despite considerable change, R. H. Tawney's remark about inequality, made in 1931 and looking back to the nineteenth century, still holds true for Britain for the past forty years: 'Institutions which have died as creeds sometimes continue nevertheless, to survive as habits' (1964: 34).

EDUCATION AND INDUSTRIALISATION IN BRITAIN

The class character of British education is not simply a product of modern times. It can be traced much further back to the seventeenth and eighteenth centuries. But for my purpose the significant developments occurred after the turn of the eighteenth century and throughout the nineteenth century. It is during this period that the pace of industrial capitalist development accelerated and Britain became the most modern society in the world laying the industrial base for a far-flung colonial empire and showing the rest of the world an image of its own future. In any case, it was only during the nineteenth century, as Laqueur has stressed that a 'rationalised, disciplined, highly structured, profession-ally staffed, and essentially public organisation which is the modern school came into being' (1977: 193).

Many factors made the development of capitalist society in Britain possible. They include the fact that Britain did not have a large subsistence peasantry to hold industrialisation back (Hobsbawm, 1968). There was a growing population. By the middle of the eighteenth century Britain had come to dominate international trade so there was a good market for British exports. And finally, successive British governments actively encouraged industrial and commercial development bending foreign policy and military strategy precisely to this end. The role of education in speeding up this process is, therefore, difficult to assess in any quantitative sense. In any case, as I have already indicated, the industrial revolution in Britain did not depend upon complex technical changes (see Chapter 1). Educational change was not, therefore, a major requirement for technical change in industry to occur.

The importance of education lay more in the fashioning of an industrial labour force willing to subject itself to the disciplines of factory production *in the context of a particular form of society, industrial capitalism* (see Flynn, 1967; Johnson, 1976a, 1976b). And, in the light of recent research by Johnson (1976a, 1976b 1970), Colls (1976), and Laqueur (1977), it is essential to note that the growth of a state system of education is only one side of the equation. The state and, earlier in the nineteenth century, the voluntary bodies and churches had *supplied* various forms of mass education. But working people themselves in the period before 1850 had both *demanded* education and, through the ramshackle network of dame schools and private schools, had moved a long way in supplying their own educational needs according to their own conceptions of a proper education.

The supply side of the equation is much more easily documented, however. From its origins in the charity school and Sunday school movements in the eighteenth century the dominant conception of mass education was based on the themes of social control and industrial discipline and the division of society into mutually exclusive class groups whose boundaries were not to be crossed. Flynn has argued (1967: 14) that the charity and Sunday schools of the late eighteenth century 'were the principal channels through which the middle and upper classes sought to impose their social ideas upon the working class'. And G. M. Trevelyan, the great social historian, concurs with another historian that the charity schools applied what Defoe termed 'the great law of subordination' (1944: 368).

The subordination of the lower orders had several aims in view—political control, the suppression of crime and drunkenness, the propagation of Christian morality—but above all others was that of fitting people securely into their 'station of life' (Flynn, 1967), which for the lower orders was a life of industry and toil. The *Gentleman's Magazine* of the 1790s pressed the view that 'Industry is the great principle of duty that ought to be inculcated on the lowest class of people' (Flynn, 1967: 17). In their prayers children were to ask God to 'grant me industry'. And the schoolbooks of the period were saturated with moral injunctions to sobriety and submissiveness. One of the more well-known schoolbook writers of the period, Mrs S. Trimmer, defined a good servant in the following way:

> The duty of a servant is to be obedient, diligent, sober, just, honest, frugal, orderly in his behaviour, submissive and respectful towards his master and mistress, and kind to his fellow servants; he must also be contented in his station . . . (Goldstrom, 1972: 25).

The gradual extension of schooling to the masses was not something unequivocally welcomed. Some considered education, even by the end of the eighteenth century, to have gone too far. Bernard Mandeville satirised this viewpoint when he wrote in 1772:

> . . . going to school, in comparison with working is idleness, and the longer boys continue in this easy state of life, the more unfit they will be when grown up for downright labour, both as to strength and to inclination (Middleton and Weitzman, 1976: 27).

And some Tory high churchmen felt that mass education would subvert proper authority and make workers unfit for their occupational destinies. John Weyland wrote in 1808 of the second possibility: 'every step in the scale of society is already full, the temporal condition of the lower orders cannot be exalted but at the expense of the higher' (C. F. Kaestle, 1977: 36). But by the 1820s this kind of opposition had mostly petered out. By the 1820s the monitorial schools under the guidance of principles formulated by Joseph Lancaster and Andrew Bell had developed extensively and the conception of mass elementary education which they embodied set the pattern for later developments. Richard Johnson argues that the monitorial school can be recognised as 'prefiguring the essence of the mass school' and that its central concern was with the morality of the lower orders and their 'obstinately ungovernable behaviour' (1976a: 49).

Another historian has said of this form of schooling:

> It was the factory put into an educational setting. Every characteristic was there; minute division of labour . . . a complicated system of incentives to good work; an impersonal system of inspection and finally an attention to cost-efficiency and the economic use of plant which was carried to far greater lengths than even its most modern advocates would recommend (Wardle, 1976: 87).

There was no concern here with social mobility or personal social advancement through education. Teaching in such schools was itself mechanical and heavily based upon rote learning and drills admitting little room for the interests or creativity of the child. Instead there was the conviction, pervasive among Victorian social commentators, that through discipline, obedience, frugality and thrift, the life of the lower orders would improve and that as industrial progress itself was achieved general living standards of all the people would be raised.

This is the theme of the essential benevolence of modern industrial society. Such themes were expressed strongly by those early Victorians like Dr Kay-Shuttleworth who were most actively involved in developing a system of schools. Kay-Shuttleworth put it succinctly himself when he wrote: 'A system, which promotes the advance of civilization, and diffuses it over the world . . . cannot be inconsistent with the happiness of the great mass of the people' (Johnson, 1970: 101).

The organised provision of education in the first part of the nineteenth century (the state itself made its first financial allocation in 1833) can thus be seen to flow from several motives. But it represented also something of a pre-emptive strike at independently organised working-class education. Johnson argues, for instance, that by the early 1840s there was what he calls, following the Italian Marxist, Antonio Gramsci, a 'crisis of hegemony' (1976a: 50). This is a crisis of control, an unresolved state in which it is no longer clear which group will achieve intellectual dominance. In a later article Johnson indicates something of the tenor of working-class radical demands for education with a quotation from the *Poor Man's Guardian*, the radical Chartist newspaper which compared knowledge to manure:

> If manure be suffered to lie in idle heaps, it breeds stink and vermin. If properly diffused it vivifies and fertilizes. The same is true of capital and of knowledge. A monopoly of either breeds filth and abomination. A proper diffusion of them fills a country with joy and abundance (Johnson, 1976b: 22).

Such arguments are not compatible with the standard education diet of the early Victorian common school and there is growing evidence that such rhetoric was not simply confined to the theoreticians but that, in an inarticulate way, it was believed in by working people themselves, their beliefs being reflected in their choices among different schools for their children. Laqueur (1977) has emphasised the essential selectivity of working-class demand for education noting that publicly provided schools were held in much suspicion and were, in any case, tainted by the hateful smell of charity. He quotes a *Manchester Guardian* report of 1849 in which state interference in schools was condemned because it would lead to higher taxes 'which, like all taxes, would be wrung from the working man' (1977: 200). And he makes further reference to a study of education in London in which it was claimed that East Londoners resisted school board officers as if they were the advanced legions of an invading army (1977: 200).

By 1870, however, whatever resistance there was had been overcome. Successive Factory Acts limiting the employment of young children were followed by increases in state expenditure on education. In 1853 a Science and Art department of the Board of Trade was set up to act as a central co-ordinating body for education. In 1858 the Education Department was set up. By 1861 the Newcastle Commission noted that one in seven children were attending schools of one sort or another (Middleton and Weitzman, 1976: 43). In 1862 the notorious system of allocating funds to schools—the system of payments by results was implemented. The system was, however, uneven in both its funding and its coverage and in many of the industrial towns the schools were in a very depressed state indeed and badly attended.

Administrative change, an increasing school population, the growth of a teaching labour force, an extension of the franchise, widespread concern at the quality of education in Britain—a concern fuelled by the growing awareness of German superiority in technology, with the poor quality of the army following the Indian Mutiny and the Crimean war and the awesome successes of the Prussian military machine in the Austro-Prussian war of 1866—all combined to force through the Forster Education Act of 1870 (see Middleton and Weitzman, 1976). This Act, following the principles of local administration which evolved with the poor law, set up a national network of school boards to provide universal primary education. It was the legal framework of public elementary education until 1902. Robert Lowe's famous comment following the 1867 Reform Act which gave the vote to urban workers that, 'Now we must educate our masters' merely emphasises a continuing theme in the story of elementary education for the working classes in Victorian England, the theme of social control.

But by the last quarter of the century an organised working class was itself to inject a new dynamic into education politics—a demand for secondary education opportunities. In the language of Bowles and Gintis (1976) it is during this period, at least so far as education is concerned, that the dilemma of accumulation and reproduction begins to exert itself in a significant way. A mature working class, organised into Trades Unions, expanding with the addition of Irish immigrants, those evacuated by the Highland Clearances, by immigration from the continent of Europe and, more pertinently, reproducing itself at a faster rate than the middle classes, pressed their demands for a better system of schools than the state had been so far willing to concede.

For the middle and upper classes of Britain education during the Victorian period had a different form and a different rationale. For the middle classes and aristocracy it took three main forms. The first was attendance at public or endowed grammar schools. Until the 1850s private tuition was of equal importance in the home but this became increasingly expensive. Finally, there evolved a network of private schools of varying quality. From the 1850s onwards, however, the status of the public schools increased—an improvement often attributed to the reforms at Rugby school initiated by Dr Arnold. During the mid-Victorian period middle-class demand for a good general, classically based education to fit their children for careers in the army, the civil service, and for service in the Empire increased. Haileybury school, for instance, was founded to train boys for service in India. The status of these schools increased in the eyes of a growing commercial and industrial middle class because they were patronised by the aristocracy and, alongside the grammar schools which emerged later in the century, they increasingly offered examinations which led to a university education. These schools, with the legal status of independent foundations and therefore beyond the control of the state, have played a unique role in modern British society.

They have educated a very high proportion of British statesmen and politicians. When Baldwin formed his first cabinet in 1923 he determined to have a cabinet of which Harrow—his old school—would be proud (see Guttsman, 1963). They have supplied the greatest proportion of senior civil servants and still continue to do so (Halsey, 1971). Their curriculum, which throughout the nineteenth century placed greatest value on an all round classical education, lay at the root of the stilted development of science and technology teaching in Britain.

This does not mean that the education they offered was in some sense technically useless. The opposite, in fact, was true. As J. A. Mangan has pointed out, the 'essential attractiveness' of such schools was that 'they offered their own kind of technical training which was available nowhere else—a training in the style of a traditional, leisured elite rather than the skills of an industrial society' (1975: 154).

Other aspects of their curriculum filtered through to the growth of state secondary schools after the turn of the century and arguably still exert an influence on secondary education. These include the prefect system, the notion of a school *esprit de corps*, athleticism, manliness, the school uniform, the morning assembly with its heavy overlay of religious piety. Above all else, however, is the sense which such schools bred that somehow their pupils were an elite, destined for the leadership of other men and for important positions in the state (see Simon and Bradley, 1975). Their exclusiveness and elitism, guaranteed by high fees, family nepotism and even by ways of pronouncing English—the clipped intonation and distinctive vowel sounds of English upper-class speech (once described by Dylan Thomas as speaking as though the Elgin marbles were in the mouth) is an enduring sign of class membership which still encourages the upwardly mobile to farcical and never-quite-successful imitations—is the paradigm for all educational elitism in Britain. Such an education was, however, costly and by the 1870s middle-class incomes were not so high that it could be easily met.

G. M. Trevelyan notes that the search for such an education, and especially for the fees to pay for it, was one of the principal factors acting to reduce middle-class fertility at the end of the nineteenth century and the education of their sons was one of their deepest anxieties. Here, of course, lies the importance of what Bourdieu and Passeron call 'cultural capital' (1977). As the opportunities to gain access to the professions and civil service depended increasingly on education the most important legacy to bequeath to children was an ability, carefully nurtured in childhood, to succeed at school.

The great gap in this system, so far as the economic needs of the nation were concerned was, of course, technical education. And the failure of technical education to develop here as successfully as it did, say, in Germany is a salutary reminder that systems of education are not simply a response to economic requirements. Had this been so Britain would have developed a much more systematic system of industrial training both in science and technology and in the practical instruction of artisans.

From the 1880s onwards the provision of various forms of technical education increased. City and Guilds courses were extended into a wider range of subjects. The London Polytechnics began to offer trade courses. The Royal Commission on Scientific Instruction in 1884 had urged the development of more effective science education in Britain. The Commission heard a great deal of evidence that better-educated artisans had fewer accidents and produced more efficiently (Musgrave, 1967). The Technical Commission had also linked better technical education to the need to extend elementary education to higher levels. This particular suggestion both reflected a growing level of demand for, and of provision among some school boards, of so-called 'higher grade schools' which, historically, represent the first major step both towards the ordinary secondary school and secondary education for the working classes.

The higher grade schools represented the educational aspirations of the skilled working class but they were also perceived, certainly by the Royal Commission of 1884, as the recruiting ground for better-educated foremen and managers. Industrial needs, increasing through the threat of German competition, thus dovetailed with working-class aspirations for social mobility. But the secondary schools and public schools still clung to a liberal curriculum and many British firms, not being based on science and technology as a means of increasing productivity, still continued to prefer craft-trained artisans for the factory floor and public school graduates and relatives for the manager's office (Cotgrove, 1958).

The higher grade schools had, however, a short history. What may well have been an institution upon which to base a common system of secondary education was stifled in its growth by a court case brought against the London School Board by its District Auditor, Mr Cockerton, charging the Board with the illegal application of rate revenues to higher education when they were only properly empowered to provide elementary schools. By this legal gambit the higher elementary school movement was, in the opinion of Middleton and Weitzmann 'sacrificed to prevent it competing with the traditional grammar schools' (1976: 99).

By 1900 the class contours of education had been very sharply drawn. A system had been established which reflected directly the social and religious divisions of British society and which set the horizons both of social advance and intellectual awareness of the different social classes. The divisions of this society between the rich and the poor are too well known to dwell on. Sufficient to note that, through their forays into what General Booth of the Salvation Army called 'darkest England', the late Victorian social reformers revealed vast reservoirs of unrelieved poverty and squalor, of slum living conditions and demoralisation. Set against what is now known about the social determinants of educability and the importance of a secure material environment and nourishment for any learning to take place one can only speculate about the benefit of those barrack-like board schools for the poor and often reluctant children who attended them. One small fact indicates the enormity of the gulf between the classes. In the 1870s children of the upper and middle classes at the age of eleven were on average five inches taller than children of workers (Hobsbawn, 1969: 164).

Britain entered the twentieth century, therefore, with an education system which was built very much on early nineteenth century achievements and class alliances, and which was already not in keeping with the technical needs of modern capitalist production or with growing working-class demands for better opportunities. Its weaknesses were, however, much more glaringly exposed by military failure overseas, than by either social protest or social research—particularly in South Africa where a British army could not quickly bring rebel Boer farmers to heel. Growing German industrial competition was the solvent of educational complacency. Both facts together created a new climate of opinion from which the 1902 Education Act was fashioned (see van der Eyken, 1973).

EDUCATION IN THE TWENTIETH CENTURY: THE INTERWAR YEARS

If the class character of British education in late Victorian England is best emphasised through an account of its dual structure and stilted curricula the theme for the first half of the twentieth century must be its extremes of wealth and poverty. And if the overlying political problem of the late nineteenth century was the conflict between collectivism and individualism the problem for the twentieth century is the precise form collectivism should take.

The period from after the First World War until the Education Act of 1944 is dominated by the growth of secondary grammar schools and a massive failure to improve the quality of elementary schools. Educational development for the mass of the people was during this period severely handicapped by the meanness of successive governments and by the inability of local authorities to improve schools from their own resources.

In 1902 an Education Act was passed which gave over effective control of schools, both state and voluntary, to elected local authorities. It gave local authorities the power to develop appropriate forms of higher elementary and secondary education in their area. In 1906 an alliance of Liberals and Labour MPs passed a Bill to allow local authorities to provide free school meals. In 1907 new regulations were issued from the Board of Education. Grants were given to secondary schools which offered twenty-five per cent of their places to children from elementary schools.

Both events are of great significance. The first, as Middleton and Weitzman point out (1976: 120), illustrates a difference among working-class people themselves. The Labour Party, representing at this point the unskilled working class, pressed for the alleviation of hardship, thirteen per cent of London children being at this point in a state of semi-starvation. The skilled workers, on the other hand, the labour aristocrats—described by Middleton and Weitzman as 'ignorant and bigoted . . . with Billycock hats and heavy watch chains' (1976: 117)—wanted secondary education. The 1907 Regulations appeased the latter and in so doing focused the Labour Party's attention onto the provision of secondary education and the longer-term goal of equal opportunity (Barker, 1972). In Barker's analysis this period is particularly significant in the history of the Labour Party for the party's commitment to the idea of equality of opportunity and its neglect over a much longer subsequent period of questions concerning the content of education:

The goals and ethos of the existing schools were seldom criticised; the nature and quality of the instruction given to children was accepted without question. What mattered was the accessibility of this instruction and hence the shape and size of the educational structure (1972: 136).

Barker's point, of course, is that the curriculum and the structure was class-loaded and had been so for years. The validity of this general argument is unquestionable. The Elementary Code which governed the curriculum presupposed a rigid division between elementary and secondary education. It reflected a Whig view of history and society—the history syllabus, for example was to comprise 'a geneal knowledge of the great persons and events in English history and of the growth of the British Empire' (van der Eyken, 1973: 96). And the young Labour Party itself, while offering a general approval of collectivism and social reform, remained committed to an evolutionary parliamentarianism—'The essential demand was for fairness rather than for revolution or reconstruction' (Barker, 1972: 6). In this respect it differed greatly from its sister party in Germany which expressed its political hopes in strictly Marxist terms.

The dual system with a limited though extending 'ladder of oppor tunity' persisted through the First World War and during this time, through participation in the wartime coalition, the Labour Party's determination to seek reform within existiig political structures was strengthened.

In the period from 1914 to 1921 the proportion of elementary school children staying on to a secondary school education increased from fifty-six to ninety-seven per thousand (Wardle, 1976: 132). In 1918 the House of Commons passed the Fisher Education Act which, in the face of much opposition from industry, local authorities and some religious bodies, raised the school leaving age to fourteen, abolished part-time education, encouraged a widening in the scope of the elementary school curriculum and urged the provision of day continuation schools for those over fourteen.

Financial restrictions in the 1920s meant that this act was hardly implemented but cutbacks in expenditure are never simply dictated by economic emergencies; they also reflect dominant political attitudes and priorities. In the 1920s there was still a very powerful body of conservative opinion that further extensions of secondary education to the working people were unjustified. In the debate following H. A. L. Fisher's Education Bill in 1917, Lieutenant-Commander J. C. Wedgewood, a Conservative MP tried to relate the raising of the school-leaving age to the reduction of the incomes of the working class: 'If you curtail the wage earning power of these children you are doing serious injury to the working classes as a whole' (van der Eyken, 1973: 236). Working-class children were in this man's view destined to early work. And he showed a deep suspicion of the scholarship boy who might go on to university study. Such men, he stressed, would no longer be 'cabbages'. 'All this has developed in these men the theory of the anarchist, the hatred of the social injustice under which we live to-day' (1973: 237). In the most objectionable part of his speech he stressed the point that, 'If you make the cattle think they will become dangerous . . .'(1973: 237).

Even as late as 1929 Sir Cyril Norwood felt it necessary to remind the House that education had prevented:

Bolshevism, Communism, and theories of revolt from obtaining any real hold upon the people of this country. I hope that those who attribute the scarcity of domestic servants to the unreasonable institution of elementary education, by which they are made to pay for the education of other people's children, will lay in this other scale this other service, which has made of Bolshevism only a bogy which sits by their pillows and frightens them in the night (quoted by Glass, 1975: 199).

In such an atmosphere it would have been, in any case, difficult to press successfully for further extensions of secondary education and being forced back through a growing economic crisis to attend to more immediate matters such as housing and employment the Labour Party did not question the basic assumptions of the system. Their policy from 1922 onwards—expressed in the document *Secondary Education for All*—was for an extension of the free place system and to endorse the recommendations of the Hadow report of 1926 to separate elementary and secondary education at the age of eleven and then to offer different types of schools (secondary modern schools for the less able, and grammar schools for brighter children) on the principle of 'selection by differentiation' rather than 'selection by elimination' (Barker, 1972: 57).

The year 1931, above all others, symbolises the sorry state both of the British economy in the interwar period and the low priority which politically dominant groups placed on education. The economic crisis of that year—so severe that some people, of which Harold Macmillan (Conservative MP and later Prime Minister) was one, felt that 'the structure of capitalist society in its old form had broken down . . . something like a revolutionary situation had developed' (quoted in Branson and Heinemann, 1971: 6)—prompted immediate cutbacks in educational expenditure and, slightly later, a partial modification of the free place system which had been such a shibboleth of Labour politics. There was a reduction of fifteen per cent in teachers' salaries; Exchequer grants to local authorities were reduced. To hold expenditure levels local authorities were forced into the impossible trap of increasing rates although, of course, this was not done. School-building schemes were put back and the school-leaving age was not increased until after the Second World War. R. H. Tawney's reaction to all of this is worth recording for he linked the cuts directly to the class system (1964: 143):

> If the elementary school boy is no longer taught by his masters that the world has been divided by Providence into the rich, who are the ends of civilization, and the poor, who are its instruments, he is frequently taught a not very different lesson by the character of the surroundings which his countrymen provide for him.
> He is taught it by mean, and in some cases unhealthy buildings . . . by persistent understaffing . . . by his premature plunge into wage-earning employment . . . He is taught it by recurrent gusts of educational economy, with their ostentatious insistence that it is his happiness and his welfare which, when the ship is labouring, are the superfluity to be jettisoned.

Such cuts, among other factors, not only limited the educational life-chances of working-class children in comparison to children from the middle and upper classes, they also confirmed differences among different parts of the country and some of the older industrial areas—the so-called depressed areas—suffered badly in not being able to improve the quality of their education. By the late 1930s for example, industrial Tyneside still taught forty-five per cent of its elementary school pupils in classes with more than forty pupils. The figure for the mining county of Durham was thirty-four per cent, and for England and Wales as a whole thirty per cent (Goodfellow, 1941). The local tax base of some of the smaller industrial authorities was such that they could never hope to recover central government expenditure cuts from their own resources. In this way the financial mechanism acted directly on educational life-chances and this at a time when, as Paul Henderson has pointed out (1976), local education authorities were using intelligence tests to identify bright children and distinguish them from the rest on criteria which were thought to be scientifically valid. The significance of this point is, that intelligence testing in the 1920s and 1930s gave a precise meaning to what parents and teachers alike understood as ability in education and served to justify the view that those who managed to gain access to the limited secondary school places available were in some way different from their schoolmates. In retrospect it is now clear that this was no more than a clever rationing device but its ideological importance then as now was overwhelming. It allowed for the 'cooling-out' of able working-class children on ostensibly fair grounds; it converted social hierarchies into academic hierarchies while not appearing to do so and it lent support to the educational aspirations of the skilled working class for an elitist secondary education which still exerts a retarding influence on the growth of genuine secondary schools for all.

For those who could pay for the private education of their children the intelligence test at the age of eleven held out no terror. The public schools were still the route to universities. Even as late as 1938 only one out of two hundred and fifty elementary school children could get to university and the public schools supplied fifty-four per cent of undergraduates (Middleton and Weitzman, 1976: 197). Britain entered the Second World War with a population still rigidly stratified along social class lines and the war itself did little to change it.

One of the most significant effects of the Second World War was the widespread acceptance of the idea that the state should intervene positively to manage the economy in a reformed capitalist society. Angus Calder may be right in his view that, contrary to those who saw the war as giving birth to a new kind of society, 'the effect of war was not to sweep society on a new course, but to hasten its progress along old grooves' and to accelerate the emergence of a new 'capitalism of paternalistic corporations meshed with state bureaucracy' (1971: 22). But what is certain is that the possibility of governments returning to the economic policies of the 1930s had been finally pre-empted. The cost to the state of 'total war' was a long-term obligation to reward the population with better social welfare and greater opportunities for a better standard of living (see Addison, 1975).

Britain faced a postwar future than would be fashioned by a model of development which was markedly collectivist and which implied a permanent state involvement in the economy and the building of a comprehensive 'welfare state'. The Education Act of 1944, based on the 1943 White Paper on Educational Reconstruction was an essential component of these postwar aspirations. It laid the basis for a system of free secondary education for all and held out the promise of equality of opportunity in education irrespective of a child's social background.

In this respect the Act represents the final achievement of a half-century of agitation by the labour movement. But as an egalitarian measure it had several defects. Following on the recommendations of the Spens Report of 1938 and The Norwood Report of 1943 (Board of Education 1938, 1943) the Act together with instructions to local education authorities which followed it, effectively stopped the growth of an ordinary secondary school—referred to usually at the time as a multilateral school and now as a comprehensive school—and lent support to a tripartite system of schools based on the very mistaken view that there were three different types of children.

The Norwood Report of 1943, in fact, had identified three different types of children requiring three different types of school. There were pupils who were said to be 'interested in learning for its own sake', 'sensitive to language as expression of thought', 'commonly associated with the grammar school' and who 'have entered the learned professions or have taken up higher administrative or business posts' (Van der Eyken, 1973: 373–4).

The technically minded pupil was held to have 'an uncanny insight into the intracacies of mechanism whereas the subtleties of language construction are too delicate for him'. What appeals to this child most, the report argued, was the control of material things (van der Eyken, 1973: 374). Finally, in a Platonic sequence downwards from the men of gold to the men of silver come the men of bronze. Here is the child who 'deals more easily with concrete things . . . he finds little attraction in the past . . . interested only in the moment . . . abstractions mean little to him . . . (who) . . . may not be good with his hands or sensitive to music or art' (Van der Eyken, 1973: 375). The committee then went on to specify three different types of curriculum in three different types of school—grammar schools, secondary schools and secondary technical schools.

This division in English education reflects, of course, the social divisions of English society and the lifestyles, attitudes and pre-occupations of the different social strata. But these are not the malevolent distinctions of an elite. As Barker has shown they repre-sented the outlook of one powerful section of the Labour Party which, since the 1907 regulations, had associated secondary schools, not with a common school for all, but with social mobility. Equality of opportunity in this tradition is far more important than equality. Indeed, many Labour-controlled local authorities after the war moved rapidly in the development of grammar schools. In so doing they became the improbable heirs to an educational tradition which extended back to Dr Arnold and his early nineteenth-century reforms of the public schools. The new framework of education was the scaffold for old social formations, and during the 1950s there was a growing recognition of this.

During the 1950s it became clear that many children were leaving the selective secondary schools before completing the full course and many of these early leavers were working-class children (Central Advisory Council for Education, 1954). The *Early Leaving* Report of 1954 was quite explicit that this was a wastage of ability. There was, too, a growing realisation that the division of schools into grammar schools and secondary modern schools was inconsistent with the idea that all secondary schools should have parity of esteem (Banks, 1955). As Banks argued, the status of schools depended upon the status of the occupations for which they typically prepared children. It was, there-fore, inevitable that the secondary modern schools would bear the mark of Cain as elementary schools preparing children for manual work. In any case, as Taylor was later to point out, the secondary modern schools just did not make the same call on educational resources as the grammar schools; grammar schools not only had a greater status, they also got more money (Taylor, 1963).

In the early 1960s further weaknesses in the educational system were identified. The Central Advisory Committee for Education Report (the Crowther Report) exposed several deficiencies in the educational provision for those aged fifteen to eighteen years (1959). Too many pupils, the report argued, left school without any prospect for further part-time education when it was clear that they required it. The report urged the immediate raising of the school-leaving age to sixteen years although this was not done until 1973, after several postponements.

In 1963 the Central Advisory Council for Education's Newsom Report gave a critical account of provision for the less able thirteen to sixteen-year-olds (HMSO, 1963). The report was guardedly optimistic about the success of the secondary modern school but showed that many of these schools, particularly in the big cities suffered badly from the handicaps of old buildings, high teacher turnover and often complacency and fatalism among teaching staff.

In 1963 the famous Robbins Report on higher education urged the immediate expansion of the university sector (HMSO, 1963). The rationale for this was the need to meet an anticipated growing demand for such education, a consequence of the immediate postwar baby boom and of changing industrial needs. The report, in retrospect, grossly underestimated the number of places that would be needed but what it did reveal in its massive statistical appendixes was a pool of untapped ability in education which could both benefit from a massive expansion in higher education and from which the country itself could expect enormous economic rewards.

Still in retrospect it seems also clear that the Robbins expansion of the university sector was a mistake. Universities were not capable either of coping with students' demands for higher education or relating their courses as directly to industrial needs as a changing occupational structure required. The growth of the binary system of higher education around the polytechnics from 1966 onwards is a recognition of this fact although it is not clear that the polytechnics have taken on the role which they were given. The high status value of the academic degree is eagerly sought in the polytechnics and while the unit cost of their students may be cheaper than that of a university student, their graduates are indistinguishable from one another.

This series of major reports revealed the old-fashioned structure of education in Britain. Typically, however, they did so without questioning some of the fundamental values and ends of education itself. What the committee of enquiry sought was, therefore, reform and modernisation rather than major structural change.

By 1965 sufficient sociological evidence had been amassed by such writers as J. W. B. Douglas (1964; 1968) to show that despite twenty years of growth the class gradient of educational opportunities in Britain was still inconsistent with social justice. The structure of differentiated school provision, social differences in values and attitudes to education and teaching methods aimed at distinguishing the bright from the dull rather than developing the strengths of all children, were shown to interact with one another to perpetuate social divisions in educational opportunity (see Byrne, Williamson and Fletcher, 1975).

In 1965 the Minister of Education, Anthony Crosland, issued a circular—circular 10/65—which required local authorities to submit plans for comprehensive reorganisation of secondary education. The aim was, of course, to achieve equality of provision for all children but with typical reluctance to challenge inequalities in a fundamental way, the private sector of public schools was left untouched and the autonomy of the local authority in matters of policy was not seriously challenged. The growth of comprehensive schools has, therefore, been patchy and although by the mid-1970s something like eighty per cent of secondary school children are taught in such schools there is considerable evidence of more subtle forms of educational differentiation taking place within the schools themselves (see Ford, 1969; Benn and Simon, 1972; Bellaby, 1977). Finally, although by no means exhaustively, yet another major enquiry, the Plowden Report (Central Advisory Council for Education, 1967), examined the state of primary school provision in England and Wales. In the midst of an otherwise sound system of innovating schools the report uncovered areas of special need and special deprivation in the inner cities. In such educational priority areas (EPAs) in comparison with the country as a whole, child mortality rates were higher, housing standards lower, health standards lower (the report noted the appearance of rickets in some parts of Glasgow) and the cumulative impact of this held back the intellectual development of children. The report insisted the schools had a role to play in combating these problems and recommended a policy of positive discrimination in their favour. But the report typically struck a cautious note:

> We propose a nationwide scheme for helping those schools and neighbourhoods which are most severely handicapped. . . . It must not be put into practice simply by robbing the more fortunate areas of all the opportunities for progress to which they have been looking

forward; it can only succeed if a larger share of the nation's resources is devoted to education (W. Van der Eyken, 1973: 484).

The report was successful. The Government accepted its recommendations and began to allocate funds to areas of special need and in the wake of the report several pieces of research and experiment sought to prove the value of positive discrimination (Halsey, 1971).

In a short space of just over ten years, therefore, every part of the educational system had been carefully inspected and found wanting and as the 1960s petered out and the ice-cold 1970s gripped the country in an economic vice, it became clearer that pragmatism and piecemeal changes are insufficient to meet the challenges of a new phase of economic history.

The changes and developments of educational policy in the 1960s—comprehensive schools, the expansion of higher education, positive discrimination for poor areas and an increase in the number of children taking examinations of various sorts—represent a continuation of certain trends, particularly that of meeting the educational aspirations of the organised, skilled working class. These developments did not question fundamentally the structures of the system itself and the values institutionalised in its curricula, teaching methods and aims. Nor was it ever doubted that the system could continue to grow in line with the economy itself. Even so, these very modest reforms had to be fought for through a thicket of political and educational opposition worried about standards, traditions, progressive education and money. The most articulate expression of this came with the publication of the so-called Black Papers (Cox and Dyson, 1969).

Such complacency is now dangerous. The British economy in the 1970s, and perhaps the 1980s too, will be characterised by a careful control on public expenditure, high levels of unemployment, particularly among young people and whatever manufacturing investment takes place will take place in industries which are not labour-intensive. In the fight for international competitiveness only high productivity industries can be successful.

Such developments have a direct bearing on the educational system. As the centre of society—to adopt Habermas's terms (1976)—which includes the organised working class, the middle classes and traditional elite groups, because of its political and economic clout, continues to enjoy reasonable expectation of a decent education and a reasonable standard of living, the costs are transferred to the periphery, to the unskilled, the unorganised, the poor and minority groups. These are the groups which are least likely to have children who will succeed at school. And such children are increasingly unlikely to find employment. the recent report of the Manpower Services Commission underlined this fact pointing to the long-term decline of unskilled employment in the economy with the effect that skilled jobs are now being taken by people who, even a few years ago, would never have dreamed of taking them.

> The impact of unemployment is most severe on those young people who have few or no qualifications. In comparison with the better qualified they suffer longer duration of unemployment, are more frequently unemployed and when employed tend to work in lower status jobs . . . Moreover when there is a high level of unemployment, people with poor qualifications encounter increased competition for jobs from those of higher ability and with better qualifications (1977: 17).

The sociology of this situation is bewildering. As the importance of cultural capital increases groups which already possess it will cultivate it anxiously, those without it might very well reject the system from which they can derive little real benefit. The result can be only further social polarisation of an increasingly intractable kind.

Bowles and Gintis have pointed out that, 'The economic and educational systems possess fairly distinct and independent internal dynamics of reproduction and development' (1977: 204). Educational systems do not change as rapidly as economic systems and because of this there is a possibility of what they call 'mismatch' arising between the two. They further argue that the mismatch is accommodated through one of two main processes. The first, indicating piecemeal adjustments where people adjust their individual hopes and aspirations to circumstances, they call 'pluralist accommodation'.

The second adjustment is a concrete political struggle in which competing social classes seek to achieve the ends openly and directly. They argue that the major phases of educational reform in the USA have followed in the wake of political struggles in which education was shaped to fit the needs of a changing system of capitalist production.

From this perspective Britain is clearly in a transitional phase. Whether the second process will supersede the first depends on how educational processes are understood. At the moment it is still possible to conceive of many of the educational problems discussed—equality, efficiency and relevance—as having educational solutions. But it is perhaps only a matter of time before these discussions recognise the full force of the fact that the problems with which they are concerned are those of a changing economy and of a new social formation struggling to be born.

THE FEDERAL REPUBLIC OF GERMANY

Educational discussion in the Federal Republic of Germany has been dominated since the mid-1960s by an overwhelming sense of crisis. Germans themselves speak freely of an education catastrophe (*Bildungskatastrophe*) (Pick, 1964). Views on the precise nature of Germany's educational problems vary considerably, but in the wide debates which have opened up, no area of the educational system has escaped critical treatment. The 1972 OECD report on Germany set out some of the principal issues of the debate in this way (1972: 55):

> In spirit and structure, schooling in Germany remains old-fashioned, as it does in several other European countries. In an age when secondary and higher education are being rapidly developed in the other advanced states, Germany has made do with a system that until now has effectively shut off some 90 % of the children from the possibility of entering university-level education; that experiences great difficulty in remodelling curricula to suit modern conditions; in which teachers appear to follow authoritarian models in their classroom behaviour; and that is bureaucratically administered; lacking essential minimum elements of public, teacher and student participation in decision-making.

The report of the Federal Government of Education (*Bildungsbericht, 1970*) in which the Federal Government set out what it would like to see in terms of educational reform was also extremely critical of the educational system. Having pointed out that 'it [the educational system] neither contributes to implementing the right education nor does it fulfil the demands of modernisation and democratisation'.

There is considerable disquiet too, about the character of the curriculum and organisation of schools. Ralf Dahrendorf has strongly expressed the view that German schools do little to discourage a rather inflexible adherence to the *status quo* in society. Indeed, he has argued (1967) that 'educational defeatism' and a 'fatalistic attitude' to human beings is one of the reasons for the high rates of dropout from German educational institutions. Dahrendorf has also argued elsewhere (1965) that German educational institutions have historically been deeply implicated in the development and transmission of non-liberal attitudes in German society. In this respect Dahrendorf's criticisms are similar to those made during the war by Karl Mannheim (1963).

Mannheim argued that the classical liberal curriculum with its respect for authority, disciplinary rigidity and hard individual effort— characteristics institutionalised in the classical gymnasium—reduced the 'mental resistance' of Germans to the appeals of Nazism. The case is clearly arguable, but current disquiet at the German educational system reflects itself in an intense concern with the relevance and meaning of the curriculum. As recently as May 1974 Katrin Fitzherbert castigated German primary schools for their authoritarianism and uniformity (1974: 311):

> What students of the German education system find most striking about the traditional primary classrooms is the 'seen one, seen 'em all' uniformity of the ritual and content . . . Their character has been the same for nearly a century.

And referring to the fears which some people in Germany have about liberalising tendencies on society as a whole, Katrin Fitzherbert writes (1974: 312):

> Although the frightened senior citizens will regard any liberalisation in primary schools as yet another step towards total collapse, I got the impression myself that stable Democracy in Germany is not safe until that Bastille of authoritarianism, the primary school classroom, has fallen.

The roots of the sense of crisis extend deeply into wider criticisms of the nature and development of West Germany itself. Indeed it is hardly surprising that the educational system crystallises many of these disagreements and that the issue of equality of opportunity in education (*chancengleicheit*) has become the focus of such discussions.

The organisation and control and content of education of schooling are a product of decisions taken from 1945 onwards to construct a democratic German State. But the education models adopted were drawn from Germany of the Weimar period and, indeed, of the Empire. It is hardly surprising therefore, that education has become a focus of strong political struggle particularly during the 1960s when, as Robin-sohn and Kuhlmann (1967) have put it 'two decades of non-reform' have accentuated weaknesses in an educational system already evident in 1949.

In what follows I shall take up some of these themes and relate them to the historical form of capitalist development in Germany. The problems of equality, efficiency and relevance can then be shown to take their unique German form because of the way in which different social groups in Germany developed. The special problems of the 1960s and 1970s can then be related to the claims which different social groups have been making upon education in the special economic circumstances of the postwar world. And the issue which has to be assessed is whether the so-called crisis of the system can be planned away through modernisation or whether its roots are so deep in the fabric of German society that much more radical solutions would be necessary to overcome it.

GERMAN INDUSTRIAL DEVELOPMENT

German industrialisation was, as Borchardt has put it, 'derived' rather than 'autonomous' (1973: 82). The importance of this lies not simply in the fact that Germany could borrow ideas from the British experience or that, since little capital was tied up in 'old' industries, industrialisation could proceed rapidly and successfully in new industries such as steel, chemicals and engineering. Rather it is that, occurring late, German industralisation followed the logic of a particular political economy, the political economy of backwardness (Gerschenkron, 1962). As Gerschenkron has analysed it, the speed, form and ideology of industrialisation are different in backward countries in comparison to the advanced countries. Germany for most of the nineteenth century was an economically backward country. Its industrialisation came late and when it came it was rapid, necessarily rapid. Unlike Britain, industrialisation in Germany was organised by the state itself, dominated by a traditional landed ruling elite of *Junkers* in co-operation with industrial and finance capital, itself controlled through the banking system (Gerschenkron, 1962). Under these conditions it was vital that, in order to face the industrial competition of the advanced countries, particularly Britain, the most modern forms of technology had to be employed as well as the most effective forms of control. In the German case this involved reaping the benefits of large-scale production and of cartelisation through the banking system (Gerschenkron, 1962: 15).

Two developments need to be specially underlined. The first is the growth of an alliance between German agriculture and German industry based on a protectionist tariff policy. This alliance of 'iron and rye' in the late 1870s 'meant a perpetuation of the feudal element in German society through preservation of the traditional economic basis of the Junkers' (Gerschenkron, 1966: 47). Golo Mann has referred to the same process noting that in the course of Germany's rapid industrialisation, the landowners 'refurbished their nobility with the glitter from coal and iron' (1974: 335). In Germany, therefore, industrialisation did not destroy the traditional aristocracy and its feudal attitudes. An economically declining class was therefore able to hold on to political power and the values to which that class adhered retained their credence into the twentieth century.

The second development is the rapid growth of an urban proletariat which, in the years before and immediately after the First World War was to become the most revolutionary working class in Europe. Rapid industrialisation and urbanisation provided many opportunities for speculative investment in non-agricultural housing to house this growing industrial proletariat (Borchardt, 1973). Golo Mann puts it very evocatively when he writes 'Vast suburbs grew up around the old streets, named after the battles of the Franco-German wars, but lived in by people who cared little about the glory of the fatherland' (1974: 333).

This was the group to which Lasalle's General German Workers' Association and Bebel's Social Democratic Workers' Party appealed. In 1875 these two groups combined to form the *Sozialistische Arbeiterpartei Deutschlands*—the Social Democrats. This was the main source of political education for German workers; its analysis was Marxist, it was, as Mann describes it (1974: 357), 'The negative force in the Kaiser's Reich . . . superbly organised . . . deeply rooted in the people . . . yet outside the real political game'.

Between these two groups stood a small, but growing industrial bourgeoisie which, since the revolutionary failure of 1848, sought its own improvement through industry and scientific education and a *Bildungsburgertum* (an academic bourgeoisie) of academics and state officials who saw themselves as being very different from the industrial bourgeoisie. Fritz Ringer has described this group as the 'mandarins' (1969). They were a group 'haunted' by the spectre of a 'soulless age', 'a kind of nobility of the educated', 'heroes and symbols of a broad and mildly esoteric culture' threatened by what they understood as the materialism of the modern age (1969: 6–16). They were the carriers of classical learning in Germany and their institutional base was in the university.

Each of these groups received a distinctive education and each played a distinctive political role in German society. In the relationship among these groups several writers have seen the roots of the authoritarianism and illiberalism which wrecked the Weimar Republic, provided such fertile ground for Adolf Hitler and which is perhaps not yet fully expunged from the Federal Republic itself (Grunberger, 1974; Grosser, 1974; Bracher, 1973).

The political economy of backwardness forced the state into mobilising industrial development but some of the seedbed conditions for its success existed in Germany before the 1860s, particularly in the field of education.

As early as 1817 Prussia had set up a distinct Ministry of Education with separate divisions for elementary and secondary education. At the beginning of the nineteenth century and following Prussia's defeat by Napoleon, a framework of elementary schools was set up (*Volksschulen*) with a military rationale, to create a disciplined population (Samuel and Thomas, 1948: 36). Secondary education in the form of the *Gymnasium* was also a product of this period, as was the University of Berlin. All of these reforms were directed by Wilhelm von Humbolt who conceived of secondary and higher education in broadly humanistic terms requiring a great stress on Latin, Greek and the study of the classics. In this respect, Humboldt's views can be traced back to the medieval synthesis of classical Aristotelian philosophy and Christian thought—the so-called Thomist synthesis with its stress on general learning (Rowlinson, 1974).

Behind such developments in the Prussian Ministry of Education, however, was the philosophical ghost of Hegel insistent that education should serve the higher goals of the state itself and not just the needs of the individual. Indeed, as early as the 1840s an English visitor to Germany said of secondary school students that they were 'too early taught to feel their responsibility to some other power than of their parents and teachers, and the natural and happy thoughtlessness of children gives way too soon to a careful consideration of future consequences' (Samuel and Thomas, 1948: 4).

These concerns with a general, disciplined, classical education were reflected in the *Abitur* examination which has been such an important part of German education since those who possess it have traditionally had the right of a university education.

From the 1840s onwards there developed, too, a number of intermediary secondary schools called *Realschulen*. Less prestigious than the *Gymnasium* they nonetheless met the growing educational demands of the German middle class, emphasising the natural sciences and the study of modern languages. These schools were officially recognised in school reforms of 1892 and 1901 but for much of the second half of the nineteenth century they were considered vulgar examples of an unwelcome modernism (Rowlinson, 1974; Ringer, 1969). Alongside the school system there developed a system of technical institutes and polytechnics to produce the technical labour for industrial development. By the end of the century they had acquired, as *Technische Hochschulen*, the status of universities. By the end of the century, too, there had developed a number of continuation schools which offered a two-year course for workers beyond the elementary school.

Two features of this system need to be noted. The first is that, as Musgrave has emphasised (1967: 67–8), German education contributed in a direct way to industrialisation.

Germany entered the steel age with an organised educational system whose whole aim suited industry whether one considers its demand for qualified manpower or for docile workers. The principles governing the system had been decided upon and a strong central administration, especially in Prussia, was working out the details of an agreed policy. The sound basic education given met the needs at each level of the labour force and allowed the development of advanced or further education.

The second is that this system was rigidly stratified along the lines of social class. The universities were at the top of the system closely connected with the state bureaucracy and recruiting their students from an elite stratum of society. In 1890 less than two in a thousand students came from a working-class background (Ringer, 1969: 41). The *Gymnasium* was at the base of the university.

The *Volksschulen* prepared people for practical duty in the factory and aimed further, at least in the late nineteenth century, to wean workers away from the doctrines of Social Democracy. As in Britain, workers organised into trades unions had begun to evolve their own forms of adult education (Musgrave, 1967: 109). The state responded by further emphasising the political role of elementary education. An Imperial Cabinet order of 1 May 1889 underlines this:

I cannot ignore the fact that at a time when the errors and false doctrine of Social Democracy are being disseminated with increasing zeal, it is the business of the school to make greater efforts to further the recognition of what is true, what is real, and what is possible in the world. It must exert itself to bring home the conviction to the young that the teachings of Social Democracy are not only at variance with Divine Commands and Christian morality, but are truly impracticable, and ruinous in their consequences to the individual and the community alike (Musgrave, 1967: 109).

Dominant groups in German society were not unanimous that the best instrument for achieving such docility was the school. Discussing a bill in the Brunswick Diet to introduce continuation schools, one deputy insisted:

> I do not see why a man who is destined to perform menial work should burden his brain with much knowledge. He is much happier if he is ignorant of all that nonsense. Things will not improve so long as this humanitarian balderdash persists. We shall not need continuation schools if teachers are not at long last permitted to use the whip. I must insist on my point of view, that God rules the world and the truncheon rules mankind (Samuel and Thomas, 1948: 6).

Nonetheless, despite the resistance of landowners, there was by 1914 a well-developed system of elementary, secondary, technical and higher education which was the envy of Europe, which consolidated class differences of attitude and outlook and which had played a positive role in the rapid growth of Germany's modern industry. It had done so by training people for particular positions in the division of labour. The system had, therefore, acquired very early the function of occupational selection which it still retains in modern Germany in the so-called *laufbahn* system, that is, the system which matches up jobs and particular types of education.

The dominant values of the system were elitist but the elite groups which they reflected were precapitalist groups in economic and political decline. The *Junkers* were afraid of democracy and the labour movement.

In the years immediately before 1914 the attitudes and values which fostered authoritarianism, illiberalism and a unique irrational nationalism, and which were to play such an important part in wrecking Weimar's delicate democracy, were quite firmly embedded in Germany's schools.

THE WEIMAR REPUBLIC AND THE THIRD REICH

The period following the First World War up to Hitler's suicide in a Berlin Bunker in 1945 is something of an interlude in the development of Germany's educational system. The Weimar Republic was, for its short life from 1918 to 1933, far too preoccupied with political and economic problems to attend to education. The Weimar Republic did, however, make limited efforts to overcome the class character of German education. Control of education was given over to the *Länder*. Article 146 of the constitution envisaged the development of a common elementary school with the possibility of students going on into secondary and higher education. This was a possibility which had never really existed in German education but it had little success in breaching the walls of class privilege. The Social Democrats pressed for seven years of common schooling, university education for all teachers and the abolition of religious instruction in school (Ringer, 1969). But many of these reforms met with the opposition of reactionary governments at *Land* level and the basic character of the system changed little.

The Nazis, however, achieved something of a revolution in education. Education was unequivocally co-ordinated (*gleichgeschaltet*) with the state itself. It was tightly controlled from Berlin. The schools were required to preach Nazi propaganda, to teach children, as a famous Nazi slogan had it, 'to think with their blood'. Teachers were required to join the Nazi Teacher Association (*Nationalsozialistische Lehrerbund*) and most did so willingly (Grunberger, 1974). The schools taught Nazi history, Nazi biology and Nazi geography. Children and youth were forced into Nazi youth organisations all of which emphasised the Aryan myth and military virtues (Becker, 1946). The Nazi 'co-ordination' of the universities met with little resistance. The Weimar Republic had failed completely to democratise the universities and the combination of traditional elitist values with academic unemployment served only to radicalise university students to the right. As Fritz Ringer put it, 'mandarin scholarship was overrun by National Socialism' (1969: 442).

The exodus of scholars and artists during this period impoverished German intellectual and cultural life. Heavy military expenditure, loss of personnel to the armed forces, the running down of secondary schools, all served to erode further the system of schools which developed with Weimar. Nazism forced German education into a ghastly distorted mould and the war left Germany in ruins. The Allies who ruled Germany in 1945 faced, therefore, a novel task: to build up a system of education which would serve the needs of a democratic state, something which had not previously existed on German soil.

POSTWAR DEVELOPMENTS

In comparison to other Western European societies Germany's problems of postwar educational reconstruction were very severe. While other European societies could get straight down to the business of postwar reform, Germany had to wait four years to be able to do so since between 1945 and 1949 political life was dominated by the Allied Control Commission's efforts at denazification. During this time neither the institutions, resources nor the will existed to push forward with reform in education. The notion of the historical legacy as an explanation of the current educational crisis is a compelling one since the fabric of German society had been destroyed in the war. But great care is needed in interpreting that legacy. It is quite false to believe that physical destruction and low resources are the problem; the latter, certainly, is a symptom rather than a cause. Alfred Grosser nonetheless gives some indication of the extent of the wreckage. Of Germany in 1945 he has this to say (1974: 57):

> The towns were in ruins. Of Frankfurt's 177,000 houses, only 44,000 still stood; in Nurenberg, scarcely one house in ten was undamaged; 53 % of the buildings in Hamburg had been turned into 43 million cubic metres of rubble. Not one of the great cities had escaped the pitiless bombings, for which the Luftwaffe had set the pattern in its raids on Rotterdam and Coventry . . . 1,650,000 men had been killed in action, 2 million were prisoners and 1,600,000 were missing. Food supplies and transport had completely broken down; there were no mails or newspapers; administration had collapsed and chaos was unchallenged.

Added to these problems were millions of refugees from lands East of the Oder–Neisse line and other countries of Eastern Europe. A large number of schools had been destroyed and there were acute shortages of teaching materials and staff. In addition, the requirements of denazification had reduced the size of the teaching force considerably since nearly all teachers had joined the Nazi Teacher Association and had to be carefully vetted before being allowed to resume their duties. Many, of course, were not allowed to return.

The war thus left Germany with an increased population and few material means to barely feed them, let alone educate them. It was perhaps inevitable in the context that greater priorities would be accorded to building economic institutions and providing basic things like housing than to building up education. Massive investment in education was needed, but this did not happen in the dark years between 1945 and 1949.

These years should not be underestimated, but great care is needed in deciding how they should be understood. Grosser has argued (1974: 84):

The penury and demoralisation of those days had two lasting consequences. First, many Germans in the next decade retained a vivid memory of what they had been through and judged economic and social conditions by reference to the immediate post-war periods, so that they were relatively contented with their lot. Second, each individual felt a deep longing to forget the humiliation and degra dation of attitude and behaviour that had been forced upon him and to make sure that others forgot it also. The effect of this was a desire to multiply the external signs of prestige and respectability in a recrudescence of outdated values that became one of the more unattractive features of the Federal Republic.

It is perhaps understandable in this context that the German people did not demand much from education; they were far too preoccupied with much shorter-term goals. Given this context, too, it is hardly surprising that the Federal Government now envisages a much higher rate of planned educational investment into the 1980s to meet what it considers to be the crisis in German education. The reason is, simply, that education in Germany has been underemphasised and underresourced since the war.

The figures on educational expenditure for selected Western European societies since 1950 are as shown in Table 3.2. While in all the cases listed the annual growth rate in educational expenditure has exceeded the annual growth rate in the Gross Domestic Product (GDP) the difference in the two figures is smallest in the case of Germany. Put differently, a smaller proportion of the annual increase in the Gross Domestic Product has been devoted to educational expenditure than any other country listed. The increase in the percentage of the Gross National Product (GNP) which is devoted to education is also smallest in West Germany.

Germany's public expenditure as a percentage of the Gross National

TABLE 3.2
Public expenditure on education 1950–67

	Period	Annual growth rate for expenditure on education	Annual growth rate GDP 1955–67	Public expenditure on education as per cent GNP 1955	1965
Germany	1950–66	9.3	5.1	2.17	2.93
France	1952–67	11.0	4.9	2.83	4.55
United Kingdom	1953–65	7.8	3.0	2.67	4.17
Sweden	1957–65	10.0	4.3	4.14	6.41
Netherlands	1950–67	11.4	4.4	3.57	6.19

Source: Williamson (1977)

Product has not increased as much as in other European societies. This probably reflects two political factors. Firstly the philosophy of the social market economy which underlay Germany's economic policy in the 1950s put little stress on high public expenditure other than in the field of social security. German economic philosophy during this period has been described as 'neo-liberal' (Hardach, 1976). As early as 1947 the principles of a free market economy for the Federal Republic were agreed upon as a counterbalance to plans evolving in the East for a planned economy. The economic forces which explain the West German economic miracle are too complex to analyse here (see Hardach, 1976). They ranged from an undervalued currency, the Korean war, Marshall Aid and the fact, vitally important, that German expertise had not been destroyed by the war. But it was cold-war economics which set West Germany on a path of development which was unashamedly capitalist in its orientation. Such a model of development places a small premium on public investment in education.

Secondly, economic development in the 1950s was not held back at all by shortages of educated manpower. In this respect the West German economy has not *required* major transformations in education. Between 1953 and 1961 two million people left the German Democratic Republic (DDR) for the West bringing skills and work motivation. This flow of refugees together with the 7.6 million refugees from East of the Oder–Neisse who settled in the West up to 1949 and the 1.4 million from other European states, ensured a reservoir of human capital which the educational system had not been required to produce.

In this respect, it can be argued, the German Democratic Republic subsidised the Federal Republic with manpower just as in the 1960s Turkey, Yugoslavia, Italy and Spain were to supply the buoyant economy of Germany with a supply of cheap unskilled labour in the late 1950s and 1960s (*Gastarbeiter*).

In addition, despite the options available to build up a new pattern of schools, perhaps along comprehensive lines as the Americans had urged, West German education, as Rowlinson put it 'turned to a comforting past tradition and the old system from Weimar and before, with its organisation and assumptions, was reinstated' (1974: 29). What evolved was a framework of basic education followed by three types of secondary school, the *Gymnasium*, the *Realschule* and the *Hauptschule*, each catering for different social class groups. The educational forms of an earlier period were thus fused into the fabric of a dynamic modern economy. This development met with little opposition. Cold-war politics turned the Allies' attention too, from education to strategic matters. Foreign policy issues diverted the reformed, yet transformed Social Democratic Party from hammering away at domestic issues (Hiscocks, 1963). And Federalism as a set of constitutional principles, reduced the power of the Bonn Government in cultural policy.

It is, however, the social mechanisms of such a society, as they operate on patterns of learning, child rearing, resource distribution and in the organisation of schools themselves which eventually translate themselves into academic hierarchies and class inequalities in educational opportunity. Such inequalities have, indeed, been severe and what is more, have only been challenged in Germany from the mid-1960s onwards, from when affluence, a falling off in the rate of economic growth, and the political maturation of the Social Democrats, rising expectations and, particularly, the success of the German Democratic Republic, all combined to articulate a challenge to the educational system. The German educational system entered its crisis period, although clearly it had been in crisis since 1890.

SOCIAL SELECTIVITY IN EDUCATION

German secondary schools are intensely selective, and while results of selection and form of school organisation vary amongst the *Länder*, it is generally the case that social selection for education takes place extensively. In 1965, as the OECD report pointed out (1972: 57), when workers comprised 45.2 per cent of the gainfully employed males in the

Federal Republic and only ten per cent of pupils enrolled in the sixth grade of the *Gymnasia*, 6.4 per cent of those enrolled in the last grade were workers' children. What is more, considerable evidence exists to show that even when those enrolled in the *Gymnasia* are examined success rates at the *Abitur* exam are strongly linked to the occupation of the pupils' fathers. Peisert and Dahrendorf found the following pattern of *Abitur* successes in Baden-Württemberg between 1953 and 1963 (Table 3.3).

TABLE 3.3
Success in the *Abitur* versus occupation in 1953–63

Occupation of father	Per cent success in Abitur
Higher grade administrative workers	84
Professional	60
Clerical workers	33
Craftsman	31
Manual worker	24

Adapted from OECD (1972: 61)

The *Gymnasium* course is an extremely taxing one, as it always has been and in addition to the process of sifting out of students as the course proceeds, there is the phenomenon of grade repeating and this, too, is linked with the social class background of pupils.

The OECD report (1972) further points out that Germany, like Britain and France, exhibits gross inequalities in educational opportunity according to sex, religion and place of residence.

The *Bildungsbericht, 1970* showed that while the Federal average for university entrance was 9.2 per cent of the relevant age group in 1968, it was as high as 11.9 per cent in Bremen and as low as 7.5 per cent in Catholic Bavaria. Even within the different *Länder* educational chances are unevenly distributed, reflecting the uneven economic development of the country itself. The percentage of *Abitur* successes in Hesse in 1968 was 11.7. As Geipel discovered (1965), nearly one-third of all the local communities in Hesse had failed to produce one single *Abitur* success in the last ten years. Similar results have been reported for Baden-Württemberg by Peisert (1965).

Such results can be inspected from another angle, that of the social class distribution of opportunities. It then can be seen that, although rates of staying on at school have almost doubled between 1961 and 1970, there are clear gradients to this participation by social class and income. The Table 3.4 illustrates this. Children from the lower income groups are more likely to attend the *Hauptschule*, thus following a pattern of education dating from before the First World War. Attendance at a *Gymnasium* and university follows the same pattern. Table 3.5 makes this clear.

TABLE 3.4

School attendance of 10–15 year-olds by income of family head (1972)

Monthly net income (DM)	Recent school attendance of 10–15 year-old: per cent		
	Hauptschule	Realschule	Gymnasium
Under 600	84.6	—	—
600–1000	79.3	13.4	7.3
1000–1400	72.6	16.3	11.1
1400–1800	59.6	18.3	22.2
1800 and more	37.2	12.9	49.9
Self-employed Land workers	75.2	—	—
Total	67.1	15.2	17.7

Source: Williamson (1977)

TABLE 3.5

Gymnasium students and first year undergraduates by social status and age-specific transfer rates

Occupational status	Per cent 10-year-olds transferring to Gymnasium	Per cent 13-year-olds transferring to Gymnasium	Per cent first-year university students
Worker	2.8	1.1	1.8
White collar worker	20.1	11.7	10.2
Official	36.0	24.0	18.8
Self-employed	16.7	10.6	7.8
Total	12.8	7.6	6.9

Source: Williamson (1977)

The crisis in German education is inextricably bound up with the question of equal opportunities. In any analysis of this phenomenon in Germany and elsewhere it is important to be constantly aware of the political and historical context in which different social groups make demands of education.

The crisis in German education can be seen as a political fracture line in which the opposing forces stem from long-term social changes in the structure of German society. The OECD report argued, on the other hand, that the crisis is in the main one of system modernisation (1972: 103):

We have emphasised throughout this report our conviction that the task facing education in Germany is, in general terms, one of modernisation. The economic, social and political realities in Germany have changed fundamentally since the 1920s. Yet, in most important respects the education system has remained as it was recast after the Hitler period in the mould of those earlier times. Bringing education into closer congruence with the new social and political facts of German life is one of the great tasks facing the people in Germany in the 1970s.

These two views are not necessarily in conflict with one another, but in practice they tend to be.

The modernisation-of-the-system theory leads to political responses of a kind which do not challenge the operating assumptions of the system in question. Thus the OECD report stressed the need to reform teacher training, the curriculum, the administration of the system, and to remove the inflexibility in German education deriving from the *Laufbahn* system. The OECD document is not wholly unpolitical. It says of the changes it recommends that they should not be thought of exclusively as the responsibility of those concerned with education: 'These matters must, in the end, be political decisions made with an eye to a democratic nation's social needs' (1972: 103). A little later in the report the limits of the political decision-making processes of the sort the report would like to see are, almost by accident, quite heavily underlined. Of reform in the *Laufbahn* system, which 'tracks' people in careers and makes paper qualifications vitally important in job selection, the report says (1972: 106):

However, we would judge the reform of the *Laufbahn* system will be so difficult that it will make reform of education itself look like child's play. The attitude that support it are embedded so deeply in society that only a major change in perspectives will succeed in opening up careers to demonstrated ability and free from their present enslavement to paper qualifications.

The report at this point clearly recognises one of the most important inertia factors in German education, and recognises too that it is not capable of change through educational means. Educational modernisation can thus only go so far before it becomes inconsistent with the social and economic organisation of work and the distribution of power in society. Both factors interact to define a particular model of development for the Fderal Republic. Until that changes little else can be expected to change.

4 Education in State Socialist Societies The Soviet Union and the German Democratic Republic

The aim of this chapter is to examine the educational systems of two highly developed socialist industrial societies, the Soviet Union and East Germany. It seeks to relate changes in the educational systems of the two societies to changes in their economic systems and to describe the changing social structures which their educational systems are required to reproduce. I hope to show that such societies, in contrast to the industrial societies of the West, face special problems of reproduction which stem from their commitment to the ideology of Marxism. They not only have to reproduce economic skills; the major rationale for their existence is that they are building a new form of society and forging a new type of socialist man. They therefore, have to produce people committed to the revolutionary values of Marxism, people with a socialist consciousness. As I have already argued, however, (in Chapter 2) the particular form of their socialist development produces dilemmas which they have so far found great difficulty in resolving. These dilemmas—between equality and efficiency, involvement and control—are acute in the field of production where they articulate new forms of social stratification. But they are also acute in the field of education. The efficiency–equality dilemma raises questions about who shall be educated, the problem of *selection* and of what should be taught in schools, the problem of *curriculum*. The involvement and control dilemma raises the issue of who should control education. Should the control of education be in the hands of workers and peasants themselves—a view strongly expressed by one group of Bolsheviks between 1917 and 1928—or in the hands of the state?

89

There have been no easy solutions to those questions in either the Soviet Union or East Germany. In the case studies which follow I shall describe how each society has adapted its educational system to fit development goals and how the dilemmas mentioned above actually penetrate education. My main argument is that both societies display the common problems of socialist construction under the Soviet model. The Soviet model of educational development which evolved under Stalin was only one of many possible types of educational development within Marxism.

Nevertheless, this model was implanted into East Germany after the Second World War as a coherent philosophy of socialist education, a point once bemoaned by Bertholt Brecht when speaking about East Germany; he said, 'It is the great misfortune of our history that we have to build the "new" without having taken part in the destruction of the old'.

In the description of educational development in the Soviet Union I place great emphasis on the fact that socialist development has no clear blueprint and that, particularly in the field of education, a distinctively Marxist programme of development had to be built up from scratch. The problem is quite simple. Karl Marx wrote virtually nothing about education. He made comments on education in *The German Ideology* and in one or two pamphlets such as *The Civil War in France* and the *Critique of the Gotha Programme* (see Lane, 1970; Young, 1971; Cosin, 1972). The principles of a socialist education have, therefore, had to be deduced from Marxist social theory and because this is the case different deductions were possible.

The broad outlines of a Marxist theory of education are, however, clear enough, and follow from the Marxist theory of class society, the state and of ideology. They are succinctly stated in *The German Ideology*:

> The ideas of the ruling class are in every epoch the ruling ideas: i.e. the class which is the ruling *material* force of society, is at the same time its ruling *intellectual* force . . . The ruling ideas are nothing more than the ideal expression of the dominant material relationships, the dominant material relationships grasped ideas (quoted Lane, 1970: 489).

From such a position it is inconceivable that Marx would have felt sanguine about the nature of state provision for education; such provision he saw as part of a scheme of class domination. In the *Critique of the Gotha Programme*, his acidic criticism of the party programme of the German Social Democrats in 1875, Marx drew a distinction between 'elementary education by the state' and the need for the state to receive 'a very stern education by the people' (Marx, 1972: 31). He felt that the German Social Democrats grouped around Lassalle had a 'servile belief in the state' an attitude which he argued was 'remote from socialism' (1972: 31).

But what a socialist education programme would look like is not stated very clearly by Marx although he does state that 'an early combination of productive labour with education is one of the most potent means for the transformation of present-day society' (1972: 32). This comment implies a reference back to his own views concerning human alienation which he had set out as early as 1844, and in which he saw the division between intellectual and manual labour as one of the basic features of capitalist production and one which denied the labourer an understanding of his work reducing him thereby to being a mere 'appendage of a machine' (Avineri, 1968: 120).

Marxist analysis also sustains a very rigorous critical analysis of education under capitalism, a potentiality fully exploited by Lenin and subsequent Marxists. It is therefore, quite easy to say what is wrong with bourgeois education but quite another matter to say what a socialist education programme would look like except in the most general of terms. A socialist programme would provide education freely; the education provided would be common to all children. It would integrate the theoretical with the practical. It would offer children the theoretical means to understand the evolution of human society towards socialism. It would overcome the 'contradiction' between town and country. It would be an instrument for the emancipation of the working-class as a whole. It would cultivate the growth of science and technology and harness both to the task of building a socialist society. All of these themes can be traced directly to the massive body of writing which is classical Marxism. But it is still not clear what all this should mean in practice.

The experience of the Soviet Union is important here because in the shifts and turns of its educational development answers which are at least satisfactory to the Soviet view of socialism have been arrived at and have been exported both to Eastern Europe and to other parts of the world, sometimes successfully as in the Cuban case, sometimes un- successfully as in China. Without doubt, however, Soviet education practice is a powerful model for all socialist societies to consider.

THE SOVIET UNION

> Education is a kind of stepson. Everything gets taken away from it and the Party people think it below their dignity to be concerned with education (N. Krupskaya (Lenin's wife) in 1919 quoted by Fitzpatrick, 1970: 56).

Krupskaya wrote these words while visiting schools in the Volga-Kama region of Russia to see how far local authorities were developing *Unified Labour Schools* according to the declared principles worked out by *Narkompros*—the People's Commissariat of Enlightenment. Her conclusions were, on the whole, disappointing. What she discovered was teacher hostility to the new concepts of education, Party indifference, poor organisation and a widespread lack of understanding of what polytechnical, participatory education might look like. This was a matter of great concern to Krupskaya. She had been actively involved in adult education before the revolution; she was a dedicated Marxist and, like Lenin, she believed firmly that education had a key role to play in consolidating the revolution itself. What is more she believed that a revolutionary education could not be imposed on people; people had to construct it for themselves. 'Our job', she once wrote, 'is to help the people, *in fact* to take their fate into their own hands' (Fitzpatrick, 1970: 28).

At the Twentieth Party Congress of the Soviet Union in 1956 Nikita Khrushchev castigated modern educated youth for its indifference to the problems of working people, for 'running away at the sight of a cow' and for 'mistaking the claws of a hammer for its handle' (Charlton, 1968: 52). The reforms of 1958 and, in particular, the passing of the Law on the Strengthening of the Ties of School and Life, represents an attempt to revive the ideas of polytechnical education which had dominated early Bolshevik education policy.

Between these two dates, 1919 and 1958, the Soviet Union underwent a massive social and economic transformation, recording *en route* some notable scientific and technological achievements and a general growth in the standard of living of the Russian people. In the face of civil war, famine, foreign intervention and the loss of some twenty million people in the Second World War, the results have been little less than miraculous. This is especially so in the field of education. Judged quantitatively the Soviet Union has succeeded in providing primary education for all children. In fact, this particular aim was achieved as early as 1932. It has taken much longer to fulfil early aspirations about secondary education, particularly the aim of providing secondary education up to the age of seventeen for all children, but this will be achieved in the course of the current five-year plan (Tomiak, 1974). Illiteracy has been abolished and the growth of higher education has been one of the most spectacular achievements of the revolution. The number of students taking courses up to degree level (by British standards) is, as a proportion of the overall population, greater than many advanced countries in Western Europe (Lane, 1970: 502).

Conceived of as an evolving system, education in the Soviet Union has achieved some spectacular successes and some of the problems which remain, for example, patterns of social inequality, imbalance in the spatial distribution of school opportunities, uncertainty about the content of courses and the rigidities of highly centralised patterns of control, might all be thought of as temporary problems which will be overcome in the transition to communism. On the other hand, it could be argued that Soviet education suffers from a deeper malaise and that some of the currently visible problems—particularly those relating to patterns of inequality—are not simply residual but essential aspects of a particular form of society and state. This point has been made, for instance, by Oskar Anweiler (1972). He argues that the needs of modern industrial economy for highly qualified personnel in science and technology conflict with the requirements of an egalitarian ideology.

'Herein lies the Soviet dilemma', writes Anweiler. 'An "elite education" based on ability rather than on political considerations is essential and is in conflict with the egalitarian ideology' (1972: 202). But this particular analysis, like so many others which follow the logic of the so-called convergence thesis, underplays the role of political choice among different educational goals even in the same society. But in addition, it suffers from the mistake of taking technology and hierarchical forms of the division of labour for granted as if in some way, which is not fully explained, technological development along Soviet lines was the only option open to the Soviet state; that, in fact, political values need inevitably to be put in cold storage while technological problems are solved. But as I have already argued in the case of industrialisation policies (see Chapter 2) the Soviet Union faced real choices among different programmes of development.

RUSSIA IN 1917

Russian economic development in the last quarter of the nineteenth century, like that of Germany, was state directed. The political economy of backwardness rendered this necessary (Gerschenkron, 1962). Tariff-protection policies, massive foreign capital investment and a deliberate policy of industrialisation—policies associated with the Tsarist Finance Minister, Count Witte—all combined to increase the pace of Russian industrialisation up to the period before the First World War. As a strategy or model of development it was clearly of the type described earlier (see Chapter 2) as a dependency strategy but it was, nonetheless appreciable (Nove, 1972). Between 1891 and 1900 the output of pig iron trebled; industrial production as a whole doubled and by 1900 Russia was the greatest oil producer in the world. Railway track increased by seventy-five per cent and a Soviet textbook in economic history has estimated that Russia's industrial production between 1860 and 1910 increased by 10.5 times in comparison with Britain's 2.5 and Germany's 6.0 (Nove, 1972: 13). But Russia was still backward, even in comparison with Spain and Italy; her development was uneven and it generated awesome social tensions from which the October revolution was, in part at least, the outcome.

This spurt of industrial change reflected itself in education policy. Before the First World War Russia had predominantly an illiterate population although most people in urban areas were literate (Pennar, Bakalo and Bereday, 1971: 4). But there was a coherent recognition that illiteracy and low levels of education were an obstacle to economic development. Pennar *et al.* (1971: 7) quote a Tsarist economist, I. I. Yanzhul, to the effect that '. . . in order to make proper use of the fruits of technical genius, every country must prepare not only technicians, but the entire population to the new conditions generated by machine production'. The economist went on to express the common sentiment of nineteenth-century ruling groups that, 'Work with machines demands order, precision, accuracy, quickness of mind i.e. qualities which, of course, are very rarely found in an uneducated person' (Pennar *et al.*, 1971: 7).

Some groups opposed the spread of literacy or the extension of schools for the masses but others, the 'liberally oriented upper crust of Russian society' (Pennar *et al.*, 1971) pressed for it. Organisations like the Petersburg Committee for Literacy and the Moscow Literacy Committee, representing the tip of a veritable iceberg of societies of this type campaigned actively for public primary education. The motives were of course mixed, a blend of European-oriented humanitarianism with an unequivocal recognition of the economic benefits of schooling. One such prominent campaigner, V. P. Vakhterov, told an all-Russian congress of the Technical Society in 1895 that universal compulsory education was necessary because of its effect on the quality and productivity of labour. 'A trained worker', he said 'requires less supervision, does not damage equipment as often as an unskilled worker, learns faster, wastes less materials and time on the job' (Pennar *et al.*, 1971: 8).

By 1915 there were plans for a national system of primary schools leading on to forms of secondary and higher education. But the educational system was still highly stratified, even caste-like with the secondary *Gymnasium* being only available to the children of the well-to-do. In rural areas schools were often non-existent and if there were any they were most likely under the control of the Church. But from 1908 the Government began a programme of subsidies to local authorities to build schools and develop a national school network and by 1914 primary education was nearly universal although of very uneven quality and duration, and secondary and technical education was developing rapidly but in an haphazard way and with many unintended consequences (Pennar *et al.*, 1971).

The rapid development of schools did not produce a docile population. There were student riots and a flowering of social and educational criticism. Teacher organisations urged the growth of free, democratic education in which control of education was highly decentralised (Tomiak, 1974). And the broad spectrum of the political left, not simply the Marxists, evolved a critique of the schools which drew on the radical traditions of the most progressive European philosophies in education, those of Rousseau, Pestalozzi, Froebel, Dewey and Montessori (Tomiak, 1974). The Marxists, of course, were armed with the additional weapon of class analysis. Lenin, for instance, spoke of the Tsarist education system in this way, addressing a *Komsomol* Congress in 1920:

The old school declared that it wants to create a man with an all-round education, that it promotes studies in general. We know that this was an all-out lie because society was founded on the division of people into classes, into the exploiters and the oppressed. Naturally, the old school imbued as it was with class consciousness, taught only the children of the bourgeoisie. In these schools the younger generation of workers and peasants was not taught but rather trained in the interests of the same bourgeoisie and to contribute to its welfare without disturbing its peace and idleness (Pennar *et al.*, 1971: 21).

When the revolution finally came in October 1917 the Bolsheviks faced a situation in which an old order was, quite apart from war, collapsing in on itself and several different new orders were struggling to be born. What form of society should evolve was, of course, the decisive question and who should control it the most urgent practical task to attend to. But both questions needed specific answers also in the field of education. As with broader strategies of development classical Marxism did not provide any blueprints, only principles.

EARLY SOVIET EDUCATION

From the beginning the Bolsheviks understood education in class terms and sought, as Lenin had directed, to graft an overtly political function onto education. Lenin wrote in 1920:

> All educational work in the Soviet Republic of workers and peasants, in the field of political education in general and in the field of art in particular, should be imbued with the spirit of the class struggle being waged by the proletariat for the successful achievement of the aims of its dictatorship i.e. the overthrow of the bourgeoisie, the abolition of classes, and the elimination of all forms of exploitation of man by man (quoted by Lane, 1970: 490).

Much more circumspectly Lenin had told Lunacharsky, his People's Commisar of Enlightenment, that he had not thought much about education and that Lunascharsky should consult with, among others, Krupskaya to work out an education programme (Fitzpatrick, 1970).
    Some of the aims were, however, quite clear. David Lane lists (1970: 490) the three major ones—abolish illiteracy, inculcate socialist attitudes and develop science and technology. These three aims were, of course, interconnected. Illiteracy was a problem because it held back science and technology. But it also held back political consciousness. Lenin once noted that, in respect to the political education of workers there are three main enemies, 'Communist conceit, illiteracy and bribes' (Fitzpatrick, 1970: 252). In their efforts to abolish illiteracy the Soviets organised schools for adults and used existing schools on a shift basis. By 1930 compulsory school education was a reality and illiteracy completely abolished by the end of the 1930s (Lane, 1970: 490). Although, as Lane points out, much of the credit for this must be given to the regime before 1917.

The aim of inculcating socialist attitudes and of developing science and technology were reflected in the development of the so-called Unified Labour School. This was conceived of as an integral part of an education which would be comprehensive, open to all and absolutely free (Tomiak, 1974). These principles were heavily endorsed at the Eighth Congress of the Russian Communist Party in 1919 and were followed by the famous Declaration on the Unified Labour School in which the principles of polytechnical education were built in to Soviet Education. In 1918 access to universities was opened to everyone and workers and peasant faculties were set up to help workers make higher education. These were the so-called *rabfaks*. Their aim was to produce 'Red' specialists and they admitted people only of proletarian origin who had been specially selected by the Party organisations (Pennar *et al.*, 1971). By 1927 one-quarter of the intake to all forms of higher education came from the *rabfaks* (Lane, 1973: 244); and by 1923–24 only 0.6 per cent of students came from the so-called 'non-working elements' in the population (Lane, 1973: 244).

As Krupskaya understood it polytechnical education was not simply vocational study but the combination of theoretical and practical work across the whole curriculum.

Polytechnicism is not a separate teaching subject, but should permeate every disipline, be reflected in the choice of subject matter whether physics or chemistry, natural science or social science. These disciplines must be linked with each other, with practical activity and especially with labour instruction. Only thus can labour and instruction be given a polytechnical character (quoted by Charlton, 1968: 49).

And like many others Krupskaya was very ready to admit that much experimentation was needed to discover the best form of polytechnical education. *Narkompros*, in fact encouraged experimentation. There were special schools for the arts. Shatsky, a follower of Tolstoy, ran a children's colony called the 'Good Life' and Makarenko, the great Russian educationist, organised his children's colony in the Ukraine (Fitzpatrick, 1970).

As Fitzpatrick writes (1970: 50) indicating something of the hopes of the time:

In the worst period of the Civil War Lunacharsky, Krupskaya and on occasions Lenin visited the kindergartens and the children's colonies and felt that they saw the beginning of a new world: these were 'corners full of joy, full of the morning light portending future socialism; light grains of the future for which we struggle against the twilight, cruelly battle coloured backdrop of our suffering land'.

But such ideas met with organised teacher resistance and often could not overcome the basic lack of resources necessary for their implementation. Polytechnical education in one school involved inviting a local villager—a carpenter—to teach his trade to the children but all he could bring to his task was a bag of old tools (Fitzpatrick, 1970: 53). There was opposition too, within the Party itself. At a party congress in December 1920 the views of Lunacharsky and Krupskaya were opposed by another group who wished to promote specific technical education along the lines of the German technical schools as the most urgent immediate step (Charlton, 1968). Such opposition, together with the general chaos of the country during the Civil War scuppered polytechnical education.

On the issue of science and technology the principles of *Narkompros* were also eroded during the 1920s. *Narkompros* had been greatly worried by the growth of technical education under the various economic commisariats and had sought to gain control of technical education to avoid what it understood as 'narrow professionalism' (Fitzpatrick, 1970: 63). And Krupskaya expressed the view forcefully at an all Russia Congress of Trades Unions:

> From our point of view, professional education must not cripple a man by making him a narrow specialist from an early age, must not narrow his horizon, but must help all aspects of his whole development. A professional education must now prepare not only the executant, the mechanical worker—it must also prepare the worker to become the master of industry (Fitzpatrick, 1970: 66).

By 1928, however, a new leadership felt that a much improved system of technical education was required if Russia was to overtake the West. In Stalin's view what was needed was a highly trained technical intelligentsia—'Bolshevik experts in metallurgy, textiles, fuel, chemistry agriculture, transport, trade accountancy and so forth' (Charlton, 1968: 50). In 1931 Lunacharsky was replaced. The progressive teaching practices in some Unified Labour schools were denounced as 'undisciplined freedom'.

In 1923 school fees were reintroduced into Soviet schools. In 1935 the *rabfaks* were closed down and the number of schools themselves declined in the early 1920s. Many of the labour schools were transferred to the appropriate economic commissariat and some of the universities were split up into specialised institutes. By 1937 polytechnical education was removed from the Party programme.

Thus by the beginning of the Second World War education in the Soviet Union, although highly successful from the point of view of Stalin's industrialisation plans, was far removed from the principles sought by *Narkompros* in 1918. Sheila Fitzpatrick has suggested (1970: 288) that there were four main stages in the retreat from 1918. The first was the retreat from organising education on the basis of popular participation. Stalin centralised the school system. The second was the abandonment of polytechnical principles in a desperate search for specialists. The third was the Government's withdrawal of financial support, leaving the financing of schools to the local authorities. The fourth retreat was the reintroduction of fees at all levels. Nonetheless, a Soviet regime in extremely adverse conditions had nurtured the hope of an education system greatly unlike anything which had gone before or since materialised in Russia.

MODERN SOVIET EDUCATION

By the end of the Second World War the Soviet Union had evolved a form of education which reflected the manpower needs of massive industrial mobilisation of both capital and labour and which was to remain more or less unchanged until the late 1950s.

The educational system, under Stalin, had been given the task of producing quickly a body of technicians and skilled workers. The legitimating values of the system became, increasingly, those of ability and *socialist competition* under which the most successful pupils would be awarded medals. In factories there was, during this period the equivalent phenomenon of Stakhanovism, an economic movement to increase labour output norms and named after a coal miner—Alexei Stakhanov—who exceeded his work norms by a factor of fourteen. The overall aim was higher productivity and this was heavily underlined as a political value in its own right.

The academic content of general schooling was upgraded. During the early Bolshevik period school-leaving examinations had been abolished. In 1944 these were reintroduced. This old Tsarist institution made access to higher education dependent on a formal test of ability. And as

Matthews says (1972: 292), 'This signified a final rejection of the proletarian informalism of the early thirties . . . (which) . . . strengthened the position of the socially favoured pupils, if only because they had better conditions for studying'.

In 1943 special military cadet schools were set up for the sons of officers. Coeducational schools were gradually broken up into single sex schools during the 1940s. In the 1940s, too, the concept of polytechnical education was finally buried with the setting up of state labour reserves to train young people directly for production and using the official power of the draft to do so (Pennar *et al.*, 1971: 55). The immediate rationale for this was an economic one but the sociological importance of it was that the link between general school and higher education which *Narkompros* had sought to effect was broken. The children of workers and peasants were confined to the world of industrial and agricultural production.

Coupled with the introduction of fees in secondary and higher education and the adoption of formal academic measures of ability as the criteria for entrance to higher education, the basis was laid for social differentiation in Soviet society along strictly educational lines. Anweiler has written of these changes sardonically (1972: 185):

> Even if one is not inclined to regard these regulations, which remained in force until 1956, as clear evidence of a conscious plan to install a new Soviet upper class, the fee requirement alone implied that the size of a family's income would henceforth very largely determine who would attend higher institutions of learning, and suggested the abandonment of the egalitarian principles of 1918 as well as a serious breach in the ideology of socialist equality.

Once again, however, great care is needed when making interpretations of this kind. And it is important too, to distinguish between the period before the Second World War and the period after it for the constraints on the Soviet model of development were radically different in the two periods.

The form of the Soviet education system under Stalin—a basic four-year school followed by either seven or ten-year secondary school leading to various forms of craft and technical education and to higher education, itself differentiated into universities and special institutes—was clearly fashioned towards specialisation and the production of human capital along lines dictated by the framework of five-year plans. In this respect education policy was consistent with Stalin's industrialisation plans and, in particular, his views of socialist construction, a view which, stressing the importance of building socialism in one country, implied an effort to outstrip the West technologically (Corrigan, Ramsay and Sayer, 1978). But in the period after the Second World War, decisions which affected the issue of equality in Soviet education and which had formerly been based on political and economic values became increasingly subordinated to questions of functional necessity. Anweiler's use of the word 'abandonment of egalitarian principles is therefore slightly misleading. Stalin justified his so-called cadre policy on strictly Bolshevist lines. What appears, therefore, in the Soviet Union of the 1930s as (at least to Stalin) the strictly functional problem of socialist construction was, in fact, the strictly political problem of choosing among alternative forms of socialist development.

But what appears in the late 1940s and early 1950s as political choice among different educational ends is, in fact, the problem of restocking a shattered industrial economy with highly trained manpower. That was a functional necessity foisted on the Soviet Union by Hitler's war and the havoc and destruction that war brought. Quite apart from the wholesale destruction of the Ukraine, the loss of life (and estimates here vary from twenty million to thirty-five million people) some 82,000 schools were destroyed, the teaching labour force drastically reduced and some fifteen million schools places were lost (Grant, 1964: 19). In such circumstances it was absolutely essential to have a cadre policy and to suspend longer-term political ideals till the immediate problems of the aftermath of war had been solved.

In any case, inequality is not a unidimensional concept. One aspect of Soviet education policy during the 1930s and throughout the war was that of reducing sex inequalities in education. The Soviet Union has managed to eliminate sex inequalities in education opportunity. In 1939, eighty-five per thousand women had completed secondary education when 116 per thousand men did so. In 1970 the figures were, for women, 415 and for men, 474 per thousand (Tomiak, 1974:47). In higher education there has been a similar movement. In 1939, eleven out of every 1000 men had completed higher education and only five out of every 1000 women had done so. By 1970 the figures were forty-eight and thirty-seven respectively. These figures do not, of course, show that inequalities in one realm are compensated for by greater equality in another. Rather they emphasise the need to consider the issue of inequality in a broader context. In a Soviet context the problems which Anweiler raises are less significant than they are in a western context. Certainly, in the period from 1935 till the death of Stalin the issue of equality had little ideological importance since it was subservient to the higher goal of efficient production. In that sense, the standard of equality is not one against which the Soviet education system should be judged or, at least, not yet. The Soviet view of equality is a teleological one. Equality is something which will be gradually realised as 'mature socialism' gives way to communism at some unspecified point in the future.

Similar problems about evaluative criteria are raised if the broader political goals of Soviet education are examined. Soviet education has been conceived of right from the beginning as having an explicitly political role. Lenin, for example, understood the basic task of overcoming illiteracy in political terms. In a short political tract on ideological education V. Baikova quotes Lenin on the question of the level of literacy in the Soviet Union (1975: 9):

> This is not a political problem, it is a condition without which it is useless to talk about politics. An illiterate person stands outside politics, he must first learn his ABC. Without that there can be no politics; without that there are rumours, gossip, fairy tales and prejudices but not politics.

And Lenin is quoted by Tomiak (1974: 41) in the following way:

> Education is one of the component parts of the struggle we are now waging . . . The schools must become an instrument of the dictatorship of the proletariat, i.e. a vehicle not merely of the general principles of communism, but also of the ideological, organisational and educational influence of the proletariat on the semi-proletarian and non-proletarian sections of the working people with the object . . . of building the communist system.

This theme in Soviet education has continued right up to the present and is given as the major rationale of civic education whenever Soviet politicians pronounce on education. Direct political instruction is everywhere evident especially so in higher education and Soviet principles penetrate the curriculum at all levels (Grant, 1964). I shall discuss the way in which this is done shortly. For the moment it is necessary only to emphasise that in making judgments about Soviet education it is important to employ criteria appropriate to the system itself and one set of criteria is precisely this: how far have Soviet efforts to forge a 'new socialist man' been successful, given the form and organisation of the Soviet school and the type of work for which it prepares its pupils?

The form and content of Soviet education reflects these broad economic and political goals but in doing so the system also had to face up to the dilemmas discussed in Chapter 2—those of efficiency and equality and involvement and control. Once the broad outlines of the Soviet system had been settled—and this had been achieved by the end of the Second World War—a new logic took over, the logic of the system itself responding to its own internal constraints and to the hopes and aspirations of pupils who were increasingly led to expect a great deal from education in a socialist society. In the period from 1945 to 1958 there were developments of practice and attitude which some sections of the Soviet leadership felt ran contrary to the goals of an efficient socialist state and the failure of Khrushchev to 'correct these tendencies indicates both something of the resilience or, perhaps, inertia of all education systems to respond to shifts in political opinion. There is a politics of education which is not under the control even of the most highly centralised and disciplined political system.

A discussion of the two dilemmas illustrates some of these points quite well and illustrates in doing so some of the urgent issues of educational policy in the Soviet Union.

INVOLVEMENT AND CONTROL

This particular dilemma, as I have already made clear, (see Chapter 2) arises from the contrast between official ideology which stresses collectivist participatory social values and the actual control of work in factories and farms which, in the Soviet case, is heavily saturated with managerial methods stressing the need for hierarchy, efficiency and incentives and in which managers have a great deal of power. It is a dilemma because Soviet citizens are led, through their family upbringing, their education, their participation in youth organisations and through their exposure to the dominant legitimating values of the state itself to realise social values in their own lives which are inconsistent with the organisation of work and of learning itself. The education system, paradoxically, both reflects this dilemma and serves to sharpen it.

Education sharpens the dilemma because it is organised to develop a socialist consciousness among its pupils. Social values acquired in school can thus come into conflict with the values of authority in the world of work. Education reflects the dilemma because the organisation of learning in the Soviet Union is formal and hierarchical and is geared to producing specific types of expertise. This is at variance with the Marxian rhetoric of developing human potentialities to the full and of producing people with a *critical* awareness of the world.

The aim of consolidating the growth of a socialist consciousness is pursued through several different policies. In the first place Soviet education is very tightly controlled by the state, all aspects of education being planned in detail and carefully inspected (Grant, 1964). The administration of the school system is in the hands of Republic Ministries of Education and higher education is under the control of an all-Union Ministry. But administrative decentralisation is not the same as decentralised control. The planning of schools, the distribution of resources, the determination of the curriculum and the manpower quotas which the technical schools are required to meet are all planned centrally by *Gosplan*, the Soviet planning authority.

Secondly, the school system is all-embracing both in its coverage and its intentions. There is an explicit commitment in the Soviet Union to the moral development of the child and this penetrates both to the social relationships of teacher and pupil and among pupils themselves to the specific content of school syllabuses. Every child, for instance, must learn the twenty standard 'Rules for Pupils' (Grant, 1964). These rules express the general principles of discipline in Soviet education and include such rules as 'To acquire knowledge persistently in order to become an educated and cultured citizen and to be of the greatest possible service to his country', 'To stand to attention when answering the teacher; to sit down only with the teacher's permission; to raise his hand if he wishes to ask or answer a question', 'To be polite to his elders', 'To protect school property', 'Not to use coarse expressions' (Grant, 1964: 47). The aim of such tight rule specification is to build in to the daily encounters of the school the precepts of public morality with their emphasis on collective values. Such practices even penetrate to the kindergarten where even very small children are positively rewarded for behaviour such as helpfulness, co-operativeness and obedience (see Bronfenbrenner, 1970).

The values which the school must seek to realise are, in fact, highly codified. Bronfenbrenner discusses the code under the following headings basing his description on the instructions of the Moscow Pedagogical Institute (1970: 30–1). The main categories are concerned with communist morality (for example, socialist humanism) attitudes to learning (initiative, hard work) cultured conduct (good manners) aesthetic culture (creativity) physical culture (maximising development of physical skills). And the discipline and punishment rules which operate in Soviet classrooms are, in Bronfenbrenner's account, very different from those which operate in schools in Western Europe or the United States. Children are encouraged to monitor one another's behaviour and to help one another behave properly. They are encouraged to think that wayward colleagues are their own problem and that the school class itself has a responsibility to keep its own members in check. Bronfenbrenner's assessment of the effects of this process is positive. He writes:

> Taken together the results of these . . . strongly indicate that collective upbringing does achieve some of its intended effects—at least at the school age level. Not only does the peer group in the U.S.S.R. act to support behaviour consistent with the values of adult society, but it also succeeds in inducing its members to take personal initiative and responsibility for developing and maintaining such behaviour in others.

He points out, finally, that Soviet children, in school and in the family, are confronted with fewer divergent views and in consequence are more likely to conform to a more homogeneous set of social standards.

Such collectivity-oriented behaviour is reinforced by the youth movement. Indeed, the youth movement is conceived of as an integral part of the educational system. The youth movement is organised into three levels. For younger children there is the *Octobrists*. For those between ten and fifteen there is the *Pioneers* and for the older ones up to the age of twenty-five, the *Komsomol*. This latter organisation is an all-Union organisation with its own newspaper; it organises work experience programmes for its members as well as social events and political education. The recommendation of the *Komsomol* group is important to students seeking higher education.

Political principles penetrate the content of courses in a very direct way, too. In an obvious way this is reflected in the heavy emphasis which Soviet schools place on science and technology with particular pride of place given to the study of mathematics. The emphasis on science in Soviet education is to encourage the growth of a scientific (that is, on their terms, materialist) social outlook as well as to prepare students for scientific and technical work. In this respect, science education is, like so much else in the Soviet Union, consistent with their view of what it is to construct socialism. But the same penetration is equally evident in the study of literature. The aim here is to inculcate a Marxist–Leninist belief system (see Hopkins, 1974). And Soviet courses in history are designed with the same ends in view. Charles Carey quotes a Russian source on the principles behind history syllabuses (1976: 12–13):

> The formation of an idea about the historical process, that is, about the natural movement of a society toward the highest social-economic structure, and the development of a deep conviction in the victory of communism in the entire world can be accomplished by means of the study not of individual historical periods but of the whole course of history from ancient times to the present. The content of history education in the school is arranged accordingly.

Carey notes also (1976) that there is a developmental pattern to the inclusion of ideological themes into school courses; older children are expected to become directly familiar with Marxist social theory, younger ones less so, and the ideological emphasis varies among subjects. History is much more explicitly fashioned according to ideological precepts than geography.

The authority of the school and the values it supports is reinforced also in Soviet teaching methods. There are central guidelines covering teaching methods and teachers are regularly inspected both by school directors and by Ministry officials. Nigel Grant argues (1964) that Soviet teaching methods are, in comparison with those in the West extremely formal. Little value is placed on activity methods of learning. He claims a great deal of importance is placed on rote-learning methods. The pupil role is almost entirely a passive one. Teachers are trained in separate teacher institutes and some twenty per cent of their time is spent on courses on educational theory. The psychological basis of Soviet pedagogy is, however, still Pavlovian and in that respect it emphasises the need for the teacher to be firmly in control of the learning process and in setting the ongoing aims of day-to-day learning. Here, of course, is another area in which modern Soviet practice differs from some of the ideas of the early period of the revolution. Under *Narkompros* great efforts were made to develop activity methods of learning and Soviet psychology, particularly that associated with Vygotsky opened up a vast range of questions concerning the mechanisms and processes of human learning, language development and concept formation (see Holly, 1973). Under Stalin such methods were supressed and the extent of the return to formal teaching methods in the Soviet Union has led to a debate which continues today: is education in the Soviet Union Soviet or Russian? (See Tudge, 1975).

The precepts of Soviet socialism are therefore, built in to the social organisation of the Soviet school and the classification and framing of educational knowledge (Bernstein, 1973). It is not possible, however, to be sure about the effects. Carey (1976: 28) refers to some Russian research on the effects of courses in geography, history and social studies in developing a Marxist–Leninist belief system and claims that, while school students do come to know a great deal about Marxism, instruction in these areas is not very effective in developing their personal belief systems. And at the level of personal conduct there is the suggestion from Bronfenbrenner that while Russian children are much better behaved than children in the West (these conclusions follow from a comparative study of children in England, Switzerland, the Soviet Union and the USA) they 'gave less weight than the subjects from the other countries to telling the truth and seeking intellectual understanding' (1970: 81). J. M. D. Higgins (1976) has suggested that in the field of higher education student teachers in the Soviet Union have a very strong achievement-oriented attitude to their studies. Higher education in the Soviet Union is mainly vocational but Higgins claims that students wanted it for its status value. And Pospielovsky (1976) quotes Soviet sources concerned about students in higher education showing more interest in various brands of neo-positivist and existentialist philosophy than in the ideological struggle with capitalism and that these same students claim that their teaching in philosophy and social studies did not relate to real life.

It might be argued on the basis of such suggestions that ideological claims of the state are not yet fully rooted in the beliefs and sentiments of its citizens. But to do so would both be to accept a very trivialised view of the socialisation process—such evidence can give only the barest glimpse of how Soviet students think, act and feel—and to expect too much of Soviet socialism. The framework of the Soviet economy and the social relationships of work encourage the kind of achievement motivation which these studies have picked up. To explore this theme further it is necessary to consider the second dilemma mentioned earlier, that of efficiency and equality.

EFFICIENCY AND EQUALITY

Not all Soviet citizens have the same access to schooling. Children in rural areas typically do less time at school than children in urban areas and educational participation is higher for social groups higher up the social scale. In this respect, not all Soviet citizens undergo the same process of socialisation. For some the expectation is high that they will achieve at school and seek higher education and benefit from the privileges this undoubtedly brings. For others the expectation is that they will leave early and become workers. There is considerable evidence, too, that educational stratification follows directly the contours of social stratification and that the closer this link becomes the more competitive some sections of Soviet society become thus, perhaps, eroding somewhat the ideology of the solidaristic society. Indeed, it was to overcome these problems that the school reforms of 1958 were introduced but it is these very same problems which render those reforms ineffective.

The issue of inequality in Soviet education can be examined from several different angles. To begin with there are great differences between rural and urban areas. Rural areas typically have smaller schools and eight-year general schools rather than the more prestigious and important ten-year general schools. Mervyn Matthews quotes Soviet sources which express great concern at the state of rural schooling. One such source reports in this way (1972: 261): ' . . .a significant number of children taught in rural eight and ten year schools, in their level of development, breadth of outlook, depth and quality of knowledge, are still behind urban school leavers'. Nor do such children have the same *de facto* access to higher education. Matthews quotes research by the Soviet sociologist, V. N. Shubkin, which showed that, in 1963 in Novosibirsk *oblast* only twenty-eight per cent of ten-year school-leavers from villages went on to higher education in comparison with forty-six percent of children from urban areas (1972: 263).

Overlying such differences are hierarchical differences among social groups. Research carried out by the Soviet sociologist Osipov showed, for the Gorki *oblast*, that the children of workers are more likely to leave education at the first opportunity and not go on to higher work. Something like forty-three per cent of children in the forth class of schooling in this area were the children of workers. By the eleventh class the figure had dropped to twenty-three per cent (Matthews, 1972: 265). In the field of higher education these inequalities are amplified. Higher education in the Soviet Union is still a scarce commodity and from 1958 onwards Soviet leaders have been publicly concerned at the gross under-representation of workers and agricultural worker's children in higher education in higher education.

The importance of such figures, sociologically, is that they indicate something of the background against which the expectations of Soviet pupils are formed. It appears in this respect, as Yanowitch and Dodge report (1968), that Soviet youth has very high educational aspirations. Quoting Soviet social surveys they claim that seventy to eighty per cent of Soviet students wish to study beyond the eighth grade and that such aspirations are directly linked to social class position. Children from technical, specialist backgrounds—the intelligentsia—are much more highly motivated to achieve than children from other groups. Yanowitch and Dodge summarise their argument in this way (1968: 263):

> The studies just reviewed reveal the emergence of two problems associated with the integration of youth into the established structure of Soviet society. The first of these is the existence of a significant gap between the educational and career aspirations of Soviet youth generally and the opportunities for their realisation. The second involves the presence of considerable inequalities among social groups in their access to advanced education and thus to preferred work careers.

The conjunction of these two features of Soviet education could either lead to considerable dissatisfaction or to passive resignation and acceptance of social position. Neither response is in any sense consistent with dominant ideological position. Indeed, the Khrushchev reform of 1958 was an attempt to overcome some of the problems which this discrepancy was producing.

From 1955 onwards Khrushchev sought to refashion the educational system both to make it more egalitarian and more relevant to what he took to be the needs of Soviet society. But he was not simply responding to the dictates of ideology, there were some severe practical problems to be solved which had their roots in the academic form of education as this had evolved with Stalin. These were high levels of dissatisfaction over educational opportunities, elitist social attitudes and growing levels of voluntary unemployment among educated youth either through waiting for higher education or through an unwillingless to take jobs they thought to be beneath their abilities. Khrushchev responded on a broad front with five main objectives. He sought to revive the polytechnical principle, to reduce the length of general schooling from ten years to eight, to increase part-time education, to upgrade the status of trade schools and to change the basis of selection for higher education.

Under Stalin the ten-year general school course lacked any practical element. Khrushchev thought to change this through polytechnical education, thus resurrecting an idea which had once been absolutely central to early Bolshevik thinking on education. The aim was, eventually, to give all school students a trade and to upgrade the practical content of all school courses.

He aimed, too, to reduce the length of schooling to eight years. By 1963–64 some eighty per cent of pupils were reported to be provided with workplaces where they learned trades. But Matthews contends that these courses were badly co-ordinated and that 'school leavers usually did not wish to take the job they had learned even when these were available' (1972: 269). Additionally, parents, teachers and factory managers were opposed to the reform and the regulations were rescinded in 1966. Matthews refers to the whole period of polytechnical reform as, simply, an 'episode' (1972: 220).

The failure of polytechnical policy to change the school curriculum on a long-term basis must be seen against another development during this period which actually reinforced the patterns of inequality polytechnical education had, in part, at least, been designed to eradicate. This was the growth of highly specialised schools for children who were thought to be specially gifted. From 1966 onwards these schools have been specially developed but many of them, in fact, emerged after 1958. Anweiler (1972: 202) points out, for instance, that:

> When educational reform was being debated in 1958, various groups, scientists especially, underscored the importance of setting up special schools for children who early manifest mathematical or scientific aptitudes; Khrushchev, along with the Central Committee of the party, also endorsed the legitimacy of such schools.

Although there have been no published sociological studies of the social background of children in these schools Anweiler (1972) insists that, on the basis of visits to them made by westerners, they are schools primarily for an elite urban intelligentsia. And Pospielovsky (1976) refers to them as 'ghetto schools for the gifted'. Such schools clearly depend on a stock of 'cultural capital' possessed by a narrow stratum of Soviet society and function to reinforce the distinctive exclusivity of such groups. It appears, therefore, that while greater equality of educational opportunity was the main political aim, contradictory forces which legitimised even greater inequality were also being fostered.

The social pressures unleashed by Stalin's expansion of higher education in the 1940s reflected themselves in very high levels of demand which far outstripped the supply of places. Matthews suggests that this pressure produced press condemnation of bribery of admissions officials and other problems such as voluntary unemployment among school leavers. From 1955 onwards, therefore, Khrushchev changed entrance requirements to higher education. Only people who had worked for two years could be considered for admission. Quota places were reserved for such so-called 'production candidates'. In 1956 all fees were abolished in an effort to encourage more of the children of workers and agricultural workers to pursue higher education. Great efforts were also made to shift the balance in Soviet higher education to part-time education where work and study could be combined over a longer period and embrace more people than full-time education ever could hope to.

The results of these reforms are limited however. Matthews argues that they have done little to alter the position of the intelligentsia. Nor, could it be argued, did they receive widespread support. Certainly, since 1966 many of the reforms have been reversed. Part-time education has been officially criticised for its inefficiency. The academic community bemoaned the lowering of academic standards as the number of production candidates increased and the quota policy here has since been completely reversed. The Soviet government plans to extend the ten-year school throughout the Union and plans to reduce general education to eight years have been abandoned. Finally, though by no means exhaustively, steps have been taken to upgrade the academic content of school courses.

Such shifts cannot be understood simply as shifts in political opinion. They reflect rather more fundamental class alignments in the Soviet Union and such alignments have a distinctive history. They are therefore rooted in the historically evolving structure of Soviet society itself. That structure, during the time of Stalin up to the present has evolved a pattern of social inequality based on education but reflecting the organisation of work. It is patterned according to the historical underdevelopment of Soviet society. In this respect the rural—urban difference in the density of educational provision is critical for it symbolises one of the greatest failures of the Soviet regime, in other words the failure to reduce the gap between the towns and the countryside.

Such historical forces translate themselves into the kinds of claims different sections of Soviet society make upon education and it is here, in the expectations of different groups, that the logic of the educational system itself intercedes between the logic of the economy and even of the political system. The failure of Khrushchev to change attitudes towards education and work is a consequence of this. Education in the Soviet

Union has become the only realistic channel of social and occupational mobility, the vehicle *par excellence* through which people can acquire higher incomes and material rewards. The intergenerational transfer of cultural capital has replaced the inheritance of economic capital as the main mechanism of social differentiation. Success in education under these condition becomes a major personal goal, educational failure a tragedy. The danger for the state is that such personal outcomes are much more clearly the consequence of political decisions in this kind of society and unless the selection process is carefully managed education discontent could acquire a political form. The educational system is thus the main carrier of attitudes which are likely to subvert the dominant political and still collectivistic values of the society as a whole.

The sociology of this situation is necessarily uncertain and the options available to the Soviet leadership for further changes in education are not all clear. Perhaps the most they can hope for is that the progress which has been made in education since the Second World War might be maintained. Even if they do not achieve the development of a new socialist man their achievements will nonetheless have been remarkable. And those achievements will, for a long time, be a source of inspiration for many modern underdeveloped societies seeking a way to construct a socialist future.

THE GERMAN DEMOCRATIC REPUBLIC

> Goethe created the prototype of man in the form of Faust. He is a seeker, a man who thirsts for knowledge, who wants the last secrets and, continuously enquiring after the meaning of human life, finally realises that man's supreme happiness lies in free, creative work done for the benefit of the community. The aim of the socialist school is educating people who are the heirs of Goethe's Faust . . . this is the kind of man socialism needs. (1967)

The above statement comes from an official publication of the Ministry of Education of the German Democratic Republic setting out the philosophy of polytechnical training and education which, since 1965, has become a central component of the educational policy of the DDR.

The aim of this section is to examine how far the structures of education and work evolving in the DDR permit the mature development of such Faustian men. My account seeks to show how a Soviet-based model of development and a tightly controlled cultural policy interact to constitute distinctive environments in work and education in which East Germans acquire their political culture.

The DDR emerged uncertainly from the aftermath of Hitler's war and the defeat of the Third Reich from the Soviet zone of occupied Germany. From March 1964 the political direction of the zone's affairs had been in the hands of the East German Communist Party (*Sozialistiche Einheitspartei Deutschlands*, SED), that is, the Socialist Unity Party under the direction of Walter Ulbricht. Since 1971 the DDR has been led by Erich Honecker. For practically thirty years, therefore, East Germany has been ruled by a political party which, with the reserve power of Russian tanks, had followed a programme of socialist modernisation and reconstruction.

The international environment of the DDR has remained precarious. The DDR is trapped in the front lines of cold-war conflict between the superpowers. A limited European war would turn it into a battlefield for the tanks of NATO and the Warsaw Pact. *Détente* among the great powers threatens to undermine the claims of the DDR to sovereignty as a nation state in the face of the counter-claim of the Federal Republic of Germany to be the sole representative of the German people. For thirty years the leaders of the DDR have had to cope with the uncertainties of this situation and seek approval from audiences of quite different political persuasions.

This is not the place to examine the international position of the DDR. But more so than in many other societies the salience of the international environment for internal politics needs to be taken into account. Since the mid-1950s and the Hungarian uprising, and particularly since the Russian invasion of Czechoslovakia in 1968, the leaders of the DDR have had to make sure that their plans were in accord with what Moscow expected. In any case they could not escape the fact that over 25,000 Russian troops are permanently garrisoned in the DDR. The link with Moscow has not been a stressful one. The ongoing conflict with the Federal Republic and the issue of Berlin expose the DDR to the hegemonic claims of the West, especially as these claims might influence the political aspirations of East Germans, undermining the legitimacy of SED claims to the socialist leadership of the German people. The audiences, therefore, to whom the DDR leadership must play for recognition and support are: (a) Moscow, (b) Federal Republic of Germany and, through them, to the West generally, and (c) the people of

East Germany and the legitimate claims of this group to a standard of living comparable to that which they know exists in the Federal Republic. It is hardly surprising, therefore, that the theme of 'low legitimacy' has been a central one in the political sociology of the DDR (Bayliss, 1972).

Despite this international uncertainty and the traumas of its birth as a modern state, there is now a strong international recognition that the DDR has achieved modernity in a frame work of socialism and that the economic achievements of this society have been remarkable.

As in the Federal Republic the postwar obstacles to economic growth in the DDR were severe. The Soviet Union extracted reparation payments up until 1955. In the years immediately following the end of the war the industrial plant of what had been in prewar Germany, with the exception of a textile and chemical industry, a relatively underdeveloped region, was dismantled and transported as war booty to Russia. Up until 1961 the East German economy suffered a terrible loss in manpower reserves and skills to the West which still exerts a retarding influence on economic growth.

TABLE 4.1

Refugees from the DDR, by employment and profession 1952–65 (selected groups)

	1952–59	1960	1961	1962	1963	1964	1965
Industrial workers	377,648	42,695	9,368	4,691	37,579	3,222	2,452
Technical specialists	35,625	5,255	6,218	463	399	316	283
Government and law	57,097	6,938	7,028	478	148	152	129
Total all Refugees	182,393	199,188	207,026	21,356	42,623*	41,876*	29,532*

* includes pensioners
Source: Smith (1967)

This is not the place to examine in detail the structural defects of the East German economy in the early postwar period since excellent accounts are available (see Smith, 1967; Child, 1969). It is sufficient only to note that the act of partition left the DDR in a disadvantaged position to face an industrial future. The constraints of the past were just as oppressive as those of the present since the prewar economy of East Germany had not been geared up to independent industrialisation.

Since 1964, however, the DDR has produced more industrially than the whole of prewar Germany. The economy has grown considerably since the introduction of the *New Economic System* in 1963 and the DDR is now, next to the Soviet Union, the richest industrial power of the Eastern bloc, with an economy built around the growth industries of chemicals and electronics. The DDR is the world's fourth largest exporter of machinery.

These developments have occurred within the framework of a centrally planned economy organised, it is claimed, according to scientific precepts of Marxism–Leninism. The social structure of prewar Germany has in the course of the last twenty-five years been radically transformed. State ownership of the means of production has reduced the role of private capital to a minimum in East German industry. Agricultural collectivisation has removed the last vestiges of private landowning. Changes in the laws governing education, to which I shall return later, have since 1965 created a system of schools and higher education markedly more egalitarian than that of the Federal Republic and, unlike prewar forms of education in Germany, geared directly to the needs of a modern economy. The tentative moves in the Federal Republic towards an *ostpolitik* in the late 1960s, or normalisation of the relations between the two states, are a recognition of the secure fact of East Germany's existence.

There is, then, a revolution of a type going on in East Germany. It is not necessary to agree with Dahrendorf in his assessment of the DDR as 'the first modern society on German soil . . . (in which) . . . the French Revolution has been led to its horrid extreme . . .' (1967: 424), but he is surely right when he says, 'What has happened in the DDR is more the substitution of one leadership clique for another, which owes its position to the grace of alien powers. In fact, a society with its own peculiar structure has emerged' (1967: 431). Had East Germany become part of the Federal Republic it is almost certain that economic prosperity would have been achieved earlier than it has been, but it is equally certain that the centre of industrial change would have been in the western part of Germany rather than in the east so that, comparatively, the former Soviet Zone would have remained an underdeveloped area in a larger Germany.

Dahrendorf has typified the DDR as a society of modern form and totalitarian substance (1967: 431). The use of the word 'totalitarian' is obviously perjorative in the western context. But it does direct attention to the centrally controlled nature of social and economic life and in doing so perhaps hints at a basic functional property of socialist societies of the Soviet type. R. Lowenthal (1970) has typified such societies as 'development dictatorships' claiming that the very act of central control generates polycentric forces which then require the centre to act even more strongly in a self-sustaining cycle of repression. And Gerd Hennig (1974: 42) has specifically typified the DDR as a 'bureaucratically deformed society in transition to socialism'. His reasons for this are very much the same reasons given by Lowenthal—the inability of the bureaucracy to reconcile socialist goals for society with the economic requirements of the chosen path to socialist development.

The weakness of this view, however, is that it excludes the possibility of choices among alternative ways of building up a socialist society. It therefore locates all the problems of a socialist society in the economic structure when, in fact, the political system and the values it seeks to promote are just as important.

The structure of education and opportunity in the DDR illustrates these points very well and apart from anything else indicates both the strengths and weaknesses of revolutionary process along the lines of the Russian model. For the dilemmas discussed in Chapter 2, namely those of efficiency and equality—involvement and control, have to be faced directly in the field of education.

The realisation of Marxist goals in a German context would in any case have posed difficult problems. Traditional German education was hierarchically organised, inegalitarian to the extreme.

The East German revolution not only had to transform the residual structures of such attitudes but overcome, too, the more recent effects of Nazism and defeat. Basing his account on British Naval Intelligence reports, David Child describes the position of education in the Soviet zone of Germany in 1944 in the following way (1969: 176–7):

Approximately a fourth of all school buildings had been either totally destroyed or needed extensive repairs. Many schools had hardly any teaching materials, furniture or heating facilities. Most school textbooks could not be used because of their Nazi orientation . . . The biggest single problem, however, was providing enough teachers to go round. It was decided that many of the existing staff were not fitted, because of their activities under the Nazis, to carry on shaping the minds of the young. Accordingly, 78 per cent of the teachers in the area of the present Democratic Republic were removed.

East German schools were opened again on 1 October 1945 and in 1946 a law called the 'Law for the Democratisation of the German School' was adopted by each of the *Land* governments. In Child's own words (1969: 177):

The Law sought to educate the young to be capable of thinking for themselves and acting responsibly, able and willing to serve the community. The law also determined that the new education should be free of militarist, imperialist or racialist ideology. In addition it set the educational authorities three other basic tasks: to break the educational privileges of the old propertied classes: to bridge the gap between schools in urban areas and those in the villages; to raise the pre-war level.

Child's own comment in relation to these ends is that:

It is one thing to legislate and another to put things into operation, especially in the difficult conditions of post-war Germany. But over the years the first and third of those objects have been achieved and great progress has been made on the second (1969: 177).

Child's assessment of the achievements of East German education is substantially correct but a closer examination of the structures which have realised these goals does not sustain the kind of optimism which Child possesses. In the remainder of this chapter it will be shown why this is the case.

Two ideas, closely examined, can be shown to represent the essential features of the East German educational system—universality and relevance. The first embodies the claim that all citizens, irrespective of class, sex and race should have equal access and exposure to the same system of education and that differences among citizens according to levels of schooling should depend solely on universalistic and objective measures of ability. Relevance is the principle that education at all levels should be related to the needs of society and socialist construction.

The organisational form which, since 1965, has evolved to realise universality is the ten-class comprehensive school (*Die zehnklassige, allgemeinbildende, polytechnische Oberschule*). The structures designed to realise relevance are those, dating back to 1955, of polytechnical education. The educational system has the following form, as shown in Figure 4.1.

The system is under the control of a central ministry of education and is therefore, unlike the western part of Germany where the cultural autonomy of the *Länder* is still maintained. The system also is a radical departure from the traditions of German education in that it is formally non-selective at the secondary level and very closely oriented to the pragmatic world of production. In this respect, and much more so than in Western Germany the system is geared up to a process of human capital consistent with the changing manpower needs of the East German economy.

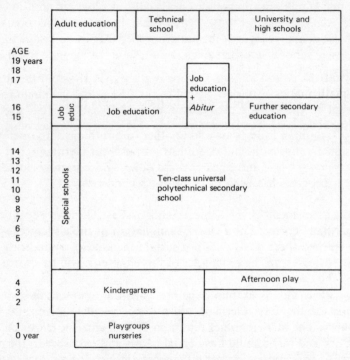

Figure 4.1 The educational system of the DDR 1975

This latter point can be illustrated quite simply by the structure of the school curriculum and the pattern of studies of students at universities. In the seventh, eighth, ninth and tenth classes of the secondary school four hours per week are devoted to a group of studies involving practical work in local factories, called *socialist production*. The school week in the eighth class is broken up as shown in Table 4.2.

TABLE 4.2
Work pattern eighth class DDR

Subject	Hours per week
German	4
Russian	3
Science + Mathematics	10
Socialist Production	4
Geography and History	4
Private Study	4
Social Studies, Sport, Music	5
Total:	34

Source: Klein (1974: 98)

By far the largest amount of time is given over to scientific subjects and mathematics—subjects geared to the formation of human capital relevant to the DDR's programme of modernisation. This scientific loading reflects itself in the distribution of students in higher education across different subjects.

TABLE 4.3
Students by subjects 1963–72 DDR

Subject area	Per cent students in higher education		
	1963	1969	1972
Mathematics and Science	11.0	8.2	9.4
Engineering Science	24.2	29.6	34.5
Medicine and Agriculture	23.4	13.4	10.4
Economic Sciences	—	14.3	15.2
Philosophy, History, Political Science and Law	—	4.3	4.1
Science of Culture, Sports and Literature	—	2.9	2.9
Art	—	1.5	1.5
Education Studies	26.1	25.3	21.6
	($n = 78,415$)	($n = 122,790$)	($n = 153,997$)

Source: DDR (1973)

The growth subjects are obviously in the field of the engineering sciences. It is not possible to read East German publications on education without being made aware forcibly of the close connection between education and what are taken to be the economic needs of a socialist state. The 1965 law which is the legal foundation of the polytechnical secondary school brings out this connection in almost every paragraph stressing all along 'the principle of the connection of education and training with life, the connection of theory with practice, the connection of learning and study with productive activity' (Hahn, 1972: 88).

Access to education, at least formally, is available to anyone with ability. There is no elite theory of manifest truth in the DDR. The achievements of this system have, too, been remarkable and in several respects the relatively underdeveloped DDR has surpassed the West German State in the field of education. This is particularly true in the field of *Kindergarten* provision and, with qualification, in the realm of equal opportunities. Both areas, in fact, illustrate the way in which, in East Germany, socialist ideology and the economic needs which are defined as a result of the ideology interact with existing social and economic conditions to shape the structure and content of education.

In addition to the formal school system there is a well-developed youth policy which engages all young people in cultural, sporting and political activities. Children from the age of six to nine are enrolled in the Young Pioneers (*Junge Pioniere*). Children from nine to fourteen are organised in the Thälemann Pioneers, named after a communist who died in the concentration camp at Buchenwald. Older children and youths can join the Free German Youth Movement (*Freie Deutsche Jugend*). It is seen as a patriotic duty to belong to such organisations (Rinvolucri-Moore, 1973). Since recommendations are important for people in pursuing their careers it is important for members to uphold the values and norms of the organisation. East German youth is in this way brought much more closely than their age peers in the West to the central legitimating values of their society.

The preschool system of the DDR is designed to achieve with small children such goals as health consciousness, imagination, attentiveness, the development of cognitive and motor skills. By 1973 there were 744 places for each thousand children in the relevant age groups in kindergartens. The 1974 economic plan envisages too that there will be 335 places per thousand children in play groups (Klein, 1974: 105). These are remarkable achievements but they reflect two important aspects of the East German revolution. The first, simply, is that education is conceived of as a state responsibility, unlike in Western Germany which is on a family responsibility. Secondly and more important, these developments reflect the manpower shortage of the DDR which requires the maximum employment of married women with young children.

Women in the DDR constitute approximately fifty-five per cent of the age group eighteen to sixty. Of those available for work, eighty-four per cent are actually employed. This is a very high proportion and explanation for it must be sought in the exodus of workers to the west up to 1961, the low proportion of men to women as a result of the war and the low birth-rate of the DDR since 1949. In these circumstances, the provision of an extended network of preschool facilities was a necessary part of expanding the labour force. It is a clear case of ideological pragmatism—doing what is desired out of necessity.

In relation to the principle of equality the same kind of ideological pragmatism can be seen to operate. In terms of overall achievement it is probably the case that the DDR has proportionately more students enrolled in various forms of higher education per size of population than the Federal Republic of Germany. Ludz's description of the DDR as a 'career society' is fully justified in this context. A large proportion of the DDR's student population is pursuing higher education on a part-time basis through a system of local tutors and evening classes. In this way the economy does not have to support a large number of completely dependent students and the State can meet its needs for higher education.

From 1947 to 1961 the State regulated very carefully the kind of student who would be given access to higher education. Working-class children were favoured, as were those people who had had an exemplary record in the fight against Nazism or who had been victims of Nazi persecution. In 1949 a system of *Workers and Peasants Faculties* were set up in each university to develop the higher education opportunities of these groups. These faculties have been dismantled and the positive discrimination programmes which went with them have been replaced simply by the performance principle.

The reason for this latter move is simply that, up until 1961, the policy of positive discrimination had a negative political and economic effect. J. E. Smith has argued (1967: 162), although without supporting evidence, that the policy of excluding children from a bourgeois background from the universities 'contributed unmeasurably to the exodus of qualified people from the east . . . and threatened to alienate all intellectuals and professionals regardless of political belief'. He goes on to quote a former Minister of Education in the DDR, Paul Wandel:

> Yes, we made a lot of mistakes in the early days. We did not know what it meant to govern a state. We were too theoretical. We did not appreciate sufficiently that a state needs more than workers and farmers; that it needs the loyalty of all its citizens (1967: 163).

Education policy has become one of the most well thought of features of the DDR but the cost of commitment has been a high one to bear in terms of equality.

As Table 4.4 makes clear there has been a decline in the percentage of students attending university from a working-class background.

TABLE 4.4
Social origins of students at universities and technical colleges

	Full-time		Part-time	
	1960	*1967*	*1960*	*1967*
Blue-collar workers	50.3	38.2	7.3	11.9
White-collar employees	19.2	23.5	61.8	30.8
Members of production Co-op	4.2	7.8	0.8	1.8
Intelligentsia	15.6	20.4	27.9	53.8
Self-employed	8.0	7.1	2.0	1.4
Others	2.7	3.0	0.2	0.3

Source: Ludz (1970: 26)

Too much should not be read into these figures. J. E. Smith has argued that 'a new intelligentsia is perpetuating itself', that 'class distinctions are becoming rigid' (1967: 171). Smith may be correct when he claims that the pressure from white-collar groups to expand educational opportunities for their children is powerful, but the growth of a middle-class society should not be read into his claims. Workers, farmers and lower white-collar workers have shared in this expansion. Women on the other hand, may not have been so fortunate. There is some slight evidence that, despite the central ideological claims, women have not achieved a social position comparable to men. They are underrepresented in higher education and suffer pressures to force them into the 'wife–mother' role rather than the 'worker–comrade' role (see Schaffer, 1976).

The notion of a 'career society' has other implications. The East Germans have not succeeded according to their own criteria of the 1950s in pressing forward to educational equality. The open door to the west up until 1961 and the need to have more trained manpower have worked together to place a high value on educational achievement as a precondition for occupational achievement. The DDR has become an achievement-oriented society and education has become an instrument of social selection according to the performance principle. Further education in circumstances of labour shortage is a highly prized commodity both for the state and the individual. The pressure to succeed is indeed intense.

In two recent East German publications, *Wirtschaftwissenschaft* and *Einheit*, great stress was laid upon improving educational qualifications to exploit new machinery and labour resources. In *Neues Deutschland*, the daily paper of the Socialist Unity Party, it was announced in February 1974, that apprentices in the consumer goods industries were to be given a differential pay rise. Those with ten years of education will receive more money than those with less than this amount. Such policies are likely to nurture high levels of achievement motivation. At the same time, however, they intensify the problem of selection since between 1967 and 1971 no more than twenty-three per cent of the age group have been able to stay on at school beyond the ten-year course.

There is no evidence yet that the structural limits on educational mobility has produced any dissatisfaction among the population; indeed, probably the opposite is true. The problem of selection is likely, however, to generate tensions in the future as more people who are qualified fail, through tight controls on manpower budgets, to realise their educational aspirations. E. Sachse, a Professor in the Bruno Leuschner School of Economics in East Berlin, has raised this problem of reconciling economic needs and individual aspirations.

Hitherto efforts have been concentrated on ensuring that the number of planned study places matched the number of graduate posts foreseen by the manpower planners. But since these procedures were established the needs felt by our young people—and by the working population too for more education have considerably increased, so that now requests for full or part-time study places exceed the economic demand for persons with the qualifications in question (1976: 382).

The reforms of the last twenty years have opened up mobility opportunities for many sections of the population. In rural areas, for instance, the rationalisation of agriculture through collective ownership has created a management and training system which has provided career opportunities for rural children where previously none existed.

But it is nonetheless true that the pattern of change in the DDR economy—towards the further rationalisation of production and control of industry—is creating a great demand for highly skilled, upwardly mobile workers who will become the managers and technicians of a modernising state. Given the historical legacy of the 'low legitimacy' of the DDR and the historical experience of that low legitimacy being transformed through economic success, it is likely that for these economic reasons the already evident selective processes in education will intensify. The interaction of economic needs, as these are defined given the East German model of industrialisation with educational planning, will intensify the dilemma 'equality–efficiency' by increasing the importance which is attached, both symbolically and financially, to higher education which, given the resources of the DDR, will not expand as rapidly to meet such demands in full.

The sociology of this situation must remain speculative. Karl Schmitt has attempted to argue recently (1975) that, on the basis of attitude surveys among East German young people, the educational system of the DDR has failed to develop 'socialist social character' and 'willingness to co-operate'. He claims that while students at all levels in the educational system express commitment to the goals of socialism their private behaviour is somewhat different. There is low participation in youth organisations and the integrity of family life is still jealously maintained. Schmitt further claims that such results are to be expected on the context of an industrial society where the technical demands of industry are likely to undermine the egalitarian claims of education philosophy. T. A. Bayliss has pursued a similar argument when he writes of the DDR (1972: 55): 'The symbols of rationality, hierarchy, and control clash with more subtle implications of individuality, equality and spontaneity'. The difficulties in such views is that they are both based upon inadequate data and inadequate theory describing societies of this type. And the 'data' to which they refer is arguably too crude to indicate much about the way in which people in East Germany actually think about the world.

How can the effects of a well-orchestrated cultural policy with respect to all forms of artistic production and even language itself be measured. Claus Mueller has argued (1973) that modern East German German is recognisably different from the German spoken in the West. He refers to it as an 'administered language' (1973: 41). On his earlier assumption that, through the acquisition of a language a person 'unintentionally assimilates the political and social values . . . of his group' (1973: 14), then, clearly, evidence about participation in youth organisations can only give the barest glimpse of the experience and thought of East Germany.

In addition neither Schmitt nor Bayliss can distinguish clearly those features of the society of the DDR which result from its unique historical experience and current international position and those which are the result of the structure of societies of the state socialist type as a whole. Until a carefully controlled programme of comparative research among East European societies is completed then it is dangerous to make generalisations about the structural consequences of the command economy for education.

There does, however, seem to be particular structural pressures working on the social system of the DDR to raise acutely the possible tension between egalitarian revolutionary ends and efficient processes of production. Unless industrial change leads to greater output, less work and therefore more opportunities for the creative use of time, fuller control of the work situation by workers themselves and the disappearance of structures which divide men from one another on dimensions of power and prestige, then the revolutionary claims made of such change will be groundless.

On each criterion the social structure of the DDR contains counter-revolutionary features and potentials. Scientific management without workers' control of decision-making, on elaborate and stratified division of labour and a stratified system of education, interact with one another to create new opportunities for social advance and higher levels of living. Whether these are the seedbed conditions of socialism is quite another matter. It would be wrong to conclude affirmatively either way. The DDR has a rapidly changing society whose future profile cannot be predicted. All that can be claimed with certainty is that the sociological analysis of this society must recognise its unique history and its international relationships.

The 'heirs of Goethe's Faust' are still in their infancy and at the moment, given their schools and jobs, it is by no means certain that they will ever grow up.

5 Education in Dependent Societies: Ghana and Tanzania

THE LOGIC OF COMPARISON

The framework of comparative study which governs the organisation of my discussion has already been set out in Chapter 2. In this section of the present chapter I want to make clear why, given the general orientation to comparison which I have adopted, a specific comparison of Tanzania and Ghana is a useful one to make. My argument has three main themes. The first is that both societies have experienced a direct form of colonial domination by Britain. The second is that, as a consequence of this colonial domination both societies experienced economic changes which tied them to the developed capitalist economies of the western world and which, even after the formal transfer of political authority in the form of independence, continue to set the constraints on what is possible in terms of further socioeconomic development. Finally, both societies, for complex historical and political reasons, face the future in different ways. They follow quite different *models of development* and these differences have a direct bearing on what is being done in the field of education and in other institutional areas. The differences between the two societies in this respect are sufficiently great to help us judge how far social changes stemming from the action of a dependent state itself can overcome the structure of economic and cultural constraints which colonial penetration left behind and which modern capitalism maintains.

Both Ghana and Tanzania were British colonies. Ghana formerly known as the Gold Coast, experienced continuous British domination from 1844 to 1957, when it became under Kwame Nkrumah the first black African state to achieve its independence. Tanzania, formally Tanganyika, achieved its independence in 1961 having been a British colony since 1918 and before that a major part of German East Africa.

126

The precise form of colonial involvement varied between the two societies. British colonial penetration of the Gold Coast was much more certain than in Tanganyika. Indeed, as David Morrison has pointed out, because of its uncertain international status, lack of exploitable resources and the absence of longstanding commercial centres—all of which distinguished Tanganyika from the Gold Coast both in the late nineteenth and twentieth centuries—the prospects for economic development of independent Tanzania were bleak (Morrison, 1976). Ghana, on the other hand, as Samir Amin has pointed out (1973), was the richest British colony in black Africa with its wealth based on cocoa production.

At the point of independence in 1957 Ghana had one of the strongest economies in black Africa with very high reserves of foreign currency, low levels of social service expenditure and a strong balance of payments. The economic promise implied in this has not been realised. Instead of steady growth Ghana has experienced a decrease in per capita incomes, a balance of trade deficit, political instability, military coups and increased foreign debts.

The post-independence economic history of Tanzania has also been unsatisfactory. Tanzania remains one of the poorest countries in the world, suffering from low incomes, high mortality rates and low levels of service provision and her economy has not developed in a way which would reduce the impact of world fluctuations in primary commodity prices or the need to decrease Tanzania's reliance on foreign aid and high levels of food imports.

Both societies have structural features which reflect their colonial history and which can only be understood if the mechanisms of that colonial penetration are identified. But at the same time the historical *constraints* of colonial dependency are being coped with in very different ways in both societies and it is here, in the models of development which each society is pursuing, that the significance of a comparison lies.

In 1967 President Julius Nyerere issued the famous *Arusha Declaration* which outlined, so he argued, a socialist development strategy for Tanzania and a policy of self-reliance. Tanzania thus sought to break the bonds of dependency through a commitment to socialism.

The generals who currently govern Ghana also have a policy of self-reliance known as 'Operation Feed Yourself'. But, unlike self-reliance policies in Tanzania it is not conceived of as an essential component of a broader programme of socialist development or code of political practice. Nor have Ghanaian development plans been so carefully worked out or tested over time. During the years since the Arusha

Declaration Ghana has had three changes of government, two of them involving military coups and even now could hardly be said to have a government with a coherent philosophy or popular support.

The direction of change in the two societies is also influenced by their different international allegiances and political reference groups. Ghana is still very much oriented to the West in its search for foreign aid, supplies and a viable development strategy, its relationships with the East, and with the Soviet Union in particular, having undergone an abrasive deterioration since the downfall of Nkrumah in 1966 (Bennet, 1975).

Tanzania, on the other hand, is positively oriented to the East and particularly to China. The building of the Tanzania–Zambia railway is the most tangible evidence of this but the longer-term political consequence of Tanzania's relations with China may be more significant then the railway in development terms. As Julius Nyerere said in a speech in Peking:

> Two things convince me that socialism can be built in Africa and that it is not a Utopian vision. For capitalism is ultimately incompatible with the real independence of African States. The second thing which encourages me is China . . . China is providing an encouragement and an inspiration for younger and smaller nations which seek to build socialist societies (quoted by M. Bailey, 1975: 42).

Such differences in political orientation are difficult to measure and their impact on the development of different forms of social structure can only be assessed in the long term. But they are real enough and help further to distinguish the development models which operate in the two states.

In the course of this historical process of colonisation metropolitan models of politics and administration and education were imposed on the people of Ghana and Tanzania. The effect was to reinforce an economic dependency by a cultural dependency on western models of education and learning. Two themes need to be emphasised in analysing this; in both cases it can be shown that Ghana and Tanzania are reacting in different ways.

The first is the role of colonial education, already noted, in causing a great gulf to exist between educated elites and the masses as a whole. When such polarisation occurs, and the colonial state fosters it, it is difficult for political elites to secure the confidence of the masses; their ability, therefore, to mobilise peasants and workers behind programmes of change after independence is seriously weakened (Mende, 1973). This problem is likely to be far more serious in Ghana than Tanzania. In Tanzania a code of leadership exists which seeks to prevent a great gap emerging between government officials, ministers and peasants. And the rhetoric of equality and service to the people at least constitutes some kind of symbolic check on the behaviour of officials. I do not wish to imply this problem has been solved in Tanzania; it has not. But Ghanaian political culture as Price has argued, sustains a different conception of leadership which he calls the 'Big Man, Small Boy Syndrome' (Price, 1974). In Ghana, he suggests, it is almost expected that officials will lead an ostentatious lifestyle and officials themselves certainly expect to do so. This generates mistrust and corruption on a massive scale, hardly the seedbed conditions for rapid development. Education is implicated in such social differentiation in so far as it is a luxury commodity and available only to the well-off and to the extent that educational qualifications are the passports to jobs in the government bureaucracy.

The second theme is the loss of cultural identity about which Fanon writes so well and which stems from having to cope with an imposed culture of education, a foreign language and only a selective exposure to the lifestyle and resources of the colonial power (F. Fanon, 1967). Remi Clignet has written about these mechanisms in the following way, claiming that Africans during the colonial period suffered from a 'double alienation' (1971: 303).

> The practices, ideologies, and philosophies imposed upon him are alien to his framework of reference and his own tradition. His first alienation results, therefore, from his exposure to educational and cultural stimuli that tend to erase the significance of his own past. But his second alienation results from the selective nature of the elements of the metropolitan culture with which he is confronted.

And Franz Fanon put it this way, writing in particular about the cultural implications of having to embrace a foreign language (1973: 14):

> Every colonized people—in other words, every people in whose soul an inferiority complex has been created by the death and burial of its local cultural originality—finds itself face to face with the language of the civilising nation; that is, with the culture of the mother country. The colonized is elevated above his jungle status in proportion to his adoption of the mother country's cultural standards. He becomes whiter as he renounces his blackness, his jungle.

Clignet, echoing Fanon, summarises this phenomenon as the 'Caliban Complex', a set of social attitudes and beliefs about the world which reinforce the sense of dependency of the colonised on the coloniser, a relationship difficult to break even after independence. But this problem, too, is less severe in Tanzania than in Ghana. Tanzania has been more successful in weaning people away from western concepts of what education is and Tanzania academics are less likely than Ghanaians to see British universities as the only model of higher education worth emulating. And there is some evidence, admittedly slight, that educated Tanzanians have begun to overcome their cultural dependence on the West. This reflects itself, for example, in changing attitudes to the use of Swahili rather than English as the language of the educated.

It is only a small indicator but it is an important one. Other indicators include the deliberate policy in Tanzania to replace expatriate teaching staff with Tanzanians and to Africanise the school curriculum. This is in sharp contrast with Ghana where education still resembles that of Britain although, of course, in an attenuated form.

Cultural dependency consolidates economic dependency to the extent that metropolitan models of education and learning are employed in the dependent society. The processes of what Carnoy (1974) has called 'cultural imperialism' and to which we have already alluded, are reflected mainly in the form and content of education institutionalised in a given state. In many African States the form of education is modelled closely on that of the metropolitan power and serves to seal further the pernicious connection between the independent state and the metropolitan power. Ali Mazrui (1975), for instance, an East African political scientist has insisted that the university, though being an 'analogue' to the multinational corporation is 'the most sophisticated instrument of cultural dependency'.

It performs this role, he believes, by cultivating a taste for western lifestyles and, therefore, western imports, and western academic values thus effectively devaluing African cultures and their cultural achievements. The case is clearly an arguable one but the strength of the western model of education can be gauged by the political difficulties African political leaders face when they attempt to encourage the growth of other forms of educational practice. This particular issue comes out very vividly in Tanzania's attempt to implement Nyerere's plans set out in *Education For Self-Reliance* and in some of the tortuous paradoxes of Ghanain education, particularly the growth of an inferior system of private secondary education, and the implacable opposition which still exists to any plans to make education more relevant to the needs of the economy.

Many West African academics emulate meticulously the practices of their European reference groups in matters of higher education and such groups have played a crucial part in various times in major political events. In the Tanzanian case, however, there is some evidence of the intellectuals showing greater allegiance to the goals of socialist development and recognising that this implies new attitudes to education.

Both societies, however have economies which, though different, are good examples of dependency and in this respect they face common problems. They face the problem of industrialising without increasing their debt, of modernising without political instability and of meeting ever-increasing demands on public expenditure without jeopardising investment plans in productive capital. And in both societies development jars against the residual structures of the colonial state and the special political forms of the successor state. The point I wish to demonstrate in this chapter is that there is still the possibility of choices being made among alternative policies even when the constraints are severe and that different choices have substantially different consequences for the form development might take. A comparison of the two states illustrates this point very well.

GHANA

At independence in 1957 Ghana had an educational system which reflected the principal historical contours of European colonisation; the distribution of schools throughout the country followed the patterns of uneven economic development which characterised the colonial economy. The social distribution of this westernised education paralleled that social hierarchy of Ghanaian society, itself having been fashioned by the structures of colonial society as a whole. And the leaders of Ghanaian independence faced the future without any clear vision of what an independent Ghana might become and their inability to conceive of this is in no small way due to the fact that they themselves were products of the colonial education system.

In what follows I shall illustrate this argument. In particular I shall illustrate that the form, content, funding and distribution of education in Ghana reflects an historical compromise between the colonial government and a Ghanaian elite and that post-independence developments have not succeeded in changing the outcome of that compromise particularly as it relates to the prevailing conception in Ghana of what education is, and what development itself ought to mean. But for a brief period during the regime of Kwame Nkrumah the prevailing conception of development in Ghana was a western model of development and even today the prevailing conception of education is a western one.

The historical form and present structure of Ghanaian education is most easily described in relation to four principal phases in Ghanaian development, each representing different models of social and economic development and each illustrating some distinctive problems inherited by a neo-colonial state. The first is the period of colonial government itself up to 1951. The second is the period from 1951 to 1961 when an independent Ghana pursued a future based on a form of capitalist development. The third is from 1961 to 1966 when Nkrumah sought to steer the country towards a socialist future. His complete failure during this period ended in a military coup and this ushered in the fourth phase which includes present-day Ghana.

GHANA UNDER COLONIAL RULE

By independence day in 1957 the Gold Coast had been under the direct influence of Britain for over one hundred years. Through missionary activity and trading, together with constitutional changes British dominance had been firmly secured by the end of Queen Victoria's reign but the most decisive changes for the social structure of modern Ghana came in the period after the turn of the century with the development of cocoa as the country's main export crop. Indeed, prior to the development of cocoa, Britain's involvement in the affairs of the Gold Coast was uncertain and hesitant, governed more by considerations of foreign policy in Europe and in particular the need to contain what were taken to be the expansionist plans of Germany and France, than by considerations of profitable economic gain. W. E. F. Ward has pointed out (1948: 226), for instance, that in 1860, 'The general opinion in England was that the West African colonies were not worth keeping; they were unhealthy, poverty-stricken and perpetually troubled with barbarian raids'. This was not, of course, the opinion of white people on the spot in the colony; as merchants and missionaries they were much more strongly convinced either of the long-term possibilities of the growth of trade or the spread of Christian civilisation and because of this were adamant about the need for a continued military and political presence in the area.

The demands of merchants and traders were, of course, longstanding. Trade with the Gold Coast had developed from the sixteenth century onwards. It expanded rapidly during the eighteenth and nineteenth centuries and the growth of commercial centres on the coast prompted the opening up of trade in the hinterland and acting as a solvent of traditional social structures well before the formal annexation of the Gold Coast by the British government.

During this period, too, social changes occurred which were later to have very profound consequences for the way in which Ghana was to achieve its independence and for the way in which education was to develop in the colony. For the early trading contacts encouraged the growth of an elite group of African merchants and traders, educated deliberately by the European merchant companies themselves to act as interpreters, soldiers and clerical subordinates. This group gradually articulated further demands for education and as C. K. Graham (1971) has shown, this demand predated the growth of mission schools which only became an important component of education in the nineteenth century. And as Graham has also shown, the rationale for education in the colony was similar to that which prevailed in Britain during the late eighteenth and nineteenth centuries.

Trade thus brought the Gold Coast into the orbit of the world capitalist economy and the educational practice of the merchant companies and missionaries imported an essential structure of that society into the Gold Coast. As I shall indicate, however, following Philip Foster (1965) that structure was to perform different functions in the colonial society to those it performed in Britain.

The pattern of African *demand* for education, particularly during the nineteenth century has been extensively discussed by Philip Foster (1965) and, more recently by C. K. Graham (1971). Both writers underline the fact that what the Africans demanded was an education which would fit them well for employment and particularly clerical employment. In the last third of the nineteenth century rapid economic growth in the colony 'gave a realistic meaning to the pressure of the Africans for more schools and for clerical forms of employment'. As Graham explains (1971: 99):

There was little need for skilled artisans because of the lack of any industrial institutions. There was evidence, too, that the skilled artisans were receiving lower wages than the clerks. No wonder, then, that there was a distaste for anything savouring of labour among upper standard boys who thought that to be a scholar was to be a gentleman and to be a gentleman precluded the possibility of gaining a livelihood except by the pen.

And Philip Foster (1965: 106) sums it up in this way referring to the failure of both the colonial government and the missions to set up a viable technical and agricultural component in the school curriculum:

> ... African pressures for academic forms of education and particularly for academic secondary education are readily under-standable. In practice the African clientele of the schools received very much the kind of education that they also reasonably desired. During the nineteenth century most British educationists on the coast had espoused the cause of technical and agricultural education as a key to economic development. African parents ... did not send their children to school to meet the need for economic growth; they sent them there to maximise their children's opportunities within the emergent occupational and prestige structure created by colonial rule.

Education in the Gold Coast thus came to be seen as an instrument of occupational mobility, an effect quite unintended by the missions and the colonial government, and not without its bizarre aspects. W. E. F. Ward has written (1948: 199) about the 'trouble from semi-educated man whose scanty stock of learning led them not to wisdom, but to arrogance or to downright rascality ... The Coast is full of stories of the misuse of odd scraps of print, of written "charms", "brain pills", magic "examination-passing pens" and the like'.

Forster (1965) has argued that the availability of education as an avenue of social mobility outside of traditional social structures and particularly the clear block which existed on such mobility due to the absence of real opportunities for higher education, were the principal factors in nurturing early nationalist movements led and organised by the educated urban groups. And Foster quotes Wallerstein with approval: 'Colonisation not only created the social conditions of its demise; it provided also the ideological weapons' (1965: 105). Thus the early efforts of the colonial government and its education ordinances, together with the activities of missionaries and merchants, resulted in a distinctively elitist western model of education becoming highly valued in the Gold Coast before the onset of the colony's most successful period of economic growth in the twentieth century and the development of cocoa production.

This model of education was reinforced by the social structure of colonial society itself. Foster argues (1965: 98) that colonial society provided Africans with a 'generalised reference group' upon which their aspirations could be modelled. Since the white people in question performed such a limited range of work it was inevitable, Foster claims, that Africans too would regard such work as the only worthwhile work for someone to do. There is, however, a further aspect to this which relates to the theme of the alienation of the educated African.

White colonial society had properties of its own which reinforced attitudes of superiority towards Africans and which set up in Africans themselves an ambiguous attitude to colonialism itself. Michael Crowder has pointed out (1968: 393), for instance, that 'colonial society' was a racist and a bourgeois society distrustful of black people: 'It is essential to appreciate the fact that colonial society was a bourgeois one, acting out an aristocratic way of life abroad, and returning on leave to middle class suburbs or country cottages in England or France. They looked upon Africans as inferiors and particularly distrusted the educated African whom they referred to as the 'savvy boy'. As Crowder says (1968: 398): 'For the British the educated African was a gaudy, despised imitator of European ways. For them the "real" African was the peasant or the traditional chief who, unlike the educated African, did not challenge their supremacy'. Crowder typifies colonial society as 'a closed society of pigmentation' which functioned successfully to help produce primary school graduates who despised their own heritage yet who could not quite cope with the new world they sought to relate to: 'They were given a brief glimpse of the Western world, but only part of the educational equipment to deal with it' (1968: 387).

I shall try to show later that the failure of Ghanaian politicians to pose the problems of development in terms other than those of capitalist development owes much to this particular aspect of colonial society.

The economic and political importance of Ghana to the British Empire increased rapidly during the twentieth century and the basis of it lay in the growth of cocoa production. As Amin has pointed out, in successive five-year periods from 1900 to 1915 cocoa production increased by thirty, twenty and ten per cent a year (Amin, 1973: 43). This rapid growth, which continued through the 1920s was at the basis of the country's prosperity for it allowed for the growth of an economic infrastructure out of the colony's own funds. Until 1929 with the setting up of the Colonial Development Fund in an attempt to reduce unemployment in Britain, self-financed growth was the only option available to British colonial government.

Cocoa production allowed for increases in population; it catalysed the growth of urban centres and it generated demands for the further development of education and other aspects of an economic infrastructure. It also accelerated changes in the social structure of Ghanaian society, fashioning even more clearly those groups who would demand independence from Britain. Tetteh Kofi (1972: 98) has put the case this way:

> The increase in exports in general and cocoa in particular brought wealth which changed the pattern and raised the level of economic activity in Ghana. A class structure different from that of the African communal societies emerged—rich peasants, poor peasants or rural proletarians, semi-proletarians, industrial or urban proletarians and the national bourgeoisie or bureaucratic capitalists . . . As the level of economic activity rose, the national bourgeoisie gained added wealth, prominence, and more importantly, self-definition.

The economic basis of this was commerce and this base expanded rapidly with the growth of cocoa production. But the warp and weft of this 'self-definition' was education binding the elites of the coastal area to a common view of the world and leading them to an articulate recognition of their obviously unjustified lack of status *vis-à-vis* government and administration. An important factor fuelling African demand for education was precisely this recognition. But education also reinforced their sense of being different from workers and peasants and the masses generally, a fact which later lay behind the failure of the United Gold Coast Convention to win elections and of the leaders of the Conventional Peoples Party to build a viable socialist development framework for Ghana.

The elite-mass gap which typifies the social structure of many underdeveloped societies can be seen, therefore, in the Ghanaian case, to have its roots in colonial education although this was not something colonial administrators intended.

Educational development in the twentieth century can perhaps best be described in terms of its principle phases; these are the period from 1892 and the education ordinance of that year to the new education ordinance of 1925. The second phase is from 1925 to the 1951 Accelerated Development Plan. The third phase is from 1951 to the present day. During each principal phase there are important shifts in education reflecting developments in colonial policy itself interacting with a changing volume and pattern of African demand for education. The period from 1892 to 1925 is typified by a growth of schools and school enrolments but on the initiative of the missions and according to principles of the 'free market', schools being provided in response to African demand for them.

Two features of this situation stand out, both reflecting the form of colonial penetration in the Gold Coast. The first is government indifference to education beyond the primary stage reflecting itself in the low direct provision of government schools, the virtual absence of any secondary provision and a high tolerance of very high levels of primary school drop-out rates. The second is the geographical distribution of schools themselves; schools developed much more quickly in the south of the country than in Ashanti or the northern territories and this uneven spread reflects directly the location and spread of economic activity and political control in the colony.

Both characteristics of the educational system had important consequences for the future. The reluctance of the colonial government to finance education led to the rapid growth of an educational structure outside of the control of the government. The second was the failure of educational expansion to match the growth of the child population (Foster, 1965: 114). Indeed, Foster reports on calculations made in 1938 which indicated that, at the rate of growth in education between 1911 and 1934 it would have taken six hundred years for all African children to be enrolled in school (1965: 116). In a sense, then, the educational system of Ghana, such as it was, was underdeveloped from the very beginning. The absence of any framework of post-primary education for the one child in ten who completed the primary school course, meant that there was a severe restriction on the growth of teachers to sustain greater growth in the schools. And the absence of a manageable structure of education meant that educational development occurred haphazardly more responsive to the immediate demands of African traders and clerks than to the needs of a developing economy.

Between 1900 and the end of the First World War the development of education in the Gold Coast accelerated. Government expenditure increased from £6,543 in 1901 to £54,000 in 1919 when Governor Guggisberg was appointed (McWilliam and Kwamena, 1975: 116). The number of primary schools increased during the same period from 135 to 234 with enrolments doubling from 12,000 pupils to 22,000. The government during this period took some tentative steps to encourage the setting up of secondary schools and a teacher-training facility at Accra, but as late as 1950 only two Government secondary schools existed. Philip Foster typifies British policy towards secondary schools during the whole of the late colonial period as 'extraordinarily cautious'

(1965: 115). Nonetheless, it can be said of the period up to 1925 that the foundations of an organised education system had been laid (Hilliard, 1956). The administration of schools had been regionalised; the government had set up four junior trade schools 'designed to meet the growing need for artisans of a reasonable general educational standard' (Hilliard, 1956: 83).

Two events of the 1920s need to be noted. The first is the report of the Phelps–Stokes Commission which prompted the British Government to set up in 1923 a permanent Advisory Committee on Native Education in the Tropical African Dependencies (Graham, 1971). The second was the report of the so-called Educationists' Committee which Governor Guggisberg had set up in 1920 to report on education in the colony. The Educationists' report emphasised the need for further expansion in the system and the immediate setting up of a teacher training college. This particular recommendation led to the setting up of Achimota college and this college came to play a significant role in the Gold Coast, not simply as a supplier of trained teachers but as a model of what a good education was to look like.

The Phelps–Stokes report served to refine government conceptions of what the aims of African education really were. The mission itself was inspired by the American Baptist Foreign Missionary Society. The conclusions of this commission (which numbered among its members Dr Aggrey, a native of the Gold Coast who had studied in America and who was to become the assistant principal of Achimota college) were accepted completely by the British Colonial Office and hailed by Governor Guggisberg as 'the book of the century, a combination of sound idealism and practical commonsense' (Foster, 1965: 156). Its main theme was the need to adapt colonial education to African conditions and particularly to the conditions of work on the land. It proposed an educational system substantially based on an agricultural curriculum supplemented by Trade schools 'to teach the simpler elements of trades required in native villages and to prepare for the less skilled occupations in industrial concerns' (Foster, 1965: 158). It recommended that tribal languages should be the language of instruction in primary schools, English only being taught in the later stages. These themes of adaption have been discussed by Foster and shown to be unrealistic in the Gold Coast context since African demand had been for a long time focused on an academic education.

But there is another theme to be found in the Phelps–Stokes report to which Foster pays little attention. This is the political importance of only a selective exposure to the values and education of white society.

The underdeveloped nature of secondary education and an inefficient primary school system meant in any case that most Africans had little direct exposure to European education tradition and skills, but the Phelps–Stokes Commission was quite clear that this selective exposure was justified, not simply because too much exposure would induce the native to leave the land but because it would also cause him to become disaffected. This particular sentiment was to dominate British policy in the area as late as 1944. The Commission had been quite clear in its view that the educated Africans constituted a potential threat to colonial rule unless, of course, their education was carefully managed. The Commission put it this way: 'The Education Commission was warned by both thoughtful leaders of both Natives and Europeans that the urban groups must be helpfully educated or they would become "poison centres" of every political area in Africa' (Scanlon, 1964: 85). And a British Government memorandum on Education in the Colonies in 1944 noted the need to control 'the explosive temper' of some groups by 'wisely directed mass education with particular stress on the development of social and civic responsibility' (Scanlon, 1964: 110).

But it was not just the requirement to control Africans for political purposes which governed colonial education policy. Colonial education policies were firmly based in a belief that African culture was inferior, that Africans required a civilisation. The Phelps–Stokes Commission is again very revealing. It reported a 'general conviction' (although not, presumably, among Africans) that 'at least the Native leaders of Africa should know a European language as a means of access to the great accomplishments of and inspirations of civilisation' (Scanlon, 1964: 68). The Commission even speculated that 'It may even be true that some one of the Native languages may be so highly developed as to make possible the translation of the great works of civilisation into that language' (Scanlon 1964: 69). The civilisation was, of course, western civilisation.

Thus the first major attempt to spell out coherently the aims of education in West Africa reflects the basic conviction that development for the African meant very much the development of a more efficient system of agricultural production in which Africans would find their employment. It was not intended that the Gold Coast should be developed as a modern industrial society in which Africans themselves might take up the key leadership positions. And the development which did take place was based on the unshakeable belief that western education and western values were both valid for and essential to West Africa.

The work of the Educationists' Committee led to the second main event of the 1920s, the setting up of Achimota college as a centre for the training of teachers with a curriculum which reflected what Governor Guggisberg thought were the needs of Africans. The intention was not to set up an English public boarding school although Achimota was conceived of as an elite institution, the pivot of secondary and post-secondary education in Ghana (Foster, 1965: 166). The philosophy of Achimota had been evolved by the governor in the early 1920s. He saw it as an institution of character training and a way of upgrading the quality of the teachers to the primary schools. Guggisberg spoke of the need for such an institution in his address to the Legislative Council in 1924:

> We are flooding the market with semi-educated youths for whom, owing to their disdain for manual labour, there is annually less employment. . . . Failing employment in an office, and strongly imbued with an unhealthy dislike for manual labour, they fall a natural victim to discontent and consequently to unhappiness (quoted in Metcalfe, 1964: 597).

And as he underlined in his pamphlet, *The Keystone*, published in 1924, 'The chief cause of these defects was that those who taught had themselves received an inferior kind of education' (Hilliard, 1957: 87). Achimota was designed to correct this.

Guggisberg, as one of his biographers has pointed out, was no education theorist. In fact, it was said of him that he would have everyone be a good boy scout: 'In Guggisberg's mind Baden-Powell was perhaps the greatest educationist of all' (Wraith, 1967: 131). Such views expressed themselves in a strict curriculum with many of the more obvious features of an English public boarding school—a house system, sporting activities (Achimota had three cricket pitches) prefects, rigorous selection, a high scale of fees and giving access to higher qualifications which would lead to university education in England. It also sustained something of the atmospheres of such schools and this reflected itself in such diverse practices as the wearing of academic gowns and initiation ceremonies for the new students. Indeed, one such student, Kwame Nkrumah, wrote of the initiation rituals that they 'seemed to last a long time, [that he] wondered whether education was really worth the misery of it all' (Nkrumah, 1957: 13). Nkrumah goes on to write about swotting, morning drill, Sunday chapel, prefects, the debating society and absolutely strict discipline.

It may have been the aim of Achimota to live up to the slogan, often used by its African vice-principal, Dr Aggrey that, 'Only the best is good enough for Africa' (Ward, 1948: 359), but one of the consequences of the school is that government support for secondary education became highly focused on this one school to the neglect of others and more, to the neglect of the much wider needs of secondary schooling in the Gold Coast. Foster has pointed out that in the period between 1920–30 some eighty-five per cent of government expenditure on schools was earmarked for Achimota (Foster, 1965: 167).

The depression of the 1930s prompted a cutback in the growth of government expenditure on education but throughout the 1930s the expansion in education was maintained although mainly outside of the government sector. During the 1940s there was a marked growth in teacher training and in October 1948 the University College of the Gold Coast was opened, housed temporarily in Achimota and offering degrees from London University.

For the full significance of these developments to be appreciated it is necessary to set them against social, economic and political development of the Gold Coast during this period and specifically the growth of nationalism. For it must be stressed that during the period of rapid educational expansion in the Gold Coast, that is from the end of the First World War, the economic development of the colony was being carefully managed to service the economic needs of the metropolitan economy in Britain and the political process which brought this about was the gradual incorporation of nascent nationalist elements into the running of the colonial state.

Several writers have stressed that the commercial and professional elites of Ghana played an important role in the colonial government. Dennis Austin has argued (1975: 354), for instance, that, 'In the interwar years . . . the country was governed by a triple elite of colonial officials, chiefs and the intelligentsia'. Bob Fitch and Mary Oppenheimer argue (1966: 13) that: 'Until 1947, Gold Coast "politics" consisted primarily of lobbying by various cliques of chiefs and lawyers for greater representation within the Gold Coast Legislative Council'. And finally, the situation up to 1948 has been summed up by Samir Amin in this way (1973: 47):

> Until 1948 British colonial policy had been uneventful. A new class of capitalist planters had been established on the basis of the old Ashanti chiefs, and political life had been reduced to intrigues by the 'lobbies' of planters and anglicised intellectuals of the coast, centred around the United Gold Coast Convention.

Such groups did not command wide popular support and what support they did have came from the more educated section of society, groups which sought a political authority outside of the traditional structures of tribe and chiefdom (Hurd, 1967). Even when the nationalist movement divided and Kwame Nkrumah founded the Convention Peoples Party to demand immediate independence in 1949, the basis of popular support was quite small and the most active groups were, as David Apter and (1963), Dennis Austin (1964) have separately pointed out, disenchanted standard seven boys aggrieved by colonialism, the traditional chiefs *and* the wealthy leaders of the United Gold Coast Convention. Their demands were not for a more equal society only that the government should be African.

During this same period the importance of the Gold Coast economy to Britain increased enormously, as indeed, did the whole colonial economic system. Colonial visionaries like Leo Amery (Secretary of State for the Colonies 1924–29) and Viscount Milner (Secretary of State 1919–21) had argued vociferously in the interwar years that colonial development would help solve Britain's economic problems and particularly unemployment (Porter, 1975). Their views were not widely accepted and met stiff resistance in the Colonial Office and the Treasury (Constantine, 1975). But if the Government was not convinced industry and commerce was. British exports to her colonies increased from thirty-seven per cent in 1920–24 to forty-nine per cent in 1935–39. British foreign investment in the colonies increased from forty-six per cent in 1911–13 to fifty-nine per cent in 1927–29 (Porter, 1975: 261). But the dividends were, perhaps, in the long term a mixed blessing. Britain's pattern of exports from 1870 onwards favoured non-industrial countries. As Porter says (1975: 263), 'The underdeveloped world was an easy refuge for inefficient and hard-pressed entrepreneurs, and its existence itself perpetuated their inefficiency'.

The dividends themselves were, nonetheless, great. Vast fortunes were made by such companies as the United Africa Company and Unilever (see Rodney, 1972). And during the late period of colonialism, including the Second World War and the period up to independence in 1957, the British Government through the mechanism of the Sterling Balances and the Cocoa Marketing Board (set up in 1948 by a Labour Government) was able to reap immense financial rewards from West Africa. The Sterling Balances represented low interest loans from the colonies to Britain—the money itself coming through the marketing networks—and played an important part, as Fitch and Oppenheimer put it (1966: 44), in 'priming the pump' of Britain's postwar economic recovery.

By the end of the colonial period, then, the Gold Coast economy was making an important contribution to the British economy and the sterling area. But it should not be forgotten that as late as 1953, some fifty per cent of the population was still involved in subsistence agriculture; twenty per cent were involved in cocoa production and only about eight per cent of the population were directly involved in the exchange economy (Foster, 1965: 139). And despite the most highly developed education system in tropical Africa outside of the Union of South Africa, functional literacy was well below twenty per cent (Foster, 1965: 171).

GHANA UNDER COLONIAL RULE FROM 1951–61

Independence was formally achieved in Ghana in 1957 but effective independence was achieved in 1951 following a period of labour unrest and the formation of the Convention Peoples Party in 1949 led by Nkrumah. The first Nkrumah government was formed in 1951.

Despite the image he was later to acquire, Nkrumah's policies in this early period were hardly radical. Fitch and Oppenheimer (1966: 32) have described them as 'reformist'. The CPP (Convention Peoples Party), they argue, sought little more than to convince the colonial government that they were ready for self-government. Robert Dowse (1973: 265) has typified the leadership of the CPP as *dirigiste*, in other words determined to provide guidance from the top, and Nkrumah's economic thinking as 'populist'. Nkrumah's aim, Dowse argues (1973), was to let the private sector of the economy grow and, through taxation and the running down of the sterling balances, the state would direct the build up of an economic infrastructure. Samir Amin (1973) has argued that in this early period (between 1951 and 1957) there was little thought of fundamental social and political changes. But it is precisely during this period that the Ghanaian economy became fragile. To meet popular demands a policy of price stability was pursued coupled with an increase in private consumption (Dowse, 1973). A great deal was invested in the public sector but the price was a running down of the sterling balances and in the mid-1960s the world price of cocoa dropped and by 1957 there was a budget deficit. These are classic symptoms of a dependent economy. They prompted Nkrumah to say informally in 1957:

The Duchess of Kent came one day and gave us our political freedom. I was strong because the price of cocoa was high . . . in two weeks the price of cocoa was fiddled by the commodity markets . . . My strength was gone and I was forced to sign away my nation's wealth. The Duchess came one day and gave me my political freedom and in two weeks I lose my economic freedom . . . Bloody clever (quoted by Harcourt-Munning, 1976).

This experience was to lead Nkrumah to pursue a different development model to the one he had followed in the 1950s, based as it was on precepts of aid, trade and capitalist-led economic growth.

Educational development during this period was governed by the 1951 Accelerated Development Plan. Its main aim was to develop primary and 'middle school' education and teacher training. Philip Foster (1965) has said of this period that many people looked to educational expansion as one of the more tangible benefits of independence. School fees were abolished in 1952 and during the whole of the 1950s educational facilities expanded rapidly. Particular emphasis was placed on the expansion of primary and middle schools and teacher-training facilities since an inadequate supply of trained teachers was an important break on further development (Graham, 1971: 178). During this period competition for scarce secondary school places became intense and by 1959 the Government had decided that only those students in the second or third year of the middle school could take the common entrance examination for secondary schools. The significance of this is that, as Foster had pointed out (1965: 195), a dual structure was emerging in Ghanaian system from what had previously been a single track school system. And this dual structure reinforced and continues to reinforce social divisions in Ghanaian society.

An Act in 1961 made primary education compulsory throughout Ghana and during the early 1960s the pressure which had been built up over the past fifteen years for an expansion of secondary schools resulted in a rapid growth of places. Fees for secondary schools were abolished in 1965. The geographical distribution of this growth, both of schools and of enrolments was uneven; areas in the North of Ghana still showed markedly lower enrolment in comparison to Ashanti and the south (Hurd, 1967). And the overall effect of the expansion was mainly to shift the problem of selection in education to the level of sixth-form entry. By the mid-1960s this was a major bottleneck to the growth of educational opportunities.

By the mid-1960s, then, a pattern of educational demand existed which placed a high value on an academic schooling leading to higher education and the social gradient of this demand paralleled the social class pattern of Ghanaian society. A survey in 1960 by Philip Foster showed that forty per cent of the children in the fifth form of secondary schools were from professional, technical and clerical family backgrounds when this group as a whole accounted for something like only seven per cent of the working population (Foster, 1963). Farmers, who comprised nearly sixty-three per cent of the population supplied only thirty-two per cent of fifth formers. Additional data from a study by Hurd and Johnson, however, shows that when the category 'farmer' is broken down further it can be shown that the rich cocoa farmers are much more likely to have sons in the fifth form than other poorer farmers and that the wealthier farmers constitute less than a third of the cocoa farmers as a whole (Hurd, 1967). Hurd and Johnson have argued (1967), in fact, that during this period educational growth contributed little to making Ghana a more open society. Noting that only 0.2 per cent of their sixth form sample and 1.6 per cent of their university sample were from semi-skilled and unskilled workers, despite the fact that, in 1960, such groups comprised thirteen per cent of the labour force, Hurd and Johnson (1967: 73) conclude that: '. . . the rigidity of the emerging class system is such that achievement through higher education is more difficult for the child of a labourer than for the child of a subsistence farmer'. For richer farmers, however, educational opportunities are considerable. There is, however, a wider significance to such results which Hurd and Johnson themselves do not emphasise. The evolving form of the Ghanaian class system, expressed in such data, reflects the evolving form of the Ghanian state and economy. The data highlight which groups were gaining in wealth and prestige and which groups were not. They also indicate the contours of political division in Ghana which were to lead eventually to Nkrumah's downfall.

Opposition to Nkrumah in Ghana had come initially from the established elites of the Gold Coast who had grouped themselves politically into the United Gold Coast Convention. In the 1950s and 1960s it was to come from big farmers, businessmen, the military and academics grouped by 1969 into the Progress Party of Dr Busia. Such were the groups which opposed Nkrumah's attempts, inept though they may have been, to build a socialist state in Ghana in response to the economic crisis of 1961.

For by 1961 the Ghanaian economy was in serious trouble. The productive base of the economy had not been significantly expanded between 1955 and 1959. Samir Amin (1973: 242) describes the pattern of investment during this period as 'traditional' in that more importance was attached to building up an infrastructure of public buildings and transport than on developing industry or agriculture. Real wages had fallen during this period and the balance of payments ran into deficit. Consumer goods not capable of being produced in Ghana accounted for over fifty per cent of Ghana's imports and something like sixty per cent of import demand is accounted for by the income of cocoa farmers (Amin, 1973: 243).

Between 1963 and 1966—a period in which Nkrumah, following his visit to the Soviet Union had decided upon what he understood as a socialist programme of development—the cost of living increased by forty-eight per cent. Nkrumah sought a tighter control of the economy and a programme of forced industrialisation. He argued vociferously that the middle class in Ghana was incapable of modernising the country. Ghana became a one-party state and Nkrumah's own ideological position became quite mystical stressing his own role as the Leader. Dowse has noted (1973: 268), somewhat cynically, that 'Ideology made palatable the nasty inevitable and put the mundane reality of everyday sacrifice into a more glorious setting'. And the 'nasty inevitable' was the need for the state to assume command of the industrialisation process since, in a dependent economy the indigenous bourgeoisie is, in fact, incapable of doing so itself.

But the results of this shift in Ghana's model of development were not up to expectation. By 1967, through heavy borrowing the foreign debt of the regime represented over thirty per cent of the Gross Domestic Product; the state was bankrupt.

Several writers, particularly those on the left, have argued that Nkrumah's failure to achieve planned socialist industrialisation was based on a failure to understand the nature of capitalism and a failure to organise a worker-based revolutionary party (see First, 1970, Fitch and Oppenheimer, 1966). Ruth First sums it up this way, writing about the failure of the CPP (1970: 187):

> Intrinsic to the failings of the CPP was Nkrumah's own character, with his limitations as theoretician and leader. He saw socialism, and economic development, as a process to be promoted by edict . . . He lived in a world of paper plans . . .

Her argument is that Nkrumah was ringed round externally by the forces of international capital, worried by his efforts to switch the direction of Ghanaian trade to the eastern bloc, and internally by those groups who saw greatest benefit to themselves through remaining tied to the west. Nkrumah, she argues, failed because he could not combat these groups. The CPP as a party was not geared up to doing so; its base was eroded by the fragile allegiances of bureaucrats, opportunists and small businessmen whose commitment to socialism was far less than their commitment to the existing social order which rewarded them well. Dowse (1973: 272) has argued a similar case insisting that the CPP leadership's commitment to socialism was mere 'verbal acquiescence'.

It is too easy, however, to attribute the coup of February 1966 which deposed Nkrumah while he was on a visit to Peking as the outcome of an organisational failure on the part of the CPP. The soldiers who took over in February 1966 were successful not because they were well organised—although that, of course, was the case—but because they reflected the demands of a different section of Ghanaian society to the section Nkrumah represented, a pro-western section. The Army itself was clearly pro-western and had been concerned about Nkrumah's plans from 1961 onwards to send Ghanaian cadets to the Soviet Union for military training. Fitch and Oppenheimer have argued (1966: 4) for instance, that the Ghanaian officer corps is permeated with 'anglophilia' and tended to judge their daily African experience by the norms and values of the British officer corps. And Ruth First (1970: 73) in her study of African military leaders refers to such men as 'Narcissus in uniform' retaining after independence the colonial pattern of army organisation, their dependence on the West for military training and their affinity for western defence policies.

But it was not just the military who opposed Nkrumah. Opposition came from businessmen and professional groups and academics. Thomas Hodgkin (1967) has argued that Ghanaian academics trained at Oxford and distrustful of Nkrumah's brand of Marxism were implacably opposed to the idea of the one-party state, to closer ties with the Soviet Union and to what they took to be indiscriminate support of national liberation movements. And Dennis Austin (1975: 236) has described the political leadership of post-independence Ghana and the educated elite as 'rival colonists'. He describes their relationship this way (1975: 236–7):

> From 1945 onwards, graduates from the universities had begun to enter the public service, local government, the professions and business enterprises, replacing the British, and becoming a new administrative elite with direct access to the resources of the state. But in laying hold of the proto-independent state, they were opposed by the power of a nationalist party in the hands of a 'political class on-the-make' which was certainly no less determined to exploit the

resources they were begining to control . . . These differences were sharpened by envy, and enlarged by what passed as ideology.

Ghanaian academics had been worried about what they took to be threats to their academic freedom. Nkrumah had, after all, been planning to inject compulsory Marxist courses into the University of Ghana and to sever the connection between the institution and its foreign external examiners. It seemed to many academics that Nkrumah sought to subject the university completely to the needs of the party. And referring to the new university council set up in 1967 after the coup, Austin, a former teacher in Ghana writes: 'The declared intention of the newly constituted university council was to return Ghana—the phrase echoes down the years from the great days of Achimota—"to the academic gold standard"' (1975: 248). Seen from this point of view, much of the opposition to Nkrumah can be traced to those social groups which were fashioned by the colonial state and educated by that state for its own purpose; they were its political heirs inculcated with a *habitus* which prevented them being critical of new forms of neo-colonial dependency.

GHANA UNDER COLONIAL RULE FROM 1966 TO THE PRESENT

The National Liberation Council which succeeded Nkrumah indicated from the beginning that its task was to return Ghana to democratic politics. Unlike many military regimes, it proceeded to do just that. Dr Busia of the Progress Party became Prime Minister in 1969, and this brought with it yet another shift in economic policy. The currency was devalued, wages were frozen, restrictions on capital transfers were lifted and many undertakings were returned to private ownership (Amin, 1973: 248). Tetteh Kofi (1972–73) has typified the development plans of the Busia regime as a 'dependency strategy' in so far as it relied heavily on foreign aid and the prospect of attracting foreign capital.

The period from 1966 onwards in the field of education has been uneventful; no great initiatives have been taken to change the system which had grown up since 1951. If anything, some of the problems of that system have merely been made more intractable. In this period the emphasis of Government policy has been on the development of secondary education and the improvement of teacher education. An Education Review Committee set up immediately after the coup showed, for instance, that over sixty-five per cent of elementary school teachers were untrained (McWilliam and Kwamena, 1975: 120).

The Review Committee aimed to produce recommendations which would improve the educational system of Ghana. It was chaired by Professor Kwapong, Vice Chancellor of the University of Ghana and it reported in 1967. The Committee began from the assumption that there had been a fall in educational standards since independence and that this was attributable to a too-rapid rate of expansion of elementary education by the Nkrumah Government. The Committee argued that an important element in the situation was the poor quality of Ghanaian teachers, and it urged the government to improve teacher training and teacher salaries. It also recommended that English teaching in Ghanaian schools should be strengthened. By 1969 many of the Committee's recommendations on teacher training had been implemented and improvements made in teachers' salaries. Table 5.1 shows the salary structure by 1970.

TABLE 5.1
Level of school times starting salary in Ghana

Level of schooling	Years of schooling	Starting salary (new cedis)
Middle school	10	359
Secondary school	14	437
Secondary school	16	756
Graduate	19	1668

Source: Williams (1974)

The logic behind this improvement was a straightforward managerial one; if teachers were better paid there would be a greater incentive for them to stay at their posts and for intending teachers to improve their qualifications.

But it is arguable just how far such an official line can be effective. Research into the social status of the teacher in Northern Ghana in 1969–70 concluded that most teachers 'were doing no more than working out their bonds after which they hoped to be able to invest their education in some more attractive enterprise; the untrained teachers hoped to get their free education and would then follow suit' (Roberts, 1975: 259). This piece of anthropological research concluded that most teachers were dissatisfied with working in rural areas and saw little satisfaction in teaching itself. It is hardly conceivable that financial incentives would modify a malaise of such magnitude.

In the field of secondary education the Committee sought to consolidate the achievements of the past few years and improve the quality of schools. Between 1966 and 1972 the number of secondary school places expanded by twenty-five per cent and the number of graduates teaching in the secondary schools was increased from 300 to 1202 (McWilliam and Kwamena, 1975: 125). The secondary school curriculum was brought firmly into line with the requirements of the West African Examinations Council Joint School Certificate regulations and aimed to produce the bulk of the middle level manpower of the economy and the 'potential top level' manpower for university courses (McWilliam and Kwamena, 1975: 124). The generals and the government of Dr Busia which followed them also sought to upgrade the quality of technical and commercial education.

But by the time of the second coup in 1972 the achievements of the two post-Nkrumah governments had been small. Changes in educational policy had done little to slow down the fall in enrolment rates in primary education or to reduce the great regional differences in education provision. Indeed, as Blakemore has shown, enrolments in the north of Ghana dropped by over a third between 1966 and 1972 and this is an area where about eighty per cent of the people have not, in any case, ever been to a school (Blakemore, 1975). There is little evidence that the system became more accessible to wider social groups (Bibby, 1973). The growth in poor-quality private secondary schools may even indicate that the situation in this respect is getting worse (Bibby and Peil, 1974). And the decision to maintain English as the main language of middle and secondary school instruction—a decision taken for the very straightforward reason that there is no other national Ghanaian language and that, in any case, as the Education Review Committee put it, English 'is the gateway to the international world' (McWilliam and Kwamena, 1975: 119)—will effectively reinforce class differences in educational attainment since only the educated speak English with any great facility. G. Omani Collison has shown (1974: 454) with a small sample of eighty-five sixth form students that, using measures of concept formation and thinking ability drawn from the work of Vygotsky, 'The bilingual problem explored from the conceptual perspective reveals consistently that when English is the language of education, the majority of the experimental subjects were not able to exercise their conceptual potential'. On the question of language, however, the final word must rest with Dennis Austin. He has referred to English in Ghana as 'the most potent force of "academic colonialism" '. He compares the colonial world, in which the English language is a 'dominant element', with the Island of Circe, 'enchanting men's minds and turning them into—what? Well, into subordinate creatures of what was once an island empire and is now a global market economy' (1975: 262). Ghana is thus trapped in a language which seals the link between the colonial past and the neo-colonial present.

The economic performance of Ghana between 1969 and the 1972 coup was indifferent, being adversely affected by a drop in cocoa prices and very high repayment schedules for foreign debts. Cheryl Payer has shown (1974: 201) that in the period between 1966 and 1972 the additional interest Ghana had to pay on foreign debts through debt rescheduling agreements amounted to forty per cent of the original debt. This is the classic 'debt trap' in which new borrowings are made to pay off old debts. And Payer quotes the Ghanaian Finance Minister when he pointed out that debt repayments were so high that per capita incomes in Ghana had fallen from 261 dollars in 1965 to 239 dollars in 1969 and unemployment was as high as thirty-five per cent of the labour force (1974: 201). Inflation was high and in 1972 the government announced a forty-eight per cent devaluation of the currency (Palmer, 1975). This was the trigger for the second coup under the leadership of Colonel Acheampong, a career soldier, devout Christian and former school teacher.

Economic policy under Acheampong has lacked a coherent thread. Initially the new government—which called itself the National Redemption Council—repudiated some of its international debts and created a great deal of international suspicion about the economic prospects of Ghana. Since 1972 the government has pursued a distinctively populist, belt-tightening policy of self-reliance which is known as Operation Feed Yourself. This involves a shift in government investment from capital-intensive state farms to smallholders who produce something approaching ninety per cent of Ghana's agricultural output (Rake, 1977). The aim is self-sufficiency in food and a phasing out of expensive import substitution industries. A second phase of Operation Feed Yourself concerns industry and aims to increase Ghana's production of various raw materials for its own industry. Success however, is still a distant hope. Domestic food prices are very high and the domestic food index is increasing at sixty-three per cent per annum (Rake, 1977: 22). Inflation is running at an annual rate of forty to fifty per cent because of very high government borrowing.

The government has allowed a partial rehabilitation of Nkrumah but is reluctant to conceive of its lurching development policy in explicitly socialist terms. In a recent Ministry of Information press release the government was at great pains to contrast the 'soldierly' 'practical' ways of General Acheampong with the 'histrionics of Nkrumah' and the 'hyperbole of exaggeration' of Busia (Ministry of Information Accra, 1977). The government is attempting to develop a framework of economic planning around five-year plans which, in words of the 1975 plan, seek to 'expand the productive base of the economy' and 'capture the commanding heights of the economy' to permit economic independence (Keesings Contemporary Archives, 1977).

But the result does not match expectation. By 1977 the inflation rate was estimated at eighty per cent. A National Reconstruction Corps was set up to involve unemployed youth in development projects. In May 1977 the government closed the country's three universities and in the midsummer had to face a general strike among professional workers demanding that the government be returned to democracy.

It can, in fact, be argued that the present government of Ghana is both economically and intellectually bankrupt, that it has lost its constituency. Ghanaian middle-class groups are ambivalent because of high prices and shortages. Ghanaian workers have suffered a gradual reduction in real living standards in the twenty years since independence since the rate of economic growth has not been commensurate with the rate of population increase, and in any case unemployment is high.

Nor has the base of educational opportunity widened or educational standards improved. Indeed a recent review of Ghana's secondary school expansion in the 1960s concluded that the expanding network of schools offers a not very relevant style of education to meet the very high demand which exists for that education (Boyd and French, 1974). The old tensions between the political elite, the military elite, and the academic elite continue. The universities are worried about their autonomy, the government is concerned at the universities' elitism (Austin, 1975). The only major change in Ghanaian education since 1972 had been the setting up of the Ghanaian Teacher Service as a device to secure greater central government control of education at all levels. In every other respect, the system responds to the constraints imposed by the economy, the class system, and the residual yet tenacious conception of a proper education bequeathed to Ghana by the British Empire.

The pattern of education in Ghana is only one factor among many which have held back the development of Ghana since independence; but in so far as it has contributed to the failure of successive governments to mobilise the people of Ghana behind a radically conceived strategy of development, its role has been a decisive one. Can Ghana, in fact, reconcile the narrow-based demands of its educated elite for an education aimed at occupational success with a development strategy out of dependency? The evidence so far invites a negative answer.

TANZANIA

Tanzania achieved its independence from Britain in 1961. Annual per capita average incomes were about £20; average life expectancy was thirty-five years of age. The economy was heavily dependent on a limited range of price-fluctuating exports and on sisal in particular (Chau and Caillods, 1975). The political system, as subsequent developments have made clear, was not geared up either ideologically or organisationally to combat the structures of dependency which lay behind Tanzania's poverty. The new state possessed all the classic characteristics of neo-colonial dependency and the educational system illustrates this very clearly.

The educational system had been an important tool of the independence movement, a focal point of political organisation through the Tanganyika African Parents Association and the demand for universal primary education had been one of the key demands of TANU (Morrison, 1976). But on independence day Tanzania inherited a school system which was racially differentiated, heavily urban in its bias, elitist and very poorly developed. Only about one quarter of all children who had access to primary schools could expect to reach the higher grades and of these only about one-third were able to go on to secondary schools. Those who attended primary schools comprised only about twenty per cent of the age group and those in secondary schools represented something like only three per cent of the total age group (Chau and Caillods, 1975). Many important posts in the government and education were held by expatriates and the educational system as it existed then was simply not geared up to replacing such people while at the same time African demands for career mobility through education were high.

These facts coalesced into an intricate political situation in which the independent government faced a series of very difficult choices in educational policy each with different, yet very serious political costs. If primary education was to be rapidly expanded to meet parental demand then this might divert resources from the more valuable forms of secondary education training people for central economic posts. If, on the other hand, secondary school provision was held back in the interests of greater equality, a situation might result in which economic development would be hindered through manpower shortage and social divisions in the country exacerbated because richer parents would buy private education (see Morrison, 1976).

Tanzania's colonial history weighed heavily on the new state's system of education. The resources available for education reflected the historic pattern of colonial education policy and economic structures. The Depression and then the Second World War held back the growth of education spending in Tanganyika. During the Depression, from 1930 to 1934 for instance, government financial assistance to mission schools, a very important part of the colonial system, was reduced by forty-five per cent and the government cut its own education staff by forty per cent (Cameron and Dodd, 1970).

At independence, therefore, Tanzania faced a system of schools which was racially divided, underresourced and incapable of meeting both popular demand for education or the needs of the economy and government for high level manpower.

The cultural legacy of colonialism with its long-term political consequences was perhaps the most difficult obstacle to overcome, for it was this legacy which had shaped the pattern of African demand for education and the prevailing conception of what it was to be educated. It has to be understood as a system which had been imposed on an already functioning indigenous pattern of education. It reflected, as Cameron and Dodd (1970: 47) have demonstrated, 'a persistent tendency to prescribe for the Africans only what an alien race thought was good for them'. Marjorie Mbilinyi has, however, stressed much more forcefully the political role of education during the colonial period. She writes (1975a: 1):

> The African formal education system under the government and missions and missionary activity in general represented the essential parts of the ideological structure of the colonial state. It served the objective function of providing the African with the skills and knowledge necessary to be productive peasant producers, workers or petty bourgeois servants of the state, shaping his willingness to accept his place in the colonial social structure.

Three themes each encountered already in the Ghanaian case illustrate the functions of colonial education, each having implications for the form, distribution, content and functioning of schools themselves.

The three themes are: firstly, education for adaptation, secondly, education for control, and finally, the devaluation of African culture.

Education for adaptation expresses the long-held conviction that Africans were destined to a life on the land as simple peasant producers and should be educated accordingly. This theme pervades colonial education policy. A small number would be required in government and administration and in clerical employment; for these an appropriate western model of education was necessary. To meet the last problem Governor Cameron set up under the educator. Travers Lacey the famous boarding school at Tabora in 1924 to educate the sons of chiefs. The so-called central schools of which Tabora was one, were set up to produce native clerks and officials who would assist in the administration of the colony and in commerce, and while the model of the school as a boarding school derived directly from the model of an English public school the central school in Tanzania was not required to produce the governing elite which its English counterpart did. As Mbilinyi stresses (1975a: 19):

> The elite of Tabora were trained to be a subordinate group of administrative officers within the colonial structure, not the ruling stratum of the dominant class. Whereas at Eton, a deliberate effort was made to develop *national* esprit de corps (group loyalty.) At Tabora the colonialist educationists intended their students to identify themselves according to tribal divisions . . . Whereas the youth of Eton learned Classics, the Tabora students learned 'bookkeeping, typing and office routine in preparation for taking up jobs in government offices'.

In addition, Tabora took on the organisational paraphernalia of the house system, prefects, the competitive spirit and school uniform. Mbilinyi claims that this structure had the paradoxical effect of reinforcing elitist attitudes which transcended the divisions of the children into tribal groups and in that respect served to fashion the group that would eventually oppose colonialism on a nationalist basis.

Primary schooling and upper primary schooling were also strongly linked to the perceived needs of the colonial labour market; primary schools were for peasants; upper primary education for clerks. Marjorie Mbilinyi quotes (1975a: 15) the annual report of the Education Department of 1923:

The development of the elementary education schemes . . . is becoming firmly established along vocational lines and in accordance with the policy of teaching the native child the three R's while keeping him as closely as possible in touch with the life he is accustomed to: and at the same time to introduce as the industrial influence during his school life the work which . . . he would do at home . . . agriculture shall be the keynote of our education programme.

This policy was not, of course, always successful. The Director of Education for Tanganyika complained in 1926 that 'A census of African children at the present time will probably reveal that . . . the vast majority look upon school as a means to become a clerk or a teacher to enter some other sedentary employment' (Morrison, 1976: 58). Even as late as 1957 the Provincial Education Officer in the Mwanza district complained in his annual report:

This is the least satisfactory aspect of the spread of schools. The authority of the sub-chiefs, elders and parents is being replaced by that of teachers, or, after children have left standard four by no authority at all. Lip service is paid by politicians and agitators to the ideal of universal primary education not for itself, but as a means towards emancipating from the drudgery of work on the land (quoted by Dubbeldam, 1970: 25).

This attitude towards primary education persists strongly in modern Tanzania as Dubbeldam has shown in his survey (1970) of parental expectations in the Mwanza district.

The juxtaposition of an underdeveloped system of education, itself hierarchically organised, with African demands for an education out of subsistence agriculture created a distinctive cultural matrix in which success in examinations became the prime aim of education and, as Morrison says (1976: 73): 'Not unnaturally, many individuals who manage to overcome difficult selection barriers began to show signs of superiority and expect privileges in recognition of their achievement'. Competitiveness, selfishness and antipathy towards elders and work on the land—all of which Julius Nyerere has severely criticised in *Education for Self-Reliance*—were the corollary of these processes in education although they should not be thought of as 'natural'; they reflect, rather, the structures of colonial education itself and the social purpose of that education.

The second theme is that of education for control.

Education policy was conceived of by successive British Governors of Tanganyika as an integral part of the policy of indirect rule. In 1925 Governor Cameron began to interpret the Mandate of the League of Nations which gave Britain control over Tanganyika as the need for Britain to rule the territory indirectly through Native Authorities. Cameron saw this as developing 'the native politically on lines suitable to the state of society in which he lives' (Cameron and Dodds, 1970: 40). Education for control had a subtle racial twist, too. Asians in East Africa formed the commercial links between Africans and metropolitan business and were educated separately. During the whole of the British Mandate this separation was maintained and a good part of the rationale for doing so was political in that a divided education encouraged group rivalries which would defuse general discontent against the British. The Director of Education, Rivers Smith, put it very clearly in 1925, alluding to the growth of Indian nationalism and the dangers of a link being formed between African and Asians:

At present we have a healthy rivalry and a growing race consciousness amongst the Africans and a certain feeling of resentment that the Asiatics get so many of the 'plums'. In my opinion co-education might conceivably weaken this healthy and natural rivalry and eventually lead to making common cause for political ends (quoted by Mbilinyi, 1975a: 7).

But control operates directly, too, on the form of the school curriculum, teaching practices, punishment procedures and in the kinds of symbols the school manipulates to legitimate its own authority. Walter Rodney has argued (1972: 270) that colonial schools were 'sublimely indifferent to the twentieth century'. Their books, methods of teaching, patterns of discipline and range of subjects were based on nineteenth-century models of what education is. Little science was taught and there was no development in the African context of a system of higher technological education. What was taught was taught in the conviction that western European values were right for Africa. This was simply taken for granted, but the necessity of these assumptions from the point of view of control was not lost sight of. Rodney (1972: 270) reports the comments of a Principal Education Officer in 1949 to the effect that Tanganyikan primary schools should be bombarded with propaganda about the British royal family. The Officer put it this way: 'The theme of the British king as a father should be stressed throughout the syllabus and mentioned in every lesson'. And he went on to urge that

African children should be shown numerous pictures of the English princesses riding on their ponies at Sandringham and Windsor castle. The cultural myopia and wilful instrumentalism of these remarks is obvious, yet such remarks have a subtle side to them. In so far as they reflect a Eurocentric view of the world, they devalue African history, culture and political authority. In fact, one of the persisting problems of school education in independent socialist Tanzania is the paucity of adequate teaching materials reflecting African history and culture and not that of Europe. Indeed the first 'modest' outline of the history of Tanzania was presented to President Nyerere in 1969 (Kimambo and Temu, 1969). The book had been written to overcome the difficulties of the fragmentary material currently available and to correct the 'distortions' of Tanzanian history so that history teachers in schools could be better placed to teach Tanzanian history. When the authors of the book presented it to President Nyerere as the first history of Tanzania written largely by Tanzanians, he apparently floored them all by asking, 'Is it good history?'

Colonial education was, therefore, not only selective in who would be given access to available schools, it was selective in its manipulation of the ideas to which Africans would be given access, and gave Africans only limited access to their own history and culture.

The third theme concerns precisely the way in which colonial education distorted the link between Africans and their culture and the problem of what Clignet (1971) has called 'double alienation'. The alienation effect was achieved by simultaneously devaluing traditional African education and imposing a foreign language as the language of the educated.

A. C. Mwingira, a Tanzanian education minister, pointed out to a conference of African Studies Association in Sussex that:

A small minority of us was given an academic education to fit us for an administrative elite, where practical knowledge, experience, character and attitude would count for little, but where survival in the school system and the resultant certificate meant everything . . . Textbooks and teachers stimulated a demand for sophisticated consumer durables, that were clearly beyond the economic means of the ordinary farmer, and promoted a general dissatisfaction with what were seen as the 'restrictions' of traditional society (1969: 66–7).

Overlying the selective exposure of Africans to western culture and the devaluation, effectively, of African culture, is the fact that, in any case, the medium of secondary school instruction in Tanzania and until recently, the language of Government, was English. Until 1918 the Germans had maintained a policy of teaching in the vernacular and had encouraged the growth of Swahili to provide a *lingua franca* for local administration. The British carried on this tradition except that English rather than German became the language of secondary education. The fact that Swahili is a common language over East Africa meant that it functioned well as a vehicle for the development of nationalism and as an instrument for the political unification of Tanzania. But it is still the language of the educated, and the ability to speak it well is one of the factors behind success at school and in this respect is one of the factors of class differentiation in education in modern Tanzania. As the second five-year plan noted, the use of English in secondary and higher education was creating a linguistic gulf between the educated and the masses and helping to sustain an 'alien atmosphere' in post-primary education (see Morrison, 1976: 273). The absence of schoolbooks written in Swahili reinforces this dependency on the English language in just the same way as the failure of the colonial education system to create sufficient schoolteachers and academics creates a dependency in Tanzania on expatriate teaching staff which Tanzania is only now beginning to overcome.

One can only speculate on the more subtle cultural effects of the hegemony of English as the language of the educated. Considerable evidence exists, however, of the symbolic importance of Swahili as the vehicle of nationalism in Tanzania. As early as 1947 the Tanganyikan African Association agreed that all its meeting ought to be conducted in Swahili and it has been TANU policy since its foundation in 1954 to promote Swahili as the national language. Some insight into the broader cultural and political significance of this is given by a comment in 1962 from Sheikh Amri Abedi, a Swahili scholar and poet, and former minister of Community Development and Culture in an address to the Tanzanian parliament following the President's Republican Day speech which had just been delivered in Swahili. What Abedi said was this, referring to President Nyerere's speech:

> That moment was truly the beginning of a new era in the history of the development of this country in the fields of language, national development and the running of the affairs of government . . . Today we have been given the freedom to talk in our own language. We shall now enter the field of discussion with confidence, with no doubt as to

the real meaning of what we are saying, nor, whether we are being correctly understood by others (quoted by Abdulaziz, 1971: 166).

'Confidence', 'freedom', 'real meaning' are all revealing words; it is as if the enforced use of English implied the absence of such qualities in the thought and speech of Tanzanians.

Colonial education, as I have indicated already, left independent Tanzania with a set of closely interwoven problems in which a basically underesourced school system, racially differentiated, urban in bias, elitist in form and culturally distant from Tanzanians themselves, had to face up to two sets of potentially inconsistent demands. The needs of the new state for manpower related to development goals had to be balanced against the demands of parents for some tangible benefit of independence, particularly increased educational opportunities. David Morrison has described these demands as the '*uhuru* complex', in other words, 'demands for rapid government action that could not possible be satisfied by the limited stock of available human and material resources (1976: 20). In fact, the period after independence was one of considerable uncertainty and instability. In 1962 Nyerere resigned to try and reorganise TANU into a more effective political instrument for development. In 1964 there was an army mutiny. In 1965 Tanzania became a one-party state and as Cameron and Dodds have written (1970: 160), 'between 1961 and 1965 more emphasis was placed on overhauling the infrastructure of the nation than on creating a new society'. Independence, of itself, solves nothing; it only offers new opportunities and until 1966–67 it was not clear just what the opportunities were.

After 1967 and the Arusha Declaration and, in the case of education policy the publication of *Education for Self-Reliance*, the government of Tanzania committed itself to a programme of socialist development and self-reliance. The Arusha Declaration signalled a change in Tanzania's *model of development* which was to have important implications for education policy. It is to these that we must now turn since it is very much the achievements of post-Arusha policies together with some of the special problems associated with them, particularly continuing problems of class differentiation and dependency, which make the Tanzanian experiment such an important one for Africa as a whole.

EDUCATION FOR SELF-RELIANCE

The aim of the policy of education for self-reliance is to evolve an education system for Tanzania which guarantees primary education as of right to all the population and which serves the needs of Tanzanian society as a whole. It is a policy which is explicit in its acknowledgement that Tanzania will have a rural economy for many years to come, that it will remain a poor society and that education in these circumstances must face the fact that most Tanzanians will spend their lives working on the land. For this reason Tanzania cannot support an education system which consumes an increasing proportion of the country's resources only to breed narrow elitism and a basic disrespect among the educated of those who have not themselves had the opportunity of education. But education for self-reliance is not simply an education policy; it is part, an essential part, of Julius Nyerere's broader image of African socialism which is embodied in the Arusha Declaration (1967) and in the document, *Socialism and Rural Development* (1967) which sets out the philosophy behind the growth of *ujamaa* villages as the basic units of agricultural production in socialist Tanzania. It is, therefore, a key document in the redefinition of Tanzania's model of development in the mid-1960s.

A number of factors came together in the mid-1960s to push the TANU leadership into a new position. The Tanzanian economy had not grown as expected and exports had been adversely affected by a drop in world prices. Political discontent, too, threatened the dominant position of TANU. Specifically in the field of education considerable parental dissatisfaction over the failure of primary school graduates to gain secondary school places resulted in demonstrations throughout the country in which many education officers were besieged by angry parents demanding school places for their children. In the field of higher education the reluctance of students to take part in the National Service campaign, a reluctance which led the President to dismiss some 300 students from the University, forced into the open the issue of elitist attitudes in Tanzanian education.

Julius Nyerere had been aware of what he understood as a mass-elite gap a long time before the actual demonstration on 22 October 1967 which led to his action. A year previously he had told students who had been complaining about their living conditions that:

Every time I come to this campus . . . I think again about our decision to build here . . . Anyone who walks off this campus into the nearby villages, or who travels up country . . . will observe the contrast in conditions here and the conditions in which the mass of our people live . . . The purpose of establishing a university is to make it possible for us to change these poverty stricken lives . . . We do not build skyscrapers here so that a very few fortunate individuals can develop their own minds and live in comfort . . . We tax the people to build these places only so that young men and women may become efficient servants to them. There is no other justification for this heavy call being made on poor peasants (quoted by Morrison, 1976: 241).

And later, while talking to members of the student delegation which accompanied the demonstration against students being involved in national service, the President angrily underlined the point that the political elite and the educated elite were 'members of the same class— the exploiting class'. He went on:

The man who gets the minimum wage and the poor peasant, they are the ones who have to pay these [i.e. the wages of high salary earner— B. W.] Everybody in this country is paid too much except the poor peasant (Morrison, 1976: 244).

The students had convinced the President that a reorientation was required in Tanzanian education and that the policy of education for self-reliance set out earlier in the year needed reinforcement and hard work if it were ever to succeed.

The policy itself was clear enough. It is based on a recognition that Tanzania will remain a poor rural society for a long time to come and that education must adapt to these realities. Specifically, a poor society could not go on pouring a large proportion of the monetary Gross National Product into a service which has an almost infinite capacity to consume scarce resources and which was clearly not meeting the needs of Tanzanian society. Nyerere detected four main weaknesses in the educational system: it was elitist; it divorced children from the world in which they would eventually have to live; it fostered a respect for book-learning only thereby despising the knowledge of people themselves; finally, it removed young people from direct productive work.

From this analysis Nyerere drew three main policy conclusions. Behind each one is the politically difficult conviction that the problem of primary school leavers could not be solved by expanding secondary school places; something different had to be attempted. Firstly, primary education needed to be a complete education without any implied promise of secondary education and modern sector employment. This implied relating education to rural life and for those few necessary for the economy who require secondary or further education, such education must be seen as helping the people as a whole and not just the individual. Secondly, schools must become communities themselves to give people the skills to live co-operatively. Nyerere argued that every school should become a farm and, where possible, should aim at self-sufficiency. Finally, the curriculum of schools should reflect the needs of peasant communities and give students themselves the skills they need to earn their own living in an egalitarian, socialist society. One component of this is a positive commitment to non-formal education. In Nyerere's analysis the problems of Tanzanian education are clearly linked up to the colonial heritage and the need to overcome that heritage in a disciplined programme of political socialisation and social reform. It is just at this point, however, that his critics have questioned the viability of his plans. For ease of exposition some of the more important criticisms can be set out under five main headings. These are: (1) the great gap between philosophy and practice; (2) the significance of agricultural education in schools; (3) the problem of curriculum reform and political socialisation; (4) the problem of equity; and (5) the problem of education in the modern Tanzanian state and class culture.

PHILOSOPHY AND PRACTICE

Education and Self-Reliance is not a blueprint for a new curriculum; it is a closely argued case for a change of direction in the development of education in Tanzania. It was not immediately clear, therefore, what precisely the implications of the new policy were for the schools themselves. Thus quite apart from the ever-present problem of few resources there was uncertainty about the concept of education for self-reliance, an uncertainty most obvious among some of the people required to implement the new policy. Lionel Cliffe (1973) reports one district council interpreting the new policy as requiring them to withdraw subsidies to poor people. Morrison describes the immediate reactions to the publication of the President's document as surprise and confusion. The education ministry had no prepared plan to act on and even took the publication of the document to be some kind of attack on the ministry itself.

Such uncertainty is understandable since there is always a difficult gulf to bridge between the immediate day-to-day preoccupations of teachers and children, politicians and bureaucrats, and the broader goals of an educational policy. Surely, S. Toroka (1973) was quite right when, writing as a teacher in a TANU youth league *ujamaa* settlement in the Ruvuma region, he pointed out that education for self-reliance 'calls for changes in the attitudes and thinking of the people towards the meaning and purpose of education *for this generation and after* (my emphasis).

He went on (1973: 264) 'It requires a complete overhaul of the attitudes of the people . . . remoulding the thinking in order to develop a socialist education which will serve a socialist people of a socialist society'. There *is* no blueprint for such a transformation; such changes can only come about gradually to the extent that they are planned and progress towards them monitored continually with special efforts being made to ensure that those whose responsibility it is to introduce the changes know clearly what they are doing. In this respect, school teachers are more important than politicians; much depends upon how this group interpret *Education for Self-Reliance* in their day-to-day contact with students and in the way they implement and organise the school curriculum.

But here another legacy of colonial education exerts itself. As late as 1964 some seventy per cent of secondary school teachers were expatriates (Von der Muhll, 1971). It cannot be assumed that this group will embrace the new values of socialism and self-reliance since they themselves were, and to a small extent still are, the prime carriers of the attitudes towards education which came under attack in 1967. But the failure of the colonial education system to train an African teaching corps of a quality sufficient for staffing the secondary schools results in the paradoxical situation that expatriates could not be quickly replaced and even if they had been the likelihood was, as Von der Muhll has pointed out, their replacements would have been even less capable, because of their inferior education and political awareness, to mobilise support behind the new policies. Nonetheless, the second five-year development plan (1969–74) sought to increase the number of children involved in primary education from 43.8 per cent in 1968 to fifty per cent during the period of the plan and to ninety-five per cent by 1989 (see Chau and Caillods, 1975: 30).

Such an expansion is consistent with the goals of *Education for Self-Reliance* to give all Tanzanians at least a primary education. But to achieve this teacher training had to be expanded, particularly the number of grade C teachers, that is those teachers who themselves have only completed primary education. A new and important function, that of vigorous political socialisation into the difficult-to-grasp values of Tanzanian socialism, is therefore to be performed by those who are perhaps less able intellectually to appreciate themselves the very values they are required to pass on to others. Admittedly, the Institute of Education at Dar es Salaam has been very active in the field of teacher training but their task is an arduous one and their results not very encouraging.

A further difficulty in the implementation of the new policy concerns the goals of equality and the problem of selection for secondary schools. The first five-year plan had envisaged a slowing down in the rate of growth of primary enrolments. Education for self-reliance policies involved an expansion of primary education and a restriction of the growth of secondary school places consistent with manpower needs. By 1966 the plans to reduce primary enrolments were beginning to work and such enrolments were dropping. Morrison (1976: 270) has calculated, in fact, that the cutback has been too severe; there were less primary places for seven-year-olds by 1970 than there were in 1965. What this means is that the problem of selection for secondary schools becomes even more severe. And one aspect of this has been a steady growth in the number of private secondary schools. The transition ratio (that is, the proportion of the age group in school going on to the next stage of schooling) between primary and secondary education in 1962 was forty per cent. By 1972 it was down to eleven per cent (Chau and Calliods, 1975: 37). The growth in private schooling—and by 1972 enrolment in grade 1 of private schools was exactly half that of enrolment in the public system— is a direct outcome of this and reflects the persistence of significant demands for education for social mobility, an attitude to education which the new policy sought to change. Looked at in a longer historical perspective, this particular problem clearly has its roots in the failure of the colonial government to expand secondary education and the continuing inability of the independent state to fund secondary expansion out of its own limited resources. In the short term, the new policy must succeed in diverting aspirations for education into patterns which the economy can, in fact, sustain and which the political system can contain. Whether it can succeed depends, in part, on what attitude Africans take to some of the changes proposed in the new policy and in particular what these policies imply for what their children will learn at school. The issue agricultural education in schools illustrates some further dilemmas the new policy must resolve.

THE SIGNIFICANCE OF AGRICULTURAL EDUCATION IN THE SCHOOLS

Julius Nyerere (1974: 100) was quite clear that schools should aim to be self-sufficient communities, reflecting the basis of social life in Tanzania itself, self-reliant villages:

> Each school should have, as an integral part of it, a farm or workshop which provides food eaten by the community, and makes some contribution to the national income.
> This is not a suggestion that a school farm or workshop should be attached to every school for training purposes. *It is a suggestion that every school should also be a farm*; that the school community should consist of people who are both teachers and farmers, and pupils and farmers [my emphasis—B. W.].

This goal has been criticised from two quite different directions. Professor Foster has argued a very cogent case, based admittedly on the premise that development can only come from a skilful injection of expertise into the economy and under conditions where producers can respond freely to market incentives, that agricultural education in this form in Tanzania will fail (Foster, 1969). There are several strands to his analysis but two stand out. The first is that parental expectations about education are expectations for an academic education. The roots of such expectations lie in the way in which the colonial education system functioned. Agricultural education will always under these circumstances be regarded as inferior and will be avoided. The second argument is a technical one; schools are not geared up to producing effectively and cannot generate the necessary expertise for really effective agricultural production. His last point need not concern us since it reflects a political attitude to development on Foster's part which runs counter to the politics of development in the case of Tanzania; Nyerere is not interested above all else in the rapid growth of a commercial agriculture since this might subvert his broader socialist policies for the development of an egalitarian society in the countryside.

A second direction from which this policy has been criticised is from the Marxist Left in Tanzania, particularly from Hirji (1974) and Mbilinyi (1975b). Hirji has argued that the new policy is idealistic in the sense that it seeks to change attitudes towards education and through that to change society itself. In addition, he argues, the emphasis on education for rural life is a tacit acceptance of the *status quo* in Tanzania, an acceptance of economic and political dependency. A direct comparison is therefore possible, he claims, between education for self-reliance policies and the policies of the colonial government which sought precisely the same ends:

> In its reliance on the changing attitudes as a principal weapon to transform social inequality, or in other words, to make a revolution by education, lies its idealism. E.S.R. is caught up in the insoluble contradiction of wishing to eliminate the class structure of Tanzanian society without any prospects for eradicating the structures of underdevelopment. It fails to perceive the fundamental interrelationship between these two structures (1974: 15).

Given, he argues, the existence of great inequalities in Tanzanian society, themselves stemming from the form of the Tanzanian state which, through its subsidiary organisations has grown faster than the productive base of the economy, it is inevitable that the pressure will still exist to demand of education a route to high status jobs. In these circumstances productive, practical agricultural work in schools will be seen and, Hirji argues realistically, as a drudge or a punishment. He then alludes to China, a society from which Tanzania has drawn a great deal of aid in recent years, to draw out the moral that education can only be a revolutionary force in a revolutionary society. Since Tanzania is not a revolutionary society then education can only maintain the *status quo*.

The Hirji argument relates education to the form of the Tanzanian state. Mbilinyi does the same but reaches slightly different conclusions. Her main point is that the new policies are different from those of the colonial state. The modern state in Tanzania is committed to socialism and education in rural areas, in an agricultural system which is collectivised, is explicitly an instrument of change rather than adaptation:

> The fact that collectivization is now taking place in the rural areas means that young people are being trained for socialist modes of production, not to be yeomen or kulak farmers (1974b: 40).

But she is not complacent about the results believing that the forms of teaching and school organisation in Tanzania, which she believes to be authoritarian and dehumanising 'remain a reflection of capitalist relations of production' (1974b: 43). Unlike Hirji she is not so emphatic about the inevitability of the faults she detects; she feels that insufficient ideological work has been done to implement *Education for Self-*

Reliance effectively. The result is that there are glaring inadaquacies in the schools, particularly in rural areas. Writing about the kinds of changes a rural peasant might perceive since 1967 in the education of his children, Mbilinyi writes (1974: 43):

> I would suggest he notices, first of all, that his children carry a hoe to school, where once they carried note books; that the chances of his children entering Form 1 are even slimmer than before, while at the same time secondary education is even more necessary for getting a job; that his children do not 'learn' (i.e. memorize) as much as before because (his own explanation) all the time is spent in hoeing on the shamba. He may therefore, conclude that it is not worth it to invest in a child's education if (1) the child will not get into secondary education; (2) he will not get a job; (3) all he learns is farming, which the old man can teach better anyway.

The solution, she feels, lies in a transformation of the Tanzanian economy and society but, specifically in the education system: 'parents and children need to *experience* a new kind of education, which emphasizes on the one hand the scientific basis for economic and technological development, and on the other hand, reinforces co-operative forms of work, learning and living' (1974: 44).

Mbilinyi therefore, recognises a greater autonomy in the educational system's relationship to society than Hirji can conceive; in her account of it, real possibilities for change exist if changes are implemented imaginatively. Mbilinyi therefore, opens up debates about the nature of the curriculum and of the processes of teaching and of teacher training whose importance is not really stressed by Hirji.

THE PROBLEM OF CURRICULUM REFORM AND POLITICAL SOCIALISATION

George Von der Muhll has argued (1971) that schools in Tanzania represent a potent force for political socialisation. But there are obstacles. Von der Muhll writes about resources starvation, expatriate teachers, the lack of teaching material and finally, school life itself. And on this last problem, aptly, he quotes Nyerere. In a speech in 1966 to the students at Morogoro Teacher Training College he said:

> Those of us who left school many years ago have forgotten many of

the facts we learned there. But we are what we are now in large part
because of the attitudes and the ideas we absorbed from our teacher.
It does not matter what the teacher says in the Civic classes or
elsewhere; his students will learn from what he does. If a teacher fawns
on visiting officials, and then treats a poor farmer as though he were
dirty, the lesson will not be lost on his pupils (quoted by Von der
Muhll, 1971: 43).

Nyerere is raising here the importance of what some sociologists call the
hidden curriculum, the structure of the organisation of teaching itself, of
interpersonal relations, attitudes and taken-for-granted assumptions
about how the world 'really is', which clothe the everyday work of
teaching and learning with a social significance which goes well beyond
the content of specific lessons.

Marjorie Mbilinyi, a teacher educator at Dar es Salaam, has written a
savage indictment of Tanzanian schools accusing them of 'alarming
conservatism' of caring little for students, of 'colonizing' children and
thus preserving a neo-colonial capitalist economy (Mbilinyi, 1975b).
She describes the schools as authoritarian, hierarchical, fostering a spirit
of competition among pupils rather than co-operation, elitist in their
selection methods, staffed by inadequate, often reluctant teachers and
organised to punish rather than to teach. Her general point is that,
'Independence and Education for Self Reliance have not led to a
fundamental transformation of the educational system' (1975b: 3). But
she insists that the schools do have a part to play in raising the
consciousness of pupils so that they can perceive the structures which
continue to oppress them and then act to change those structures. But
such a shift in perception presupposes, she argues, a transformation in
the organisation and attitudes.

THE PROBLEM OF EQUITY

Julius Nyerere was quite explicit that elitism was one of the basic faults
of the education system in Tanzania (1966: 98):

    . . . the education now provided is designed for the few who are
    intellectually stronger than their fellows; it induces among those who
    succeed a feeling of superiority, and leaves the majority of the others
    hankering after something they will never obtain. It induces a feeling
    of inferiority among the majority, and can thus not produce either the

egalitarian society we should build, nor the attitudes of mind which are conducive to an egalitarian society. On the contrary, it induces the growth of a class structure in our country.

His prescription to change this is mainly concerned with changing schools and their curricula and while his analysis relates Tanzanian education to its colonial roots it does so in an unsystematic manner and his analysis of social divisions in modern Tanzania, at least in *Education for Self-Reliance*, is primarily concerned with class attitudes rather than class structures. Class in Tanzania has, in fact, to be understood as a structure of social relationships bound in with the structure of the dependent state itself.

Mbilinyi (1974a) has documented the interaction of class, regional, sex and educational factors to produce patterns of educational inequality in Tanzania in which the children of peasants have fewer opportunities than the children of workers and that both groups are disadvantaged in comparison with traders and other elite groups. Her analysis of primary school pupils and their families in two regions of Tanzania (Mwanza, a cotton-growing area based on small peasant production and Tanga, a sisal-growing area with opportunities for wage employment) indicates an intricate network of factors which determine access to primary schooling. Her methods allowed her to distinguish three main groups in the population in these areas based on a Household Possessions Index. The groups differed from one another consistently, she claims, on the basis of occupation, education and mode of agricultural production. She describes each group in the following way (1974: 14):

> The upper strata were more likely to have off-farm sources of income, whereas all of the lower strata were full-time peasants in both districts. The upper strata had more formal education, and the numbers of the individual household heads with formal education decreased from the upper to the lower strata. The Mwanza upper strata were also more likely to use machine substitutes for labour on the farm and to own their own fox ploughs.

She then related the pattern of primary enrolment to the social class background of the parents; the results are shown in Table 5.2.

The table, admittedly based on small numbers, shows a clear stratification gradient to education. But what is more important is that Mbilinyi found some significant difference among the groups in the

TABLE 5.2
Mean proportion of educated children (girls separately) in the three stratification groups

	n	Educated children	Educated girls
Upper strata: Mwanza	24	83.3	79.1
Tanga	22	84.6	86.6
Middle strata: Mwanza	25	56.2	40.7
Tanga	23	62.3	55.4
Lower strata: Mwanza	23	25.4	13.0
Tanga	7	2.9	00.0

Source: Mbilinyi (1974a)

reasons they give for sending or not sending their children to school. Among the upper strata group intergroup differences are accounted for by differences in their perception of the value of education. In the lower strata such differences were mainly accounted for by religious differences; Christians were more likely to educate their children. The greatest differences were found among the middle strata and were directly related to differences in the form of farm production. Households which did not depend upon child labour because they had machinery were more likely to be able to dispense with child labour and educate the children. There is, therefore, some evidence of a strict economic calculation of the opportunity costs involved in sending children to school.

Mbilinyi notes, in respect of these findings, that the measures which have been taken in Tanzania to abolish school fees may not have the effect of increasing primary enrolments since the problem of low enrolment is related to the form of rural production and can only be expected to change if farming methods themselves change. At one point she notes that the *ujamaa* programme of villagisation might have the effect of freeing child labour for education.

Mbilinyi's findings need to be put in an historical perspective; her comparisons are between areas of different levels of socioeconomic development. In this respect they relate to a wider context of the way in which colonial economic policies affected the regional development of Tanzania. Another social survey illustrates my point and concerns higher education. In a survey of 264 university students at Dar es Salaam, Abel Ishumi (1974) was able to document strong regional variations in access to university as well as a materialistic motive as the dominant motive for attending university. Ishumi explains the regional inequalities—the fact that more students came from the North and South—in the following way (1974: 67):

> The pattern can be explained largely by historical factors, which have had a reinforcing (and multiplier) relationship with the present educational trend. The heavier representation in the north east, north west and south of Tanzania come from areas which have long benefited from missionary formal education. Whenever the Christian missionaries set up mission stations (with a preference for temperate-like highlands and permanently settled regions), they also established schools to provide literary skills for participation in congregational affairs but also to discourage Islam which had entrenched itself in the eastern parts, especially along the coast. The colonial administration was later to benefit from this initial educational start and to reinforce the system by providing more schools in the already privileged regions in its search for skilled and semi-skilled Africans to man the lower-cadre positions in the territory's administration and economy.

The pattern of expectations which Mbilinyi detected can thus be directly related to the historical distribution of schooling and forms of agricultural production, different strata in Tanzania coming to have different views of their own and their children's position because of their location and livelihood.

Education for self-reliance policies are not so far having a great deal of effect in reducing these differences. The people who benefit most from education in Tanzania are urban dwellers, wage workers, traders and officials. Those who benefit least are peasants in the less-developed rural areas.

There are both forces working for greater equality and forces working against it. Those working against it include the processes of class stratification in Tanzania and these work in subtle ways on education. To take a small example; children who fail the Government examinations to allow them to transfer into secondary schooling may be helped by private schools if their parents can afford it. In fact, as Mbilinyi has indicated (1975b), almost one-third of secondary school pupils have transferred into the state system from private schools. Those who cannot afford this are denied further formal education. Such possibilities do little to break the connection between family wealth and educational opportunity and, on a broader front, do not reduce the currency of education as a step towards the plumb jobs in the economy.

On the other hand, efforts are being made to modify selection procedures and to mitigate the financial burden of sending children to school. A recent change in university selection procedures, for instance, now means that sixth form students do not have an automatic right of entry to the university. They must be selected by their colleagues in the villages as being suitable. A greater premium is, therefore, being placed on students having the correct attitudes rather than necessarily the correct background. But whether further change is possible depends upon what changes can be made towards greater self-reliance and socialism, on the political resilience of the people of Tanzania to sustain the kinds of changes post-Arusha policies require. For some critics, particularly on the left, the prospects for such change remain only an agenda item and the state as presently constituted is seen as an obstacle to socialist development.

EDUCATION AND THE STATE

Two sorts of argument are common to bolster the claim that the state in Tanzania is not geared up to achieving socialist development. The first is that, since the country is poor, an even greater premium is placed on plans being imaginative and effective and that this has not always been the case. A second type of argument asserts that the nature of Tanzania's dependency, together with the growth of state structures to plan development has put the administrative control of the country in the hands of a 'national bourgeoisie' while the real control over resources, and therefore, over the form and pace of development, remains with an 'international bourgeoisie' of corporate capital (see I. Shivji, 1975). On this analysis further socialist development in Tanzania is possible only through an alliance of workers and peasants determined to build socialism and wage what Shivji has called 'the silent class struggle' as an open conflict in which the present state is an immediate enemy.

Truth, however, lies somewhere in between; in the absence of an 'open class struggle' whose results, in any case, could not be predicted, the most likely outcome being, perhaps, as elsewhere in Africa, a military takeover, educational changes can take place which do constitute a step towards a socialist society. This at least, has to be the hope of a development strategy which does not destroy its own achievements in the pursuit too rapidly of a political phantom. Whichever view is taken, however, some notion of the precise constraints faced by a dependent state in the development of education is essential.

The case that new initiatives can be taken within the present form of state has much to commend it for three main reasons. Firstly, much has been achieved in ten years. Secondly, the state is not so rigidly oppressive or inflexible that it is closed to criticism or weakened by complacency. Thirdly, the strategy of non-formal education represents a way of improving education to overcome many of the deficiencies of a formal system which itself can be changed.

The achievements of the last ten years can be measured in terms of scale and of content. A scale measure which is of crucial importance is the growth of admissions to primary schools. In 1961 the admission rate was forty per cent; in 1963 it was forty-three per cent. With the implementation of the second five-year plan in 1969 it has gone from 45.7 per cent in 1970 to more than fifty per cent in 1973 (Chau and Caillods, 1975: 32). Even more impressive is the transition ratio from lower primary to upper primary levels. In 1961 this figure was 21.4 per cent. In 1972 it was 84.2 per cent. Enrolments from primary school to secondary school have, however, gone down from about forty-six per cent in 1961 to twenty per cent in 1972. This is consistent with planning policy to restrict secondary education to manpower requirements. But despite a decrease in the transition rate the overall numbers of students enrolled has increased at an annual rate of about ten per cent from 1961 onwards. And the number of students at university has increased tenfold in the same period from 194 in 1961 to over 2000 in 1972. There has thus been an impressive quantitative growth in education provision which is geared in to the manpower needs of the economy.

Qualitatively there has been an important shift in the curriculum; there is more emphasis on rural training. In the university there is a series of courses on the problems of development and underdevelopment. Curriculum planning has been centralised and is increasingly Tanzanian in its content. And there have been some very important developments in the field of non-formal education and adult education. Solomon Odia noted in 1974, for instance that: 'Probably no country in Africa had made a greater effort than Tanzania to evolve a development strategy that is directly relevant to the practical problems confronting it' (Odia: 1974). And an integral part of this strategy is various forms of informal education and rural training.

The rationale for developing non-formal methods of teaching and learning and particularly to involve adults in such programmes is clear. Jack London (1973) has argued forcefully that adult education has a unique role to play in development and sums up that role in the following way:

In brief, the unique role of adult education is to provide learning opportunities for the highly educated to keep them up to date, for the partially trained to qualify them for medium and higher level employment, and formerly neglected pesants, workers and their families, to reduce the education and communication gap and help them become more productive and effective in their work, in their social and personal relationships and as citizens.

Adult education is cheaper than formal systems of education and has a high development payoff since learning takes place at and is directly related to, the point of production. He feels that the Tanzanian government has grasped this fact for the programme of adult education being followed covers a wide range of activities and is pursued with seriousness. The programme consists of the following elements: (a) a commitment to self-reliance policies; (b) a diploma programme of adult education in the university; (c) adult education as a component of all teacher training; (d) 1970 was declared a year of adult education; (e) an institute of correspondence study has been set up as part of the institute of adult education; and (f) a directorate of adult education in the Ministry of Education with planning responsibilities. In addition, Tanzania has initiated several experiments with teaching through radio as a way of reaching people in remote areas of the country.

Additional policies in the field of non-formal education include the setting up of rural training centres to offer training in craft skills and to lend help to *ujamaa* villages; these centres provide training for farmers. There is a Unesco-sponsored functional literacy project and during the five years from 1970–75 something like 3.8 million people registered at literacy classes and 1.9 million actually passed the literacy test at the end of the period (Nyerere, 1977). Tanzania is, too, taking some bold steps in the field of health care and the training of rural health care workers. This whole strategy is part of the broader rural development programme and, arguably, cannot be expected to succeed unless the plans for *ujamaa* villages themselves can be implemented to create conditions under which young people especially can begin to work out a future for themselves in the countryside rather than the towns. Evidence, in fact, of fundamental shifts in social attitudes is scant and it is possible to have severe doubts about the programme of villagisation. There has been some evidence that peasants have been forcibly moved into villages and that too many young people seek to work in the towns (see Morrison, 1976: 293). But as Morrison asks: what are the alternatives? At least in Tanzania criticism of existing practice and active social planning are still possible. But this is where the issue of Tanzania's dependency exerts itself again and questions must be raised of the capacity of the state to modify the social relationships of dependency.

The picture of a clear line of policy and a determined government controlling and implementing imaginative plans for socialist education in a nascent socialist society is, perhaps, in the end, too optimistic. Issa Shivji (1975) has argued very forcibly that post-Arusha policies reflect the interests of an ascendant class in Tanzania, a bureaucratic bourgeoisie which, through its wealth, political clout and education has come to supplant the commercial bourgeoisie of the initial post-independence era. It is a dominant class with direct links with what Shivji calls an international bourgeoisie and the effect of its policies in such areas as trade, aid, industrial strategy, commerce, health, education and welfare, is to bind Tanzania ever more firmly to structures of international capitalism. His argument is a complex one but his comments on rural development programmes illustrates his case quite well and if valid, force us to rethink the prospect of a self-reliant Tanzania.

His point here is that villagisation policies serve to 'integrate the non-monetarized (or the so-called "subsistence sector") within the cash economy. Given the overall neo-colonial structures of the territorial economy this means integration within the world capitalist system' (1975: 106). And he goes on to quote by Cliffe (1973) and Von Freyhold (1973) to document two further points. The first is that *ujamaa* programmes have been most enthusiastically developed in those areas only marginally involved in the cash economy, and that as a result have not offset the growth of social differentiation among the peasantry into those who are rich and employ the labour of others, and those who are poor and must sell their labour power. Secondly, since the methods employed in implementing *ujamaa* have often been bureaucratic and coercive and do not lead peasants to participate in a wider struggle against those forces of capitalism which are at the root of Tanzania's poverty, the policies can have little real effect in changing the ideas and social perception of peasants.

The beneficiaries, according to Shivji, are, in the first instance, the bureaucratic bourgeoisie; their work in para-statal organisations, government departments and the professions, despite the increasing involvement of the state in the economy, helps to bind Tanzania to the capitalism of multinational corporations. In the last analysis the beneficiaries are the multinational companies themselves. The argument here takes us too far away from education to warrant further discussion but if Shivji is right then, quite apart from the persistence of dependency the post-Arusha model of development is not being institutionalised in a way Nyerere would have hoped; socialism and self-reliance must, on this analysis, remain only an item on a political agenda.

The discussion of Tanzania can be concluded with two *caveats*. The first concerns data. Whether or not education for self-reliance policies in education have worked or not can be decided, in large part, on evidence of changed attitudes towards education on the part of peasants, workers and educators themselves. While there is a great deal of evidence that the rhetoric of self-reliance and socialism is readily embraced and heavily legitimated publicly, there is little firm evidence about attitudes and practices. On balance, it seems the broad orientation of the educational system is in the right direction; this, at least, is a considerable achievement if comparisons are made with the period before 1967.

The second *caveat* concerns the questions which have been asked about Tanzania. Julius Nyerere is very willing to admit that the achievements of the last ten years have been small. In his report, *The Arusha Declaration Ten Years After,* he was quite explicit (1977: 1–2):

Ten years after the Arusha Declaration Tanzania is certainly neither socialist, nor self reliant. The nature of the exploitation has changed, but it has not altogether been eliminated. There are still great inequalities between citizens. Our democracy is imperfect. A life of poverty is still the experience of the majority of our citizens . . . We have not reached our goal; it is not even in sight.

But by what standards ought judgements to be made? Perhaps the question should be this: what has Tanzania managed to avoid and what new opportunities have the achievements so far opened for the future? If comparisons are made with other East African states then Tanzania's tentative steps towards a socialist society cannot be so lightly dismissed.

6 Education in Underdeveloped Socialist Societies Cuba and China

The classical texts of Marxism are of little practical use in building up educational systems in socialist societies. Plans for education have to be tested against both ideological requirements and economic needs and this always involves conflict. In Chapter 4 an account was given of how such conflict in the Soviet Union fashioned Soviet education. In this chapter I want to examine two societies which face the task of constructing socialism in the shadow of Soviet claims to the leadership of the communist world. In both China and Cuba the task of educational construction has had to take into account not simply the problems of their own societies but the powerful presence of the Soviet Union itself. In the case of Cuba the Soviet model of development—for complex military and economic reasons—has become the template for Cuban educational practice. Since 1961—although the roots of the break go much further back—China has sought to build a socialism which is radically different in conception to that in the Soviet Union. An account of the Chinese educational system brings this out directly.

My aim is not so much to compare China and Cuba (that would be futile since they are so different from one another) but to illustrate that both societies face common problems. These are problems, primarily, of reconciling the ideological claim that revolution requires the full participation of all the people in education with the pragmatic constraint that neither society can afford this. In both cases, however, imaginative experimentation has produced attempted solutions to this problem from which many other Third World societies have much to learn. It is extremely difficult to assess what is happening in these societies. It is vital to avoid the dangers of both cynicism and gullibility for there is much of both in the literature about them. China, perhaps, illustrates this problem well.

Peter Worsley (1974), in his account of China has argued that unlike many other Third World Asian societies China has achieved both social development and growth. This is in contrast to societies, like South Korea or Japan which achieved amazing economic growth but in which the benefits of that growth are misappropriated and in which life for many is mean and squalid. Worsley's whole account is woven around this theme and while he finds fault with China—for intellectual dogmatism, for abysmal ignorance of other societies (and, interestingly, he singles out Cuba here), for not according women the status he feels women should have in a socialist society and so on, he nonetheless feels strongly that the Chinese are transforming social relationships so that the quality of life for the masses is measurably improving. He sees the revolution as being intrinsically open-ended and responsive to new problems.

His book, like so many others, is based on the experience of a very short visit, his own secondhand reading and his own deeply held views of socialist construction. It is a book, which is also supercharged with Worsley's own commitment and it reflects his heavy emotional investment in his visit. He says at the end of the book he crossed into Hong Kong with tears in his eyes (1974: 250):

I soon knew I was home, for Hong Kong is part of the capitalist world. When a ten-year-old girl badgered me with her tray of chewing-gum, whisky and Hong Kong newspapers, I thought to myself 'Young lady, two hundred yards away you'd be at school'.

I mention this to underline that, on my terms, this is a gullible book. This is not intended as criticism; it is, in fact, an extremely informative work but its viewpoint is partial, its evidence thin and in any case largely constructed by the Chinese themselves. His account therefore, like so many others, offers an interpretation, nothing more.

Cynical accounts must also be handled carefully. In comparison to India, China has made enormous advances in the field of education and in making China an egalitarian society. Martin King Whyte (1975: 695), however, has argued that:

. . . the distinctiveness of Chinese egalitarianism is to be found not so much in its reduction or elimination of differences in income, power and educational skills, although some of this has occurred, but in its attempt to mute the consequences in terms of matters like life styles, consumption patterns and interpersonal deference, of the inequalities that do exist.

Such a view is partial in a very different way but behind its ostensibly matter of fact, non-ideological façade there is a clear cynicism about Chinese achievements. He seems to be saying that if we lifted the ideological shroud we would find something not dissimilar to societies in the West. Such an argument, as I shall show, is absurd.

In a similar vein D. Ray (1970: 50), in commenting on the importance the Chinese attach to the fight against 'revisionism' (a fight in the educational field which manifests itself as a deep worry about social divisions based on education emerging) says that ' "Revisionism" may be far less the product of evil men than the logical outgrowth of economic development'. He then claims that as the Chinese economy grows the skill of the expert rather than the enthusiasm of the masses will be at a premium. What this comment reflects is a deep commitment to a simple form of structural-functionalism which is hardly applicable to China; he seems to imply that, contrary to the full thrust of Chinese policies, industrial development will turn China into a society like the Soviet Union.

In what follows I hope to avoid both dangers: the account I shall give, however, is as a consequence tentative and provisional, but I hope fair.

EDUCATION IN CUBA

The changes which the revolution brought about in the education of the Cuban people have been among some of the most important achievements of the revolution as a whole. 'Nowhere else in the world', write Huberman and Sweezy, 'except possibly in the socialist countries of the Soviet Union and China—has so much been done in so short a time' (1969: 23). In the course of less than twenty years Cuba has achieved virtually universal adult literacy and the provision of basic primary education for all children. In addition Cuba has developed experiments in rural education, the linking of work and study, the management and control of schools and adult education which represent a model for all underdeveloped societies to follow. Education is carefully planned to contribute directly to political socialisation and manpower formation for Cuban industry and agriculture.

At the same time, however, as Sam Bowles has emphasised (1971: 473), 'every major dilemma in the construction of a socialist society has had a counterpart in the school system'. Cuban schools are often very old-fashioned. A competitive examination system still exists and while the overall goals of the system are egalitarian, the requirement to produce rapidly a technical labour force of high calibre has led to the concentration of resources onto a number of elite institutions such as the Lenin school in Havana. Ability grouping within schools and the efforts to link up the best instructors with the best pupils so as not to dissipate scarce resources is a further manifestation of elitism in Cuban schools. The principle of correspondence between education and social structure is thus not something socialist societies can escape from. Whether, therefore, Cuba can make the breakthrough to a fully socialist society built on the 'new man' is something which has to be assessed against the real structures of Cuban society rather than its rhetoric. In Cuba those real structures which are reflected in the form, level and functioning of schools are anchored in Cuba's past and in the shifting sands of the revolution itself.

Education in prerevolutionary Cuba reflected directly the structure of Cuba's dependency. It was unevenly distributed between rural and urban areas. The great mass of children were excluded from secondary education and only about half of the age group who were eligible were actually enrolled in primary schools. This was true as late as 1958 (Bowles, 1971: 479). A survey of over 1000 households in the Cuban countryside in 1956 by Catholic students from the University of Havana (the survey was designed to gain a representative sample of the 400,000 rural families in Cuba at that time) revealed that over forty-three per cent of the adult population were illiterate (Paulston, 1974: 329). Children in non-manual salaried jobs were much more likely—Bowles (1971) suggests five times more likely—to complete the primary school course. The system was therefore very elitist and dominated by a university educating, or, as Arthur Gillette (1971) puts it 'grooming an impractical elite'. The educational system produced a mix of manpower geared not to economic development but to the ostentatious living of an urban elite.

The domination of the Cuban economy by American firms meant that the technical expertise for the economy was effectively produced in the USA itself. There was no particular requirement, therefore, to expand the technical training function of the university of Havana. In 1952, for instance, there were 6560 graduate jurists for every 1000 inhabitants but only 294 agronomist engineers and 355 veterinary surgeons. This was in a society very largely dependent on agriculture (Gillette, 1971: 5). In addition secondary school graduates sought jobs in middle-level management or teaching, or civil administration. The consequence of this was a devaluation of lower-level technical skills which might have been useful in the economy. Overlying all of this, however, was the glossy and seductive veneer of North American culture-breeding expectations and attitudes which were beyond the means of most Cubans except the urban rich.

The *fidelistas* attached a great deal of importance to the development of Cuban education and the idea of using education as the means to build a new socialist man has a resonance in Cuba which goes right back to the guerrilla war in the *sierra maestra*. In his *Reminiscences of the Cuban Revolutionary War* Che Guevara tells of the daily lessons during which illiterate rebel soldiers were taught how to read and write (Gillette, 1971). And one of the first great achievements of the revolution was the literacy campaign of 1961. During this campaign, which began in 1959 and reached its peak in 1961, thousands of students went into rural areas and taught successfully literally thousands of rural workers and peasants to read (Paulston, 1974). In the course of this campaign teachers in urban areas came to appreciate more of the problems of providing education for the rural poor.

Sam Bowles (1971) has listed the four main aims of the Cuban revolution in education, each corresponding to broader economic aims. They are: firstly, to increase educational enrolments; secondly, to eliminate Cuba's dependency on foreign expertise through an expansion of technical and scientific studies; thirdly, education was used deliberately to undermine the class structure of Cuba; and finally, they aimed to create the new man. In achieving these aims Cuba has evolved a number of new educational structures. These are: firstly, the so-called schools to the countryside; secondly, there are interest circles which aim to involve students in the extracurricular study of their subject area; and thirdly, there is the idea of collective learning and universalisation of the university. The growth of an extensive system of part-time adult education is one of the forms in which this latter idea is carried into practice. These headings are, of course, gross simplifications but they do reflect the main thrusts of Cuban educational policy and the structures they indicate are related to one another.

SCHOOLS TO THE COUNTRYSIDE

In this programme whole secondary schools are transferred to the countryside and their pupils work alongside the *campesinos* in the fields and plantations. Beginning with an experiment in 1967 '*La escuela al campo*' was judged to be a success and generalised throughout the school system. Nearly all secondary school pupils spend from six to ten weeks each year spending half of their days studying and half working. This experiment has subsequently been refined with the setting up of the Youth Columns where young people spend up to three years in a semi-military organisation doing agricultural work where and when they are required.

This particular programme is directly related to Cuba's plans to integrate manual and mental labour, to develop *conciencia* and to break down the divisions between urban and rural areas. It has, therefore, a clear ideological rationale. It is also related to labour shortages in the Cuban economy, however. The 'flight from cane' during the 1960s and a too rapid programme of industrial diversification during the first phase of the revolution resulted in labour shortages at crucial harvesting times. The schools to the countryside programme sought to fill this gap. The effectiveness of the programme is, however, in some doubt. Judged for its ideological worth this programme was probably very successful. Sam Bowles (1972:, 296) has argued that, since the leadership roles in these schools are often taken up by those who work well and not simply by those who are good at intellectual tasks, the 'occasional inversion of the school's social system teaches an additional lesson for equality'. They certainly made urban youth familiar with the problems of the countryside. Judged as economic enterprises, however, their achievements are very questionable. Firstly, not much serious study is done (Bowles, 1972). Secondly, as was pointed out at the first National Conference on Education and Culture in 1971, since the productivity of students is low and students make few meaningful contacts with *campensinos*, the overall effect of the programme is to increase unit labour costs (Paulston, 1974). In fact, the schools *to* the countryside programme has given way to a programme of schools *in* the countryside. As Castro put it:

> There will no longer be the school to the countryside: there is now the school in the countryside . . . We will combine systematically study and productive work daily . . . This type of school combines two factors. First an ideal educational type of a socialist education, a Communist education with the necessities of our own economic development. At the same time the school is not a drain on the economy but contributes to the economy and to the development of the country (quoted by Carnoy and Werthein, 1977: 579).

In 1972–73 some eleven per cent of students in the first cycle of secondary schooling were enrolled in schools of this type. Such schools have production schedules integrated with national agricultural plans. They are run democratically and place a high value on what is called in Cuba 'socialist emulation' or socialist competition to bring the best effort out of its pupils. This kind of educational Stakhanovism echoes back to Soviet incentive programmes of the 1930s.

A recent British visitor to the island sums up his experience of talking to students in such schools:

> The study/work arrangements appear popular with the pupils. All those I spoke to—freely and at random—emphasised the sense of fulfilment they got from the responsibilities they were given. It was the visible and concrete contribution they were making to the well-being of the country which seemed of most importance to them.
> Nobody was bothered about what would be—by Western standards—severe limitations on personal freedom. In particular, the tightly organised and very long day, with evening leisure pursuits supervised and planned, would hardly be acceptable to someone not trained in this way from earliest childhood (Moorman, 1976b: 15).

But, as Moorman points out, since half of Cuba's population is under the age of twenty they have, indeed, known no other way of life. There does seem some prospect, therefore, that the schools in the countryside programme will achieve more than the early schools to the countryside programmes. Both programmes, however, are distinct improvements on the state rural education in many Latin American countries.

INTEREST CIRCLES: TECHNOLOGY AND IDEOLOGY

The so-called *circulos de interes* are an important adjunct to the formal school curriculum. They involve students in study and in activities related to a particular subject area and its practical application. There are thus interest circles in agriculture, soil science, chemistry and many other subjects. Bowles (1971: 489) has written this about interest circles:

> A society which has foregone the use of wage incentives needs an alternative means of encouraging young people to enter particular occupations. Thus the *circulos de interes* provide a means of informing young people about the content of various occupations, while at the same time stimulating interest in careers that are likely to make a major contribution to national development.

The transition from school to work is, therefore, not left to chance in Cuba.

But this is just part of a wider attitude that education should serve directly the needs of the economy and of economic development. The same theme shows itself in the pattern of enrolments in Cuban higher education. Between 1958 and 1968 the number of students enrolled in higher education increased by nearly a half but within this broad expansion of places the number of places given over to the humanities and social sciences decreased markedly (Bowles, 1971: 488).

The Cubans are not, however, content with their achievements in this respect and are particularly worried about lack of student interest in agricultural studies. Schools *in* the countryside are a part response to this problem and the use of youth columns to involve students in agriculture must also be seen in this light. Both strategies, however, reflect a deep-seated problem which is not unique to Cuba. Castro himself pinpointed it when he said in 1972:

> Who wants to go to work in the countryside? The countryside is rough, it's poor. Moreover that rough, poor countryside doesn't change from one year to the next, and we'll be having a rough, poor countryside for years to come. All these factors have a bearing on each other and give rise to certain attitudes of evasion (quoted by Paulston, 1974: 253).

Cuba's response, like that of Tanzania and China is to forge strong links between study and work although until the differences between town and country are eradicated the evasiveness which worries Castro will remain a problem.

THE UNIVERSALISATION OF THE UNIVERSITY: COLLECTIVE LEARNING

Castro was asked once in the early 1960s about his attitudes to university education. His reply was that he was not too worried about the universities since by the end of a decade the whole island would be a university. It is Cuban policy to integrate the work of universities with work in the factories and the fields. There are three strands to this policy—a programme of extension, diversification and integration. The programme of extension works through both numerical expansion of higher education opportunities and the active encouragement of workers and *campesinos* to prepare themselves for university study through part-time study in so-called workers and peasant faculties. This latter policy is the policy of diversification.

The Director of Adult Education in the Cuba Ministry of Education told Moorman in 1976 that Cuba aims by 1980 to have a complete duplicate system of part-time education for workers (Moorman, 1976b). In 1976 there were 312,000 adults (of whom 40,000 were over forty years old) doing primary level work. There were 122,000 doing secondary level studies and 123,000 doing pre-university studies. If such groups are successful they automatically qualify for a part-time university course, and at the moment more than half of the students at the university of Havana are part-time (Moorman, 1976b: 15). In this way higher education in Cuba can combine expansion with the need to retain workers at their posts in production thereby lessening the cost of providing higher education.

The programme of integration works by decentralising university studies and combining studies with practical problem-solving in the economy. The plans for the future are for the universities themselves to be centres of specialised high-level research with most of their routine work—teaching and normal research—being done, as it were, in the field.

Finally, through changing the methods by which students actually learn, Cuba seeks to emphasise that knowledge itself is a collective product, a fact taken seriously in the interest circles but which is also reflected in the management of Cuban schools and university courses.

ASSESSMENT

By what criteria should Cuban education programmes be judged? Much depends upon how Cuba's *model of socialist development* itself is to be evaluated. If the changes which have occurred in that model—from an initial revolutionary millenarianism to a more tightly controlled Soviet style programme—are judged to be in some respects unfortunate then a similar judgement will have to be made about Cuban education. For the overall aim of building the new man has had to be compromised by the need to build a new economy. The rhetoric of collective achievement has increasingly given way to that of individual effort and 'socialist competition'. And the need—as the Cuba leadership sees it—to mobilise labour to higher productivity has led to the growth of a policy of incentives for work effort to replace the moral economy so favoured by Guevara. Arthur Gillette, an admirer of Cuba's achievements, has suggested (1971: 21) that this shift in the character of the revolution and in particular the integration of youth and education itself into the economy, has perhaps gone too far. He feels that the present generation of Cuban youth are not in a position to carry out their own revolution and to that extent are an alienated generation.

Some writers have expressed doubts, too, about the egalitarian goals of the revolution. Bowles (1971) has noted that children in rural areas are much more likely to drop out from schools than their urban comrades and women, although having benefited enormously from education, are still underrepresented in further and higher education. More recent data to those available to Bowles shows, for instance, that women account for 48.6 per cent of primary school enrolments, 46.0 per cent of secondary school enrolments but only 21.2 per cent and 30.3 per cent of technical and univeristy education respectively (Franco, 1975: 389). Both Paulston (1974) and Dumont (1974) have noted the problem of high school dropout rates and high rates of grade repeating, both problems reflecting basic inefficiencies in the schools themselves.

Such facts, taken alongside others about the increasing selectivity of the Cuban system—the Lenin school in Havana, for instance, takes only those pupils who achieve average grades of ninety-five marks per hundred during the last three years of primary school (Carnoy and Werthein, 1977: 587)—suggest that the goal of equality has been sacrificed to some extent in favour of efficiency. This is the consequence of the basic dilemma discussed in Chapter 2, that of producing technical cadres for socialist construction.

What success there has been in building up *el hombre nuevo* is difficult to judge. There is little doubt that the revolution itself is secure and that it has consolidated its own ideological rationale. The schools reflect this. The curriculum is based on Marxist principles and much skilful use is made of Marxist revolutionary symbolism in education. The Lenin high school, Allende College, Makarenko Teacher Training College, Ernest Thälemann College, all recall the names of socialist heroes and Che Guevara is probably a greater source of political inspiration from his grave than he ever was alive. The overall effect on the minds of young Cubans must remain a matter for speculation. Only one thing is certain and I conclude this rather brief discussion of Cuba with an observation by Paulston (1974: 256) which captures the point well:

In a larger sense, Cuba's attempts to seek salvation in schooling and in rural development provide a revealing indication of cultural con-tinuities and discontinuities in what must be Latin America's most ambitious effort to find a way out of poverty, underdevelopment and dependency.

CHINA

> The tree may prefer calm,
> but the wind will not subside.
>
> *A Favourite saying of Mao Tse-Tung*

It has been estimated that about forty per cent of China's population is under the age of sixteen (see Mauger *et al.*, 1974: 34). In 1976 there were around 150 million children attending primary schools, some forty-six million in secondary schools and some 500,000 receiving tertiary education in 380 institutions (Gardner, 1977). Such figures refer, of course, only to the formal system of education and therefore grossly underestimate the numbers engaged in non-formal programmes of study. In any case, schools as such are only one component of education in China. In the people's communes, the production brigades, factories and the People's Liberation Army, learning is a continuous process; it is woven in to the pattern of Chinese living as an integral part of its overall design. The sheer magnitude of China's educational effort is therefore not its most remarkable feature although it is, indeed, remarkable. Of much greater significance is the form which education takes in China and the way it contributes to the building of a socialist society, for the Chinese see education as the bedrock of the revolution. Mao once put it this way in a remark which, once explained reveals the whole character of the Chinese revolution: 'The important question is the education of the peasants'.

In this chapter I shall explain why this is so, tracing the Chinese conception of revolutionary education to the historical experience of the Chinese Communist Party and the Marxist thoughts of Mao Tse-Tung. I shall show that China's educational system reflects the dilemmas of and changes in the Chinese revolution itself. Its structure represents a series of compromises between revolutionary ambitions and the *constraints* of a backward peasant society.

The importance of the Chinese experience lies, for me, in three main areas. The first concerns the rural areas of China. Unlike many other Third World societies China has been very successful in developing the countryside. Land reform and the growth of the People's Communes are at the base of this but education has played a crucial role, too. The growth of school enrolments in the countryside is only a small indication of its contribution. Part-time schooling, the development of agricultural middle schools, mass literacy programmes, the Communist Labour University, public health education, and the programmes to send young people to the countryside 'to learn from the masses' are all interconnected additional factors contributing to rural development (Lee, 1974). Such developments, too, are all consistent with the Maoist view that agriculture and industry must be developed in step with one another and not simply in crude quantitative terms. In 1969, for instance Mao argued that:

It is necessary to drive all opera singers, poets, playwrights and writers from the cities to the countryside. They should be sent stage by stage and group by group to the rural areas and factories. They must not stay all the time with their organs since useful things cannot be written in this way. If you do not go to the lower level you will not be fed. You will be fed when you go to the lower level (quoted by Hsi-en Chen, 1974: 221).

Feeding, in this context clearly refers to cultural stimulation and the sentiment Mao is echoing here—that intellectuals and technical workers have much to learn from the peasants—extends into many other aspects of Chinese politics and has its own deep roots in the Yenan period. Such a cultural policy is aimed explicitly, however, at reducing the gap between urban and rural areas.

The second area concerns the question of the relevance of education to social development. Again, unlike many Third World societies China has fashioned an educational system which is directly geared to what they like to call 'the struggle for production'. The rationale for this is not simply to increase production itself but also to distinguish modern Chinese education from the classical traditions of Literati scholarship and Confucian otherworldliness. Mao returned to this theme time and again during the Cultural Revolution. In his 1969 instruction on Part-Work, Part-Study, Mao insisted that:

As far as all circumstances permit, all secondary vocational schools and skilled workers' schools should tentatively run factories or farms for carrying out production so as to become self-supporting. Students should work as they study (quoted by Hsi-en Chen, 1974: 219).

Earlier, in 1964, he had made plain his objections to current Chinese practice in a now very famous talk with a delegation from Nepal. What he said was this:

> There are many problems in our education, and the most important one is dogmatism. We are in the process of reforming the educational system. The present period of schooling is too long, there are too many courses of study, and many of the teaching methods are not good enough. The textbooks and concepts studied by the students remain to be textbooks and concepts, and the students know nothing else. They do not make diligent use of their limbs and *they are unable to distinguish the five kinds of cereal from each other* (my emphasis) (quoted by Hsi-en Chen, 1974: 223).

During the Cultural Revolution it was common for students to criticise their education saying that they could only grow rice on the blackboard.

But such arguments amount to much more than the simple proposition that learning and production both profit from being combined with one another. It is a specific application of the mass-line concept. In the same talk to the Nepalese Mao said:

> Strength comes from the masses. Without reflecting the demands of the masses, nobody is equal to his job. One should learn knowledge from the masses, lay down policies, and after that go back to educate the masses. Therefore, in order to be a teacher, one should first be a pupil. No teacher is not a pupil first (quoted by Hsi-en Chen, 1974: 224).

This is very different from the modern Soviet concept of polytechnical education although there are surface similarities. The Maoist position is characterised by a refusal to separate off questions of politics from questions of education and is deeply mistrustful of the expert since a reliance on expertise reduces the self-reliance of villages, communes and factories, and, ultimately, of China itself.

Parallel to the technical claim that education and production must be combined is the ideological insistence, less important now than during the Cultural Revolution, that the masses themselves must be in control of education. This idea is captured in the Maoist slogan 'Education must serve proletarian politics and be combined with productive labour'. During the Cultural Revolution a most sophisticated, widely discussed and emulated formulation of what this injunction means in practice was set out by the Revolutionary Committee of Lishu county in Kirin province. This is the famous Kirin programme, supported by the Maoists and published in the People's Daily on May 12th 1969. Article One of this programme states:

> In accordance with Chairman Mao's teaching, *In the countryside, schools and colleges should be managed by the poor and lower-middle peasants—the most reliable ally of the working class.* The middle schools should establish 'three-in-one' revolutionary committees which comprise poor and lower-middle peasants, who are the mainstay, commune and brigade cadres and representatives of the revolutionary teachers and students (quoted by Mauger *et al.*, 1974: 78).

Throughout China this model of school management was widely implemented; education thus became radically decentralised and responsive to the immediate needs of local areas. This is in sharp contrast to the experience of many underdeveloped societies although, not, of course, to the experience of some parts of China. In Yenan this was how education had been organised in the period from 1944–49.

The third area concerns the issue of equality. The Maoist revolution in education is radically egalitarian and careful to avoid caste-like divisions based on education emerging in China. This is another undercurrent of the Cultural Revolution where the blows for equality were struck against so-called 'bourgeois academics' and their 're-actionary' teaching methods. This group were identified as supporters, effectively, of the 'capitalist road' who cultivated a 'promotion-conscious mentality' (see Bastid, 1974).

The point of this criticism has to be appreciated in a broader international context. The struggle against 'revisionism'—of which educational elitism is, in the Maoist view, a key component—was, and is, a struggle against the Soviet model of social construction. The slogan, frequently used during the Cultural Revolution but going back to 1958, 'Better Red than Expert', symbolises the Maoist position. An educational system which fashions experts and other educated elites is effectively maintaining capitalist relations of production and this, of course, is the most fundamental criticism which the Chinese make of the Soviet Union.

The egalitarian aims of the Chinese—or, at least, of the Maoists—can best be seen in their attitude to examinations and to university admissions. Mao had told the Nepalese delegation that 'The method of examination tackles the students like enemies and launches surprise attacks on them'. During the Cultural Revolution wide publicity was given to student demands to abolish examinations on the grounds that examinations continued the old feudal system of selecting Literati and that they sustained 'reactionary' social attitudes. Additionally, it was widely claimed, examinations widened the gap between mental and manual labour, town and country, workers and peasants. Accordingly, university entrance requirements were changed to include evidence of 'good socialist consciousness'—something upon which a candidate's comrades would give judgement—and a satisfactory work period in factory or commune. Academic ability as such was not considered too significant a factor. There has been a retreat from this position since the death of Mao (Gardner, 1977) and there is certainly a continuing debate in China about admissions standards, courses and patterns of control in education (see Cleverley, 1976; and Chambers, 1977). In China since the Cultural Revolution, however, it would be extremely difficult, whichever way policy on examinations changes, to allow schools and universities to become again 'the little treasured pagodas' they once were.

These three areas are all clearly related and together they amount to a powerful model of how education can be related to a programme of total social change. How far some of the broader revolutionary goals of education have been realised is something almost impossible to assess. China is still, as the Chinese themselves regularly point out, an underdeveloped society. The educational system still faces the constraints therefore of limited resources. In addition, there is conflict within the leadership over what the immediate goals of education ought to be. Jack Gray (1976b: 246) has written about current dilemmas of Chinese education policy in this way:

> The choices are: a single system of schools *versus* a two-stream system with cheaply run popular schools and an elite stream for the training of the more intelligent as future leaders; schools which combine education with labour *versus* schools in which education is full-time; selection for higher education on the basis of 'political consciousness' *versus* selection by academic criteria. While compromise on all these issues is conceivable, in fact no compromise solution has been advocated in China . . . Education therefore arouses bitter emotions in a country where, traditionally, a youngster's academic success was almost the only ladder to fame and fortune.

Nonetheless, the area of agreement among the leadership is still great and the achievements they have to be set against the situation in China before 1949 and, indeed, before the Cultural Revolution. And to understand the parameters of the current educational debates it is essential to relate them back to what in China is known as the struggle between the 'two roads'—conflicts within the Party over the way to build socialism in China. These historical themes are important because they enter into Chinese educational policies in a direct way being at the root of the dilemmas set out by Gray.

CHINESE EDUCATION BEFORE 1949: CONFUCIUS TO MAO TSE-TUNG

The achievements of China since 1949 must be measured against both the traditional structures of Chinese education and the period from the collapse of the Manchu dynasty and the birth of the Republic in 1911 to 1949 when the communists achieved power. The contrast is between a society fully mobilised for development and one, in the case of classical China, which was feudal and autocratic and, in the case of the Republic one which was racked by warlordism, civil war and tentative attempts at industrial development. In both, education was a luxury not available to the mass of the people.

Classical China from before the time of Christ up to China's defeat in the Opium War of 1840 at the hands of Britain (a convenient date from which to trace China's subsequent incorporation into the modern world) was dominated by Confucian philosophy and, from the Tang Dynasty (AD 618) to the Quing Dynasty (as late as 1905) by a ruling bureaucracy selected on the basis of examinations and steeped in the Confucian classics.

This philosophy emphasises the harmony and stability of all relationships, the importance of filial piety, agreement between rulers and the ruled and the importance of moral and political education. Confucian philosophy does not sustain a critical scientific method; knowledge is deduced from general principles and particular events are understood in terms of these (see Hawkins, 1974; Price, 1970). The measured skills of the Literati were a wide knowledge of classical texts and an ability to compose essays using the traditional eight-paragraph form. These are the so-called 'eight-legged essays' which came in for so much criticism during the Cultural Revolution as examples of useless scholarly formalism.

From the 1860s onwards there were some efforts to improve Chinese education, particularly scientific and technical education by sending students abroad to study (particularly to the United States). China's defeat in the Sino-Japanese war of 1894–95 accelerated this process. The Chinese had up to the 1920s been influenced by the Japanese and German methods of education but after this period they drew heavily on American experience (Hawkins, 1974). Republican China from 1911 had no clear education programme. Civil war, revolutionary turmoil and economic disruption were not the background against which much could be achieved. Even as late as 1937, the beginning of the Japanese invasion, only about fifteen per cent of Chinese children had any access to primary schools and fewer still to middle and secondary schools. In any case the schools that did exist only functioned in the cities (Watson, 1975). Something like ninety per cent of the population was illiterate, more likely to be swayed in argument by appeals to religion or magic than by reason and science. For those who did go to school their education, in keeping with tradition, was formal, biased to rote learning and aimed at producing the harmonious dependence upon the rulers which had been traditionally conceived of as the aim of all education. The foreign-trained people were almost entirely absorbed into teaching and they did attempt to incorporate some of the methods of the American progressive movement in education.

It is important, too, to note that very early on in the 1920s the Chinese communists had come to a clear class analysis of education and had sensed the importance of education as part of the rural revolution which was sweeping China at that time. Mao, in a very important document, *Report on an Investigation of the Peasant Movement in Hunan*, written in 1927, said:

> In China education has always been the exclusive preserve of the landlords, and the peasants have had no access to it. But the landlord's culture is created by the peasants, for its sole source is the peasant's sweat and blood. In China ninety per cent of the people have had no education, and of these the overwhelming majority are peasants. The moment the power of the landlords was over-thrown in the rural areas, the peasant movement for education began (quoted by Hawkins, 1974: 55).

The document as a whole is a vital one in the history of the Chinese revolution because it makes clear that Mao's faith in the peasants as a revolutionary force is not a later heretical development in his Marxism but an essential component of it from the beginning.

What the communists did not have, however, were practical blueprints for a new type of education. The significance of the Yenan years following the Long March lies precisely in this: during this time in considerable hardship and without resources they built up an educational system which departed completely from the traditional system and from what was available in other societies. The experience of these years amounts to a unique Chinese model of educational development.

As late as 1944 in the communist-controlled areas only one child in every six had any access to education (Selden, 1971). From 1944 there were some bold experiments in popular education. The slogan 'develop production, expand the schools' stems from this period. Internal conflicts in the Party had led Mao to instigate a rectification campaign (the so-called *cheng-feng* movement) and some of the methods developed in this campaign—self-criticism and small group study—were transferred in education practice.

The aim of the rectification campaign had been to produce party and military units which could function consistently under highly uncertain conditions of central authority and communication. The same goal applied to education implied drastic decentralisation of school management and control. Part-time schools were set up so as not to disrupt production. Given the absence of teachers everyone and anyone capable of teaching did so. As Mark Selden says: 'Young and old, literate and illiterate, farmers and cadres could all be found among the ranks of both teachers and students' (1971: 271). The rationale for this was to instil the idea that collective action could bring a better future. One American visitor to the area, Gunther Stein, described it as a big elementary school (see Mauger *et al.*, 1974). Two universities were set up in Yenan—the North China Union University and the Yenan Resistance University. The emphasis in both was the combination of theoretical study with practical work. Jack Belden has summed up the educational philosophy of the communists referring to his own personal experiences in the Border Regions:

> Education is not a way of life in itself: it is only an instrument. Since anyone can use this instrument it has a class nature. In Chiang Kai-shek's areas, I found that education was used to forge servile followers of Chiang Kai-shek. But here in the Liberated areas, we try to use this too to make the educated people servants of the masses. There is another point. Education cannot be divorced from life but must be combined with reality. John Dewey says: 'Education is life: school is society'. But we say 'Life is education: society is a school'. That is why

we take the living material around us as subject matters for education (quoted by Mauger *et al.*, 1974: 7).

One final point about the Border Region years: the communists did not reject outright traditional concepts of learning, nor did they dismiss as old-fashioned traditional methods of agriculture and of production. They respected such methods and used them evolving an attitude which came to be described during the period of the Great Leap Forward as 'walking on two legs'. The aim was to use fully that which was of genuine value from the old society.

Much of what happened in this period could be explained as invention born of necessity, that the experiments with what is now known as 'intermediate technology' or the drive to be self-sufficient, were policies forced on a government literally fighting for its life. It should not be forgotten, however, as Mark Selden pointed out that: 'In fighting for their lives men were actively redefining those lives' (1971: 228):

CHINESE EDUCATION: 1949 TO 1966

The 'Yenan Way' was, however, more of an experiment than a fully worked out programme for the education system of a socialist state. In 1949 the communists faced the problem of consolidating their power. They opened primary and middle schools immediately and established three new universities to carry out ideological work (see D. Bodde in Schurmann and Schell (eds), 1977). But the obstacles they faced in building up a China-wide system of education were severe and there were, too, divisions in the Party ranks about the best way in which to build such a system.

Quite apart from the immediate obstacles of poor organisation underdevelopment and the sheer weight of numbers—problems rendered more difficult by the fact that the Communists had had little experience in administering urban areas (see Schurmann, 1977)—there were features peculiar to the Chinese language and to traditional social structure which inhibited rapid educational change. The complexity of the script, as Price has pointed out (1970: 74) requires that a great deal of school time must be spent on the formal learning of characters. The persistence of traditional attitudes to the family meant that people were more likely to give their loyalty to their family and immediate locality than to something—the Party or the Revolution—which transcended both. Finally, in the areas which had not been held by the communists in the period before 1949, traditional concepts of education still prevailed. Schurmann and Schell capture the essence of the problem when they point out (1977: 4) that:

> For two thousand years the state had been an intimate part of Chinese society. Every poor boy aspired to become a scholar so that he could ultimately become an official. So ingrained was the idea of 'official' in Chinese minds that even the name for the supreme deity was 'heavenly bureaucrat' (*t'ien-kuan*).

To break down such attitudes was no mean task especially since there were chronic shortages, not simply of teachers appropriately qualified ideologically to achieve the goals of the new system. The traditional teacher in China emphasised the importance of rote-learning; he commanded great respect and classrooms were authoritarian (Watson, 1975: 123). One of the more important undercurrents of the Cultural Revolution was to rid China of such teaching methods.

In the early years, however, the Party's policy of 'leaning to one side', that is, of modelling its development plans on the Soviet Union probably reinforced something of the hierarchical, formal methods of education which existed in China. An important Party slogan in these early years was 'Learn from the Soviet Union' and it was translated into practice in a number of important ways. Firstly, special preference was given in university admissions policy to the children of workers and peasants and schools were set up on the lines of the Soviet *rabfaks* to help such people with their studies. Political education became a core subject and a number of special schools offering much shortened courses for really gifted children were set up. The aim, as Hsi-en Chen has described it (1974: 16) was to turn out a 'proletarian intelligentsia'. Russian became the foreign language most commonly taught in Chinese schools. Between 1950 and 1958 some 600 Russian language teachers taught in Chinese universities and schools. Chinese students went to the Soviet Union for their training. Hundreds of Russian textbooks were translated into Chinese and Russian concepts of important areas of scientific and technological research came to dominate Chinese universities. School fees also existed; the university course was extended to five years to make it comparable to the Russian university course. There is, however, some evidence that in the period from 1952 to 1958 the number of children from worker and peasant backgrounds who gained access to university or higher education increased by only a small amount from twenty to thirty-six per cent (Watson, 1975: 128). The Red Guards were subsequently to criticise such elitism but it is important to stress that what they were effectively criticising was a whole plan of socialist development and their slogan 'Better Red than Expert' captures the essence of their argument.

By 1956 the 'leaning to one side' policy was under great strain. A very complex interaction of national and international factors explain why. Stalin had been denounced in the Soviet Union, and throughout the communist world this opened up a reappraisal of what socialist development meant. Hungary had been invaded and this articulated divisions about whether the alliance with the Soviet Union was a proper one to maintain. Inside the Party in China divisions were opening up about the role of intellectuals in Chinese political life, about the role of experts in the planning process and about the pace of agricultural modernisation. The Maoists responded with a campaign—the so-called Hundred Flowers Campaign. The slogan, 'Let a hundred flowers bloom, let a hundred schools of thought contend' was designed to encourage an upsurge in the Party against what the Maoists thought were some of its bureaucratic tendencies. This was a time, it must be remembered, when conflicts over the form and pace of agricultural mechanisation and modernisation were also intense. The campaign was followed by a rectification campaign to stifle the superabundance of criticism which had been directed against the Party. The period of the Great Leap Forward followed directly from this and Mao's essay, *On Contradiction* (where he set out the argument that ideological struggle was crucial for further socialist development), represents the philosophical justification for the economic steps taken.

The Great Leap Forward was aimed at building up a socialist industrial society rapidly and represented a dramatic departure from Soviet practice. It was a vital period for Chinese education. J. Glassman has argued (1977: 259), for instance, that the new programme of highly decentralised production (the backyard steel furnace was the symbol which the western press seized upon to characterise this development) and labour-intensive technology required a much larger number of less well-educated but more highly motivated and politically conscious workers. Since 1949 levels of urban unemployment had been creeping up. The urban population had increased from 10.6 per cent of the total in 1949 to 14.3 per cent in 1957. But during the same period, while the urban workforce was increasing by some 1.8 million per annum the number of jobs was increasing at only 1.4 million per annum (Glassman, 1977). The Chinese responded with a sending-to-the-countryside campaign and by setting up the so-called *minban* schools in the rural areas aimed at universalising primary education. Simultaneously the Party decentralised education management (a further departure from Russian methods of administration) and encouraged the growth of half-work, half-study schools.

The Great Leap Forward was accompanied by the setting up of the People's Communes to increase agricultural productivity *and* revolutionary consciousness. It is from this period, for instance, that the Chinese press began (as they still do) to praise the achievements of the Tachai commune for the use it made of both Marxist theory and collective hard work to make massive improvements to its living standards. And it was during this period, too, that the final decisions were made to open up the oil field, Taching, as a model of how to combine industry and agricultural production, thus breaking down the division between the rural areas and the towns.

The Great Leap Forward was not an economic success and it was followed by three years of bad harvests. Mao's own position in the Party weakened and intraparty disagreements about industrial strategy increased. In the educational field these disputes became evident in the so-called socialist education movement of the early 1960s to counter tendencies in the communes to increase the size of private production plots and to counter tendencies in the Party itself towards what the Maoists, at least, understood as corruption and bureaucratic practice (see Collier, 1973). The key slogan to this campaign was in injunction to workers, peasants and cadres to take part in 'Class struggle, the struggle, for production and scientific experiment'.

Hsi-en Chen sees this movement as modelled on the party rectification campaigns of the 1940s and as an extension of the anti-rightist campaign of the Hundred Flowers period. In this respect it was part of the broad strategy to remould the intellectuals. It was an education movement in that it was aimed at broad ideological and cultural changes in society as a whole. In the schools great emphasis was placed on what the Chinese call 'the histories'—a method of teaching in which peasants are brought into the classroom to recount their life histories to contrast the present with the period before liberation. The slogan governing this practice was 'To recall past bitterness and reflect on present sweetness' (Hsi-en Chen, 1974: 33). This method of teaching is still extensively used throughout China as a powerful instrument of political socialisation.

The most decisive event of the 1960s was the Cultural Revolution and it can be seen as an extension of the socialist education movement although, as I explained in Chapter 2, there were other complex causes. In the field of education it can be seen as a great effort to follow the

Yenan way and to rid the educational system of those attitudes which the Maoist group associated with the Soviet model of socialist construction.

THE GREAT PROLETARIAN CULTURAL REVOLUTION

The so-called 'sixteen-point decision' of the Central Committee of the Party concerning the cultural revolution—a decision which effectively launched it—gave the following direction to education:

> In this great cultural revolution, the phenomenon of our schools being dominated by bourgeois intellectuals must be completely changed.
> In every school we must apply thoroughly the policy advanced by Comrade Mao Tse-Tung, of education serving proletarian politics and education being combined with productive labour, so as to enable those receiving an education to develop morally, intellectually and physically and to become labourers with socialist consciousness and culture (quoted by Hsi-en Chen, 1974: 236).

The schools closed; the universities closed. Red Guard groups roamed the countryside cleansing party cadres of their false doctrines and instructing workers and peasants in the works of Mao. (For an account of how this was done in one village see Myrdal and Kessle, 1970.) The management of schools and universities was given over to 'three-in-one' revolutionary committees chaired by workers and peasants themselves. Special ideological retraining schools—the May 7th Cadre schools— were set up to re-educate Party functionaries. In 1972 over 90,000 party cadres were attending such schools in China (Macciocchi, 1972: 98). The aim of these schools is to re-engage party members, officials and other leaders with Maoist theory and to effect a fundamental change in Chinese culture. This, I know, seems a very broad aim but the cadre schools are quite explicit about it and have devised ways of doing it.

Maria Macciocchi was told in one such school that they were trying to give a 'proletarian meaning' to such aesthetic concepts as beauty, ugliness, pleasure and pain. She was told that in the past such concepts had class meanings: the poor were thought ugly and base, for instance. By involving leading cadres in the collection of 'night soil' and garbage they broke down this attitude. Similarly Peter Mauger was told during his visit to one such school in Peking that they had transformed what in Chinese jargon was a 'three-door cadre' (that is, someone who had come through the family door, through the office door, insulated from the mass of the people and even despising them) into a true revolutionary. Formerly, Mauger was told, one young woman had held her nose when she saw peasants carrying out the night soil. But, 'Now that she has seen the poor peasants treasuring it she says, "It is not the manure that is dirty, but my ideas". Now she takes a lead in the hardest and dirtiest work; we call her the iron girl' (Mauger, *et al.*, 1974: 72). Such schools, however, are clearly elite schools; Maria Macciocchi says that it is as difficult to be chosen for one as to be chosen for a space flight. Currently, however, they are the ideological guardians of the revolution.

As the schools and universities began to open from 1967 onwards (many of them being modelled on the Kirin proposals) a system began to emerge with the form, as shown in Figure 6.1. Under the draft

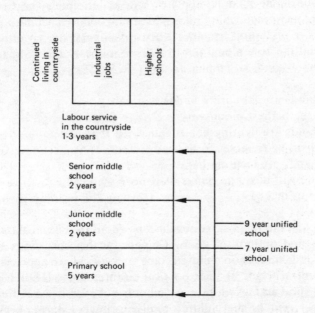

Figure 6.1   The Chinese education system

Source: Hsi-en Chen (1974: 43)

programme primary schooling was shortened and greater emphasis placed on political education and involvement with manual work although eighty per cent of the time is spent on basic learning (Watson, 1975: 134). Watson has set out the timetable of a primary school in Nanking:

8.0–8.30 am   Study the works of Mao
8.30–8.50 am   Physical exercise
8.50–11.30 am   Lessons and ten-minute break
Lunch and rest period
2.0–3.35 pm   Lessons and home

Out of a total of about twenty-seven lessons each week almost a third is given to language study since primary school graduates are expected to know about 3000 characters; to read widely a knowledge of at least 7000 characters is required (Watson, 1975: 134). An analysis of the content of Chinese textbooks in elementary schools by Roberta Martin further reveals that the themes given most emphasis are those of self-sacrifice and hard work. In contrast to such books in Taiwan the Chinese texts devalue family life thus undermining the Confucian emphasis on family loyalty. Family life is important in China but family members in textbooks are always portrayed against their other social roles. And the role model *par excellence* is the worker. She quotes a poem about hands to emphasise this (1975: 252):

Our hands are labouring hands that can
move the highest mountains
Our hands are fighting hands and when the enemy
sees them he trembles from head to toe
Our hands are creating hands
And we will have the things that those who came
before us lacked.

Martin comes to no positive conclusions about the effects of this on the attitudes and outlook of young Chinese but her suspicions are clear enough: in China schoolchildren come very quickly to appreciate some of the central tenets of their political culture. There is still a division between rural and urban primary schools but even in rural areas some ninety per cent of the children receive primary education (Watson, 1975).

Secondary education in rural areas expanded rapidly in the period after the cultural revolution but on the basis of part-time schooling and the importance of formal school tests has been devalued. This means that the transition from primary to junior middle and senior schools is easier than it once was. The organisation and functioning of secondary schools is similar in form to the primary schools although, of course, the content of the work is different. The school day extends to 6.30 pm and, reminiscent of the Soviet Union, there is a clear account given in school rules of what is expected of pupils. Rule 1 states: 'Endeavour to learn'. Rule 16 states: 'Obey public order. Take care of public property'. Rule 6 says: 'During the class assume a correct posture; listen to the lecture attentively; do not talk unless when necessary; do not do anything else besides your class work' (quoted by Watson, 1975: 141). This particular rule runs directly counter to the thoughts of Mao who once argued that 'students should be allowed to doze off . . . rather than listen to tasteless lectures' (quoted by Hsi-en Chen, 1974: 221).

The secondary schools combine study with work, often having their own workshops to do this, but perhaps to the western visitor the most intriguing feature of the schools is their attitude towards punishment. In Chinese schools pupils are represented on the Revolutionary Committee and this directly affects the power relationship between teachers and pupils. The policy on punishment is to stress what the Chinese call the 'ideological method' rather than the 'rod and slap method' (Macciocchi 1972: 453). Macciocchi (1972: 453) quotes a student in a Shanghai Middle school on this:

We think that when you brandish a rod or bang on desks we are even less convinced. We realise that if banging is the only thing a teacher knows, he lacks authority. Anyone can scream or bang on a desk. Chairman Mao teaches the opposite: to convince others you must persuade them, not force them.

This student was thirteen years old, a member of the school Revolutionary Committee and she was echoing the sentiment of a school wallposter which read, 'Can the rod and hand replace ideological work? No, they can never replace it'.

Discipline problems do arise but issues are examined in lengthy discussions where the emphasis is placed on self-criticism and helping the offender come to see the folly of his ways. As a method of changing people it goes back to the rectification campaigns of the party itself and its aim is to strengthen the authority of the group in the mind of the individual. Questions of punishment are thus not left to the professional responsibility of teachers; they are solved collectively. Punishment is therefore conceived of as an integral part of learning. We can only speculate on the effects of this but it would seem that the yawning chasm which often exists between teacher and pupil in schools in the West simply cannot exist in China. Whether this is, in fact, the case is something which we simply do not know.

The Cultural Revolution in the universities had dramatic effects. University entrance requirements changed; initial selection by commune Revolutionary Committees replaced formal academic criteria. Professors were purged for their old-fashioned teaching methods. Great efforts were made to integrate theory and practice (see Mauger *et al.*, 1974). Only glimpses of Chinese higher education are, however, available and since 1973 it is not clear what policy governs higher education since there have been several retreats from the programmes of the cultural revolution. The universities and other institutes are, however, highly selective although the criteria are very different from those which operate in the West. The universities have a very full and tight daily programme for their students. Watson quotes the timetable of Kwangtung Teacher Training College as an example of how institutes of higher learning are organised:

6.0–6.30 Reveille and Physical exercise
6.30–7.0 Breakfast
7.30–8.30 Study of Mao's works
8.30–11.30 Classes or productive labour
11.30–14.30 Free time, lunch, rest
14.30–16.30 Extracurricular activity; sport; youth league work
17.30–18.00 Dinner, free time
19.30–20.00 Newspaper reading and discussion
20.00–22.00 Private study. Lights out.

And Watson a former teacher in a language institute says this of Chinese students (1975: 146):

[They] are extremely self-disciplined and hard working. Much of this derives from the extent to which political motivation is made part of everything they do from the time they first enter school. They are all trained to feel that their work serves a greater social purpose than their individual ambitions.

As for teachers in higher education the experience of the Cultural Revolution must have been harrowing indeed. Their teaching materials were radically altered, the academic quality of their students lowered and they themselves subject to work in the countryside and constant criticism. Jacqueline Slade Tien, the wife of an American-Chinese professor reports from the University of Wuhan in 1974 that the doctrine 'laymen leading experts' was being vigorously pursued and that the students she met studying English were sharpening their revolutionary awareness on the poet, Shelley. They were studying Shelley's 'Song of the Men of England' and they were told that this poet was 'one of the advance guard of socialism' (1975). At Tsinghua University Macciocchi was enthusiastically informed by a professor of dynamics that his life and work had been 'enriched' by his contact with ordinary workers, one of whom he referred to as his teacher (1972: 70).

Other reports are less sanguine about the universities. Jan Prybla (1975), a visitor to China from Pennsylvania State University has argued that, although his trip around several institutions was like 'viewing flowers on horseback' the evidence is overwhelming that the Cultural Revolution 'has overcorrected both the real and imaginary distortions of the past'. He claims that university standards have dropped and for fear of public criticism many of China's most able academics remain passive and effectively underemployed.

And, using a similar argument to that of Glassman (1977) with respect to the Great Leap Forward period, Prybla suggests that the economic significance of the Cultural Revolution was to dampen down student expectations for high-level work since such jobs did not exist in sufficient quantity to meet the demand for them. 'Job aspirations', he says 'are nowadays nipped in the bud rather than destroyed later by the overproduction of unemployable intellectuals, as happens in many developing countries' (1975: 294). Prybla's picture of low academic morale is supported by Hsi-en Chen (1974) but it must be said that the evidence is so inconclusive no one can be sure of the real situation.

FINAL COMMENT

China is an enigma; it is a society which in many ways is sociologically impenetrable. Not only is it difficult to acquire 'hard data' on China—a real enough problem—but the student, in so far as he or she is reliant on the reports of others, perhaps drawn from visits, is dependent on some highly filtered images of life in China. They are often images which themselves are refracted through different ideological filters. It would be foolish in the circumstances to reach firm conclusions. Even the most dedicated Maoist must surely have to bear in mind Mao's own essay *Where Do Correct Ideas Come From*? He or she would then have to conclude that no-one not engaged directly in revolutionary activity in China can ever really know the validity of their conclusions.

I conclude, therefore, with my own tentative, highly refracted image. China is an underdeveloped society pursuing a unique *model of development* against a background of severe political, cultural and economic *constraints*. The model itself has undergone modification and this has involved political struggle. The successes of Chinese development have been remarkable and the comparison which should be made to emphasise this point is the comparison with India. The universalisation of primary education and the rapid extension of secondary education have been some of the most important achievements of the revolution. China has managed to bring education to the countryside in a society which is still overwhelmingly a peasant society. The Chinese communists might therefore claim considerable success in solving the problem which is basic to socialist construction in underdeveloped societies—that of mobilising and involving peasants themselves and of creating a climate in which urban cadres do not regard work in the countryside as either a waste or a punishment. The Chinese model is highly institutionalised; it penetrates their social structures directly. China has become a society fully mobilised around the political thoughts of Mao Tse-Tung. It is a society which has been *philosophied*. The Maoist slogans, philosophical argument, moral precepts and political rhetoric have been woven into the texture of everyday life and communication. Anyone who has read any of the more famous works of Mao must be startled when, on reading transcripted interviews with party cadres and workers, some of Mao's own phrases are relayed back having entered private speech.

Formal schooling is only one small part of China's educational effort and China has succeeded in marrying education to the needs and demands of production. In this respect, although the model is not transferable to other societies, many other Third World societies can learn a great deal from China.

The costs of the Chinese revolution in terms of thwarted individual ambition, of ideological coercion, even, perhaps to the speed of industrial change in China are incalculable. The revolution is certainly not yet spent. Current campaigns against the 'Gang of Four' indicate more about leadership troubles in the Party than about difficulties with the Chinese economy. A society which experienced the Cultural Revolution can hardly be expected to settle down to work to plans imposed from above. In any case, the international situation is too volatile ever to make that a possibility.

> The tree may prefer calm,
> but the wind will not subside.
>
> *A favourite saying of Mao Tse-Tung*

7 Conclusions

The case studies set out in this book contain their own conclusions so I shall not seek to repeat them here. It is sufficient to note that substantively different patterns of change and developent in education have been identified and that the differences noted among the societies discussed reflect not just their unique features but their social type.

The anaytical backbone of the book, given the complexity of the issues with which it had to cope, is however, quite crude. The account I have given has been high on description, low on comparison and often speculative in its analysis. This is only partly a consequence of the impossibility of one person having sufficient competence to cope with the range of material I have dealt with, although that, in itself, is a real problem. It is far more a question of the inadequacy of the tools of sociological analysis, of theory and of method to examine the questions raised at the beginning of this book. In what follows, therefore, I shall indicate what kind of pointers to further work my discussion has thrown up. These can be grouped together and boldly stated under three main headings—theory, method and policy.

THEORY

The arguments of this book have implications for two areas of theorising, those of cultural transmission and socioeconomic development. With respect to the former, three general points emerge. The first is that form, content and distribution of education reflects the distribution of power in society; education always reflects the compromises of politics; it follows, therefore, that change in education always follows on from changes in the distribution of power. The case of Britain illustrates this point very well; the tensions between individualism and collectivism, elitism and equality which have been so central to the evolution of education in this country can be shown to be the articulation in philosophy of interests clashing in production and politics. The British case illustrated further that the political issues penetrate directly the organisation of schooling, the content of syllabuses and the pattern of teacher–pupil interaction.

Such an observation, hardly startling, becomes theoretically interesting set against the same themes—despite differences in specific historical form—in the case of West Germany. The transposition of inequalities in the sphere of production into differences in education can then be seen to be rooted in the changing form of a particular type of social system—industrial capitalism.

Social reproduction must be studied comparatively *and* historically. Education is so heavily conditioned by constraints and compromises of the past that it has to be seen as reproducing three societies simultaneously, the past the present and the future. This point came out very clearly in the accounts of Ghana and Tanzania; in both cases the form of schooling and the social attitudes to which schools responded were firmly rooted in the colonial experience of the two states despite the altered requirements of independence. Recognition of this, not just in the case of dependent societies but in all of the case studies presented, leads to the third point, the issue of the relative autonomy of education systems from either economic requirements or political demands.

Too literal an acceptance of the correspondence principle would lead to a neglect of the high degree of autonomy and social insulation education systems can achieve under certain conditions. Indeed, in the absence of a strict regime capable of controlling student quotas, syllabus contents and the overall demand for education—conditions most readily met in the socialist states although, even then, not for continuous periods, as the failure of both Khruschev's reforms in the late 1950s and China's retreat from the Cultural Revolution both indicate—schools and colleges can display a great indifference to the world outside them. Political ideologies can so easily be neutralised by education although, when the conditions are right it can be a superbly efficient ideological instrument. What those conditions are can only be revealed on the basis of comparative studies.

The implications of my account for theorising about development are twofold. Development as opposed to growth is likely when education is widely available, geared to or at least consistent with the immediate needs of production yet embodying a vision of a better society in the future in which the benefits of growth will be widely diffused. Only when such rewards are seen as realisable can education be a force of social and economic mobilisation. Again, this is hardly a discovery; it is important, though, to examine the conditions under which such a role for education is possible.

My second point follows from this. The availability of education, its responsiveness to economic requirements or political demands varies not simply by historical circumstance but by the type of society. Different types of society allow different kinds of development to take place and societies differ radically in their capacity (something determined largely by the values of leading political groups) to overcome the constraints of the past and to conceive of new options for the future.

METHOD

There are only two points to make under this heading. Systematic comparative research requires refined typologies and standardised data. The first requirement is much more easily met than the second; it is possible to conceive of further classifications of social types from within the broad types discussed in this book. It is not so easy to conceive of a standardised data base containing material suitable to examine differences among societies in socialisation, teacher–pupil relations, pupil indentities and so on.

Perhaps all we can hope for is that, with agreement among scholars on basic theoretical approaches, empirical research will increasingly acquire a cumulative character. I hope this book provides some clues about how this might be done.

POLICY

There are two points about policy I want to make. The first is this: policy in education concerns questions of resources and priorities but is fundamentally about social ends, or, as I have put it in this book, models of development. Programmes for education cannot be discussed outside of the broader social ends they reflect. Ends themselves are not, however, disembodied; they reflect the interest and power of different social groups. Planning in education is therefore never neutral, never a matter reducible to criteria of technical efficiency. In an increasingly bureaucratised world—and only societies in the first flush of revolutionary ardour seem free of this constraint—the power of the expert is enhanced and arguments about technical expediency conceal the essential political character of planning and decision-making. The networks of international aid, the increasingly opaque workings of education ministries may mask the political issues but they exist, nevertheless.

The second point concerns the constraints on educational development. These are not simply economic or internal to a particular society; they are external and political too, reflecting the historical interconnectedness of societies and current relationships of aid, trade ideological affinity and military alliance. The education elites of Africa can only be understood in this light and the same would apply to the elites of Eastern Europe, the tutelage being of course different in both cases. The effects of these connections works both ways as the case of Britain reveals; the Empire contributed directly to social differentiation in Britain. It bolstered the economic base of a social elite and heightened its insulation in the public schools. The loss of Empire exposed the whole rickety class structure to the cold blast of capitalist competition and found it wanting. The contrast with Germany was illuminating here; without a comparable Empire Germany developed a powerful industrial base exploiting the most advanced technologies, a fact as I have shown which was directly reflected in German education, particularly in German technical education.

For poor societies the constraints which must be overcome for development to take place are not simply those, therefore, of their own poverty; they are found too, in external relationships of aid and trade which historically and together have fashioned various states of dependency.

Planning in education therefore, not only involves choices among alternative ends; it must face up to the nature of the constraints which might prevent those ends being realised. As a process it clearly requires a much more sophisticated understanding of how social structures mould education than has previously been available.

References

Abdulaziz, M. H., 'Tanzania's National Language Policies and the Rise of Swahili Political Culture', in W. H. Whiteley (ed.), *Language Use and Social Change* (London: Oxford University Press, 1971).

Addison, P., *The Road to 1945: British Politics and the Second World War* (London: Jonathan Cape, 1975).

Allen, C. and Johnson, R. W., (eds.), *African Perspectives* (London: Cambridge University Press, 1970).

Althusser, L., 'Ideology and Ideological State Apparatuses', in B. R. Cosin (ed.), *Education: Structure and Society* (London: Penguin, 1972).

Amin, S., *Neo-Colonialism in West Africa* (London: Penguin, 1973).

Anderson, C. A., The Utility of Societal Typologies in Comparative Education, *Comparative Education Review* (June 1959).

Anderson, C. A., 'Fostering and Inhibiting Factors', in C. S. Brembeck, and J. J. Thompson (eds.), *New Strategies for Educational Development: The Cross-Cultural Search for Non-formal Alternatives* (Washington, DC: Heath and Co., 1973).

Anweiler, O., 'Educational Policy and Social Structure in the Soviet Union', in B. Meissner, and D. P. Kommers (eds.), *Social Change in the Soviet Union* (Indiana: Notre Dane Press, 1972).

Apter, D., *The Gold Coast in Transition* (New York: Atheneum, 1963).

Austin, D., 'Ghana: Recent History', in *Africa South of the Sahara* (London: Europa Publications Ltd., 1975).

Austin, D., *Politics in Ghana 1946–60* (London: Oxford University Press, 1964).

Austin, D., 'Et in Arcadia Ego: Politics and Learning in Ghana', *Minerva* vol XIII no. 2 (1975).

Avineri, S., *The Social and Political Thought of Karl Marx* (London: Cambridge University Press, 1968).

Baikova, V., *Ideological Education of the Masses* (Moscow: Novosti Press Agency Publishing House, 1975).

Bailey, M., 'Tanzania and China', *African Affairs* vol. 74 (January 1975).

Balogh, T., *The Economics of Poverty* (London: Weidenfeld and Nicholson, 1974).

Banks, O., *Parity and Prestige in English Secondary Education* (London: Routledge and Kegan Paul, 1955).

Barker, R., *Education and Politics 1900–1951: A Study of the Labour Party* (Oxford: Clarendon Press, 1972).

Barraclough, G., *An Introduction to Contemporary History* (London: Penguin, 1964).

Bastid, M., 'Economic Necessity and Political Ideals in Educational Reform During the Cultural Revolution', in D. Milton, N. Milton and F. Schurmann (eds.), *People's China* (London: Penguin, 1977).

Bauman, Z., 'Twenty Years After: The Crisis of Soviet Type Systems', *Problems of Communism*, vol. 21 (1971).

Bauman, Z., 'Officialdom and Class: Bases of Inequality in Socialist Society', in F. Parkin (ed.), *The Social Analysis of Class Structure* (London: Tavistock Publications, 1974).

Bayliss, T. A., 'East Germany in Quest of Legitimacy', *Problems of Communism*, vol. 21 (1972).

Becker, H., *German Youth: Bond or Free?* (London: Routledge and Kegan Paul, 1946).

Belden, J., *China Shakes the World* (New York: Harper Row, 1949).

Bell, D., *The Coming of Post-Industrial Society* (New York: Basic Books, 1973).

Bellaby, P., *The Sociology of Comprehensive Schooling* (London: Methuen, 1977).

Bendix, R., and Roth, G., *Scholarship and Partnership: Essays on Max Weber* (London: University of California Press, 1971).

Benewick, R., Berki, R. N. and Parekh, B., *'Knowledge and Belief in Politics: The Problem of Ideology'*, (London: Allen and Unwin, 1973).

Benn, C., and Simon, B., *Half-way There* (London: Penguin, 1972).

Bennet, V. P., 'Soviet Bloc–Ghanaian Relations Since the Downfall of Nkrumah', in W. Weinstein (ed.), *Chinese and Soviet Aid to Africa* (New York: Praeger, 1975).

Berger, P., and Luckmann, T., *The Social Construction of Reality: A Treatise in the Sociology of Knowledge* (London: Penguin, 1966).

Bernstein, B., *Class Codes and Control*, vol. 1 (London: Paladin, 1974).

Bernstein, B., and Peters, R. S., 'Ritual in Education', in R. Dale *et al.*

(eds.), *School and Society* (Milton Keynes: The Open University, 1971).

Bernstein, H. (ed.), *Underdevelopment and Development: The Third World Today* (London: Penguin, 1973).

Bibby, J., 'The Social Base of Ghanaian Education. Is it Still Broadening?', *British Journal of Sociology* (no. 3, 1973).

Bibby, J., and Peil, M., 'Secondary Education in Ghana: Private Enterprise and Social Selection', *Sociology of Education*, vol. 47, (1974).

Birmingham, W., Neustadt, I., and Omaboe, E. N., *A Study of Contemporary Ghana*, vol II (London: Allen and Unwin, 1967).

Blakemore, K. P., 'Resistance to Formal Education in Ghana', *Comparative Education Review*, vol. 19, no. 2 (June 1975).

Blaug, M. (ed.), *Economics of Education, I* (London: Penguin, 1968).

Blaug, M., *An Introduction to the Economics of Education* (London: Penguin, 1970).

Board of Education, *Committee on Secondary Education* (Spens Report) (London: HMSO, 1938).

Board of Education, *Committee on Curriculum and Examinations in Secondary Schools* (Norwood Report) (London: HMSO, 1943).

Borchardt, K., 'The Industrial Revolution in Germany 1700–1914', in C. M. Cipolla (ed.), *The Emergence of Industrial Socieites* (London: Fontana, 1973).

Bornstein, M. (ed.), *Plan and Market: Economic Reform in Eastern Europe* (Yale: Yale University Press, 1973).

Bottomore, T., and Rubel, M., *Karl Marx: Selected Writings* (London: Penguin, 1963).

Boudon, R., *Education Opportunity and Social Inequality* (London: John Wiley, 1974).

Bourdieu, P., 'The School as a Conservative Force', in J. Eggleston (ed.), *Contemporary Research in the Sociology of Education* (London: Methuen, 1974).

Bourdieu, P., 'Systems of Education and Systems of Thought', in M. Young (ed.), *Knowledge and Control: New Directions for the Sociology of Education* (London: Collier-Macmillan, 1971).

Bourdieu, P., and Passeron, J. C., *Reproduction in Education Society and Culture* (London: Sage Productions, 1977).

Bowen, W. G., 'Assessing the Economic Contribution of Education', in M. Blaug (ed.), *Economics of Education, I* (London: Penguin, 1968).

Bowles, S., *Planning Educational Systems for Economic Growth* (Cambridge, Mass.: Harvard University Press, 1969).

Bowles, S., 'Cuban Education and the Revolutionary Ideology', *Harvard Education Review*, vol. 41 (November 1971).

Bowles, S., 'Education and Socialist Man in Cuba', in M. Carnoy (ed.), *Schooling in a Corporate Society* (New York: D. McKay and Co., 1972).

Bowles, S., 'Unequal Education and The Reproduction of the Social Division of Labour', in M. Carnoy (ed.), *Schooling in a Corporate Society* (New York: D. McKay and Co., 1975).

Bowles, S., and Gintis, H., *Schooling in Capitalist America: Educational Reform and the Contradictions of Economic Life* (London: Routledge and Kegan Paul, 1976).

Bowles, S., and Gintis, H., 'Capitalism and Education in the United States', in M. Young and G. Whitty (eds.), *Society, State and Schooling* (London: The Farmer Press, 1977).

Bowman, M. J., 'The Human Investment Revolution in Economic Thought', in M. Blaug (ed.), *Economics of Education, I* (London: Penguin, 1968).

Boyd, T. A., and French, S. A., 'The Performance of Ghana's Secondary Schools', *West African Journal of Education*, vol. 18 (1974).

Bracher, K. D., *The German Dictatorship: The Origins, Structure and Consequences of National Socialism* (London: Penguin, 1973).

Branson, N., and Heinemann, M., *Britain in the Nineteen Thirties* (London: Weidenfeld and Nicolson, 1971).

Brembeck, C. S., and Thompson, J. J. (eds.), *New Strategies for Educational Development: The Cross-Cultural Search for Non-Formal Alternatives* (Washington, DC: Heath and Co., 1973).

Bronfenbrenner, U., *Two Worlds of Childhood. U.S. and U.S.S.R.* (London: Allen and Unwin Ltd., 1970).

Brown, R. K. (ed.), *Knowledge, Education and Cultural Change* (London: Tavistock, 1973).

Burks, R., 'The Political Implications of Economic Reform', in M. Bornstein (ed.), *Plan and Market: Economic Reform in Eastern Europe* (Yale: Yale University Press, 1973).

Burnham, J., *The Managerial Revolution* (London: Penguin, 1941).

Burns, T., and Saul, S. B. (eds.), *Social Theory and Economic Change* (London: Tavistock, 1967).

Butterworth, E. and Weir, D. (eds.), *The Sociology of Modern Britain* (London: Fontana, 1975).

Byrne, D. S., Williamson, B. and Fletcher, B. G., *The Poverty of Education: A Study in the Politics of Opportunity* (London: Martin Robertson and Co. Ltd., 1975).

Calder, A., *The People's War Britain 1939–1945* (London: Panther, 1971).

Cameron, J., and Dodd, W. A., *Society, Schools and Progress in Tanzania* (London: Oxford University Press, 1970).

Carey, C. D., 'Patterns of Emphasis Upon Marxist–Leninist Ideology: A Computer Content Analysis of Soviet School History, Geography and Social Science Textbooks', *Comparative Education Review*, vol. 20, no. 1 (1976).

Carnoy, M. (ed.), *Schooling in a Corporate Society* (New York: David McKay, 1972).

Carnoy, M., *Education as Cultural Imperialism* (New York: David McKay, 1974).

Carnoy, M., and Werthein, J., 'Socialist Ideology and the Transformation of Cuban Education', in J. Karabel and A. H. Halsey (eds.), *Power and Ideology in Education* (New York: Oxford University Press, 1977).

Central Advisory Council for Education *Early Leaving* (London: HMSO, 1954).

Central Advisory Committee for Education, *15–18* (Crowther Report) (London: HMSO, 1959).

Central Advisory Council for Education, *Half Our Future* (Newsom Report) (London: HMSO, 1963).

Central Advisory Council for Education, *Children and Their Primary Schools* (London: HMSO, 1967).

Chambers, D. I., 'The 1975–76 Debate Over Higher Education in the People's Republic of China', *Comparative Education*, vol. 13, no. 1 (March 1977).

Chanan, G., and Gilchrist, L., *What School Is For* (London: Methuen, 1974).

Charlton, K., 'Polytechnical Education: An Idea in Motion', *International Review of Education*, vol XIV, no. 1 (1968).

Chau, Ta Ngoc, and Caillods, F., *Educational Policy and its Financial Implications in Tanzania* (Paris: The Unesco Press, 1975).

Child, D., *East Germany* (London: Ernest Benn, 1969).

Cipolla, C. M. (ed.), *The Emergence of Industrial Societies-1* (London: Fontana, 1973).

Cipolla, C. M. (ed.), *Contemporary Economies-1* (London: Fontana, 1976).

Cleverley, J., 'Succession Battle Spills Over Into Education and Starts Mass Debate', *Times Higher Education Supplement* (9 April 1976).

Cliffe, L., and Saul, J. (eds.), *Socialism in Tanzania vols I and II* (Nairobi: East Africa Publishing House, 1973).

Cliffe, L., 'Socialist Education in Tanzania', in L. Cliffe and J. Saul (eds.), *Socialism in Tanzania, vols I and II* (Nairobi: East Africa Publishing House, 1973).

Cliffe, L., 'The Policy of Ujamaa Vijijini and the Class Struggle in Tanzania', in L. Cliffe and J. Saul (eds.), *Socialism in Tanzania, vols I and II* (Nairobi: East Africa Publishing House, 1973).

Clignet, R., 'Damned If You Do, Damned If You Don't. The Dilemmas of Colonizer–Colonised Relations', *Comparative Education Review* (October 1971).

Collier, J. E., *China's Socialist Revolution* (London: Stage 1, 1973).

Collins, R., 'Functional and Conflict Theories of Educational Stratification', *American Sociological Review*, 36 (1971).

Collison, Omani, G., 'Concept Formation in a Second Language: A Study of Ghanaian School Children', *Harvard Education Review*, vol. 44 (1974).

Colls, R., 'Oh Happy English Children! Coal, Class and Education in the North East', *Past and Present* no. 75, (November 1976).

Cook, T. G. (ed.), *History of Education in Europe* (London, Methuen and Co. Ltd., 1974).

Constantine, S., 'The Imperial Government and British Colonial Development Policy in the 1920s', Mimeo: University of London Institute of Commonwealth Studies. Postgraduate Seminar (1975).

Corrigan, P., Ramsay, H., and Sayer, D., *Socialist Construction and Marxist Theory* (London: Macmillan, 1978).

Cosin, B. (ed.), *Education: Structure and Society* (London: Penguin, 1972).

Cotgrove, S. F., *Technical Education and Social Change* (London: Allen and Unwin, 1958).

Cox, C. B., and Dyson, A. E. (eds.), *Black Papers on Education* (London: Critical Quarterly Society, 1969).

Crowder, M., *West Africa Under Colonial Rule* (London: Hutchinson, 1968).

Curle, A., Education, Politics and Development, *Comparative Education Review*, vol. 17 (1964).

Dahrendorf, R., *Society and Democracy in Germany* (London: Weidenfeld and Nicolson, 1965).

Dahrendorf, R., 'The Crisis in German Education', *Journal of Contemporary History*, vol. 2, no. 3 (1967).

Dahrendorf, R., *Class and Class Conflict in Industrial Society* (London: Routledge and Kegan Paul, 1959).

Dale, R., *et al.*, *Schooling and Capitalism: a Sociological Reader* (Milton Keynes: The Open University Press, 1976).

Dalton, G., *Economic Systems and Society* (London: Penguin, 1974).

Davies, I., 'The Management of Knowledge: A Critique of the Use of Typologies in the Sociology of Education', in M. Young (ed.), *Knowledge and Control: New Directions for the Sociology of Education* (London: Collier-Macmillan, 1971).

DDR (Deutsche Democratische Republic), 'Polytechnical Training and Education in the German Democratic Republic', (Berlin: Ministry of Education of the GDR, 1967).

DDR (Deutsche Democratische Republic), *Statistiches Jahrbuch Der DDR* (1973).

Denison, F., 'Measuring the Contribution of Education (and the Residual) to Economic Growth', in OECD *Study Group in the Economics of Education: The Residual Factor in Economic Growth* (Paris, 1964).

(DES Department of Education and Science), *A New Partnership for Our Schools* (London: HMSO, 1977).

Donaldson, P., *Worlds Apart* (London: Penguin, 1971).

Dore, R., *The Diploma Disease* (London: Allen and Unwin, 1976).

Dos Santos, T., 'The Crisis of Development Theory and the Problem of Dependence in Latin America', in H. Bernstein (ed.), *Underdevelopment and Development: The Third World Today* (London: Penguin, 1973).

Douglas, J. W. B., *The Home and the School* (London: MacGibbon and Kee, 1964).

Douglas, J. W. B., *All Our Future* (London: Peter Davies, 1968).

Dowse, R., 'Industrialism and Ideology: The Ghanaian Experience', in R. Benewick, R. N. Berki and B. Parekh (eds.), *Knowledge and Belief in Politics: The Problem of Ideology* (London: Allen and Unwin, 1973).

Dubbeldam, L. F. B., *The Primary School and the Community in Mwanza District in Tanzania* (Groningen: Walters Noordhoof, 1970).

Dumont, R., *Is Cuba Socialist?* (London: Andre Deutsch, 1974).

Dumont, R., and Mazoyer, M., *Socialisms and Development* (London: Andre Deutsch, 1973).

Durkheim, E., *Education and Sociology*, in A. Giddens, *Emile Durkheim: Selected Works* (London: Cambridge University Press, 1972).

Edwards, R. C., Reich, M., and Weisskopf, T. (eds.), *The Capitalist System: A Radical Analysis of American Society* (Cambridge, Mass.: Harvard University Press, 1972).

Eggleston, J. (ed.), *Contemporary Research in the Sociology of Education* (London: Methuen, 1974).

Expenditure Committee (House of Commons), *The Attainments of the School Leaver* (London: HMSO, 1977).

Fanon, F., *The Wretched of the Earth* (London: Penguin, 1967).

Fanon, F., *Black Skins White Masks* (London: Paladin, 1973).

Federal Republic of Germany, *Bildungsbericht* (Bonn, 1970).

Fernach, D. (ed.), *Surveys from Exile* (London: Penguin, 1973).

First, R., *The Barrel of a Gun: Political Power in Africa and the Coup d' État* (London: Penguin, 1970).

Fitch, B. and Oppenheimer, M., *Ghana: End of an Illusion* (London: Monthly Review Press, 1966).

Fitzherbert, K., 'Authoritarianism in German Schools', *New Society* (9 May 1974).

Fitzpatrick, S., *The Commissariat of Enlightenment: Soviet Organisation of Education and the Arts Under Lunacharsky—October 1917–1921* (London: Cambridge University Press, 1970).

Flynn, M. W., 'Social Theory and the Industrial Revolution', in T. Burns and S. B. Saul (eds.), *Social Theory and Economic Change* (London: Tavistock, 1967).

Flude, M., and Ahier, J. (eds.), *Educability, Schools and Ideology* (London: Croom Helm Ltd., 1974).

Ford, J., *Social Class and the Comprehensive School* (London: Routledge and Kegan Paul, 1969).

Foster, P., 'Secondary Schooling and Social Mobility in a West African Nation', *Sociology of Education*, vol. 37, no. 2 (1963).

Foster, P., *Education and Social Change in Ghana* (London: Routledge and Kegan Paul, 1965).

Foster, P., 'Education for Self-Reliance: A Critical Evaluation', in R. Jolly (ed.), *Education in Africa: Research and Action* (Nairobi: East African Publishing House, 1969).

Franco, Z., 'Women in the Transformation of Cuban Education', *Prospects*, vol. 5 (Unesco, 1975).

Frank, A. G., *Capitalism and Underdevelopment in Latin America* (New York: Monthly Review Press, 1967).

Friere, P., *The Pedagogy of the Oppressed* (London: Penguin, 1972).

Galbraith, J. K., *The New Industrial State* (London: Andre Deutsch, 1971).

Gardner, J., Chinese Education: A Turbulent Decade. *New Society*, vol. 41 (28 July 1977).

Geipel, H., *Bildung und Wissenschaft Inter-Nationes*, 9 (1965).

Gerschenkron, A., *Economic Backwardness in Historical Perspective: A Book of Essays* (Cambridge, Mass.: The Belknap Press, 1962).

Gerschenkron, A., *Bread and Democracy in Germany* (New York: Howard Fertig, 1966).

Gerth, H., and Wright Mills, C., *From Max Weber: Essays in Sociology* (London: Routledge and Kegan Paul, 1948).

Giddens, A., *Emile Durkheim: Selected Works* (London: Cambridge University Press, 1972).

Gillette, A., *Cuba's Educational Revolution* (London: Fabian Society, 1971).

Glass, D. V., Education and Social Change, in E. Butterworth and D. Weir (eds.), *The Sociology of Modern Britain* (London: Fontana, 1975).

Glassman, J., 'Educational Reform and Manpower Policy in China 1955–1958', *Modern China*, vol. 3, no. 3 (1977).

Goldstrom, J. M., *The Social Content of Education 1808–1870 A Study of the Working Class School Reader in England and Ireland* (Shannon: Irish University Press, 1972).

Gonzalez, E., 'Crosscurrents in Cuba', *Problems of Communism* (January–February 1976).

Goodfellow, D. M., *Tyneside: The Social Facts* (Newcastle Upon Tyne: Co-operative Printing Society, 1941).

Goody, J. (ed.), *Changing Social Structure in Ghana: Essays in the Comparative Sociology of a New State and an Old Tradition* (London: International African Institute, 1975).

Goulet, D., and Hudson, M., *The Myth of Aid: The Agenda of the Development Reports* (New York: Idoc, 1971).

Graham, C. K., *The History of Education in Ghana from the Earliest of Times to the Declaration of Independence* (London: Frank Cass and Co. Ltd., 1971).

Grant, N., *Soviet Education* (London: University of London Press, 1964).

Gray, J., 'The Economics of Maoism', in H. Bernstein (ed.), *Underdevelopment and Development: The Third World Today* (London: Penguin, 1973a).

Gray, J., *Mao Tse-Tung* (London: Butterworth Press, 1973b).

Gray, J., 'What is the Crime of China's "Gang of Four"?', *New Society* (4 November 1976a).

Gray, J., 'Stalin, Mao and the Future of China', *New Society* (1 April 1976b).

Griffith, W., (ed.), 'Adult Basic Education II' *Literary Discussion*, vol. IV, no. 3 (September 1973).

Grosser, A., *Germany in Our Time: A Political History of the Post War Years* (London: Penguin, 1974).

Grunberger, R., *A Social History of the Third Reich* (London: Penguin, 1974).

Guttsman, W. L., *The British Political Elite* (London: MacGibbon and Kee, 1963).

Habermas, J., *The Legitimation Crisis* (London: Heinemann, 1976).

Hahn, W., 'Education in East and West Germany—A Study of Similarities and Contrasts', *Studies in Comparative Communism*, vol. 5 (1972).

Halsey, A. H., 'Empirical Advance and Theoretical Challenge', in E. Hopper (ed.), *Readings in the Theory of Educational Systems* (London: Hutchinson, 1971).

Halsey, A. H., *Educational Priority E. P. A Problems and Policies*, vol. 1 (London: HMSO, 1972).

Ham-Brucher, H., quoted in *Bildung un Wissenchaft* Inter-Nationes, 2–74 (1974).

Harcourt-Munning, F., 'Teatime Talk of how Mr Nkrumah Signed away his Gold', letter to *The Guardian* (28 June 1976).

Hardach, K., 'Germany 1914–1970', in C. M. Cipolla (ed.), *Contemporary Economics-1* (London: Fontana, 1976).

Hawkins, J. N., *Mao Tse-Tung and Education: His Thoughts and Teachings* (Hamden: Connecticut Linnet Books, 1974).

Hayter, T., *Aid as Imperialism* (London: Penguin, 1971).

Henderson, P., 'Class Structure and the Concept of Intelligence', in R. Dale *et al.* (eds.), *Schooling and Capitalism: A Sociological Reader* (Milton Keynes: The Open University Press, 1976).

Hennig, G., 'Mass Cultural Activity in the G.D.R.: on Cultural Politics in Bureaucratically Deformed Transitional Societies', *New German Critique*, no. 2 (Spring 1974).

Higgins, J. M., 'Problems of the Selection and Professional Orientation of Soviet Pedagogical Students', *Comparative Education*, vol. 12, no. 2 (1976).

Hilliard, F. H., *A Short History of Education in British West Africa* (London: Thomas Nelson and Sons Ltd., 1956).

Hinton, W., *Fanshen: A Documentary of Revolution in a Chinese Village* (London: Penguin, 1972).

Hirji, K. F., 'School Education and Underdevelopment in Tanzania', Mimeo, Education Dept. University of Dar es Salaam Tanzania (1974).

HMSO, *Committee on Higher Education* (Robbins Report) (London 1963).

HMSO, *Education in Schools: A Consultative Document*, Cmnd 6869 (London 1977).

Hiscocks, R., *Democracy in West Germany* (London: Oxford University Press, 1963).

Hobsbawn, E., *Industry and Empire* (London: Penguin, 1969).

Hodgkin, T., African Universities and the State: Another View *Comparative Education* (March 1967).

Holly, D., *Society, Schools and Humanity* (London: Paladin, 1972).

Holly, D., *Beyond Curriculum* (London: Paladin, 1973).

Holt, J., *How Children Fail* (London: Pitman, 1975).

Hopkins, E., 'Literature in the Schools of the Soviet Union', *Comparative Education*, vol. 10 (1974).

Hopper, E., 'A Typology for the Classification of Educational Systems', in E. Hopper (ed.), *Readings in the Theory of Educational Systems* (London: Hutchinson, 1971).

Hopper, E. (ed.), *Readings in the Theory of Educational Systems* (London: Hutchinson, 1971).

Hoselitz, B. F., *Sociological Aspects of Economic Growth* (Glencoe, IU.: The Free Press, 1960).

Hoyle, E., Social Theories of Education in Contemporary Britain *Social Science Information*, vol. 9, no. 4 (1969).

Hsi-en Chen, T., *The Maoist Educational Revolution* (New York: Praeger, 1974).

Huberman, L. and Sweezy, P. M., *Socialism in Cuba* (New York: Monthly Review Press, 1969).

Hurd, G., 'Education', in W. Birmingham, I. Neustadt and E. N. Omaboe (eds.), *A Study of Contemporary Ghana*, vol II (London: Allen and Unwin, 1967).

Hurd, G. and Johnson, T. J., 'Education and Mobility in Ghana', *Sociology of Education*, vol. 40 (1967).

Husen, T., *Social Background and Educational Career Research Perspectives on Equality of Opportunity* (Paris: OECD, 1972).

Illich, I., *Deschooling Society* (London: Calder and Boyars, 1971).

Illich, I., 'Outwitting the "Developed" Countries', in H. Bernstein (ed.), *Underdevelopment and Development: The Third World Today* (London: Penguin, 1973).

Ishumi, A., 'The Educated Elite: A Survey of East African Students at a Higher Institution of Learning', *Rural Africana*, no. 5 (1974).

Jencks, C., *et al.*, *Inequality: A Re-assessment of the Effect of Family and Schooling in America* (New York: Basic Books, 1972).

Johnson, R., 'Educational Policy and Social Control in Early Victorian England', *Past and Present*, no. 49 (November 1970).

Johnson, R., 'Notes on the Schooling of the English Working Class 1780–1850', in R. Dale *et al.*, *Schooling and Capitalism: A Sociological Reader* (Milton Keynes: The Open University Press, 1976a).

Johnson, R., 'Early Worker Education Movements', *Radical Education* (Winter 1976b).

Jolly, R. (ed.), *Education in Africa: Research and Action* (Nairobi: East African Publishing House, 1969).

Jolly, R., de Kadt, E., Singer, H. and Wilson, F., *Third World Employment Problems and Strategy* (London: Penguin, 1973).

Kaestle, C. F., 'Between the Scylla of Brutal Ignorance and the Charybdis of a Literary Education: Elite Attitudes Towards Mass Schooling in Early Industrial England and America', in L. Stone (ed.), *Schooling and Society: Studies in the History of Education* (Baltimore: Johns Hopkins University Press, 1977).

Karabel, J. and Halsey, A. H. (eds.), *Power and Ideology in Education* (New York: Oxford University Press, 1977).

Keesings Contemporary Archives, 'Ghana', (May–June 1977).

Kimambo, I. N. and Temu, A. J., *A History of Tanzania* (Dar es Salaam: East Africa Publishing House, 1969).

King Whyte, M., Inequality and Stratification in China *The China Quarterly*, 64 (December 1975).

Klein, H., *Bildung in der DDR: Grundlagen, Entwicklungen, Probleme* (Hamburg: Rowohlt Taschenbuch Verlag, 1974).

Kofi, T. A., The Elites and Underdevelopment in Africa: The Case of Ghana, *Berkeley Journal of Sociology*, vol XVII (1972–3).

Lane, D., *Politics and Society in the USSR* (London: Weidenfeld and Nicolson, 1970).

Lane, D., 'The Impact of Revolution: the Case of Selection of Students for Higher Education in Soviet Russia, 1917–1928', *Sociology*, vol. 7, no. 2 (May 1973).

Lane, D., *The Socialist Industrial State* (London: Allen and Unwin Ltd., 1976).

Laqueur, T. W., 'Working-Class Demand and the Growth of English Elementary Education 1750–1850', in L. Stone (ed.), *Schooling and*

Society: Studies in the History of Education (Baltimore: The Johns Hopkins University Press, 1977).

Lee, H. P., 'Education and Rural Development in China Today', in *The World Yearbook of Education* (1974).

Lehmann, D., 'The Trajectory of the Cuban Revolution', *Occasional Papers Sussex University: Institute of Development Studies* (1971).

Lenin, V. I., *Collected Works vol 31* (Moscow: Publishing House Moscow, 1920).

Lenin, V. I., *Imperialism the Highest Stage of Capitalism* (Moscow: Progress Publishers, 1975).

Levin, H., 'Educational Opportunity and Social Inequality in Western Europe', *Social Problems*, vol. 24, no. 2 (December 1976).

Lewin, M., *Russian Peasants and Soviet Power: A Study of Collectivisation* (London: Allen and Unwin Ltd., 1968).

Lister, I. (ed.), *Deschooling* (London: Cambridge University Press, 1974).

Lloyd, P. C., *Classes, Crisis and Coups* (London: Paladin, 1973).

London, J., 'A Model of a Comprehensive Programme of Adult Education in the Third World', in W. Griffith (ed.), Adult Basic Education II, *Literary Discussion*, vol IV, no. 3 (September 1973).

Lowenthal, R., 'Development versus Utopia in Communist Policy', *Survey*, no. 74/75 (1970).

Ludz, P. C., *The German Democratic Republic From the Sixties to the Seventies: A Socio-Political Analysis. Occasional Papers in International Affairs*, no. 26 (Cambridge, Mass.: Harvard University Press, 1970).

Macciocchi, M. A., *Daily Life in Revolutionary China* (New York: Monthly Review Press, 1972).

Mangan, J. A., 'Athleticism: A Case Study of the Evolution of an Educational Ideology', in B. Simon and I. Bradley (eds.), *The Victorian Public School: Studies in the Development of an Educational Institution* (London: Gill and Macmillan, 1975).

Mannheim, K., *Diagnosis of Our Time* (London: Routledge and Kegan Paul, 1963).

Mann, G., *The History of Germany Since 1789* (London: Penguin, 1974).

Manpower Services Commission, *Young People and Work* (Holland Report) (London: HMSO, 1977).

Mao Tse-Tung, *Four Essays on Philosophy* (Peking: Foreign Languages Press, 1966).

Martin, R., 'The Socialisation of Children in China and on Taiwan: An

224   *Education, Social Structure and Development*

Analysis of Elementary School Textbooks', *The China Quarterly*, 62 (June 1975).

Marx, K. and Engels, F., *The German Ideology* (1846).

Marx, K., *Das Kapital*, in T. Bottomore and M. Rubel (eds.), *Karl Marx: Selected Writings* (London: Penguin, 1963).

Marx, K., *Critique of the Gotha Programme* (Peking: Foreign Languages Press, 1972).

Matthews, M., *Class and Society in Soviet Russia* (London: Allen Lane The Penguin Press, 1972).

Mauger, P., *et al., Education in China* (London: Anglo-Chinese Educational Institute, 1974).

Mazrui, A., 'The African University as a Multi-National Corporation: Problems of Penetration and Dependency', *Harvard Education Review*, vol. 42 (2 May 1975).

McCleland, D., *The Achieving Society* (New York: van Nostrand, 1961).

McWilliam, H. O. A. and Kwamena, M. A., *The Development of Education in Ghana* (London: Longman, 1975).

Mbilinyi, M., (1974a), 'The Problems of Unequal Access to Primary Education in Tanzania', Mimeo (Tanzania: Education Department University of Dar es Salaam, 1974).

Mbilinyi, M. (1974b), 'The Decision to Educate in Rural Tanzania', Mimeo (Tanzania: Education Department University of Dar es Salaam, 1974).

Mbilinyi, M. (1975a), 'African Education in the British Colonial Period (1919–1961)', Mimeo (Tanzania: Education Department University of Dar es Salaam, 1975).

Mbilinyi, M. (1975b), 'The Colonisation Process on Our Schools', Mimeo (Tanzania: Education Department University of Dar es Salaam, 1975).

Meissner, B. and Kommers, D. P. (eds.), *Social Change in the Soviet Union* (Indiana: Notre Dame Press, 1972).

Mende, T., *From Aid to Recolonisation* (London: Harrap, 1973).

Metcalfe, G. E., *Great Britain and Ghana: Documents of Ghana History 1807–1957* (London: Thomas Nelson and Sons, 1964).

Meyer, A., 'Communist Revolution and Cultural Change', *Studies in Comparative Communism*, vol. 5 (1972).

Middleton, N. and Weitzman, S., *A Place for Everyone: A History of State Education from the Eighteenth Century to the 1970s* (London: Victor Gollanz Ltd., 1976).

Miliband, R., *The State in Capitalist Society: An Analysis of the Western System of Power* (London: Quartet Books, 1973).

Milton, D., Milton, N. and Schurmann, F. (eds.), *People's China* (London: Penguin, 1977).

Ministry of Information, Accra 'Ghana, Twenty Years of Independence', *The Times* (11 March 1977).

Moorman, P. (1976a), 'School for Life is Cornerstone of the Permanent Revolution', *Times Educational Supplement* (5 March 1976).

Moorman, P. (1976b), 'In Search of the New Man: from Ivory Tower to Factory Floor', *Times Higher Education Supplement* (5 March 1976).

Morrison, D., *Education and Politics in Africa: The Tanzanian Case* (London: C. Hurst and Company, 1976).

Mueller, C., *The Politics of Communication A Study in the Political Sociology of Language, Socialisation and Legitimation* (London: Oxford University Press, 1973).

Musgrave, P. W., *Technical Change, the Labour Force and Education: A Study of the British and German Iron and Steel Industries 1860–1964* (London: Pergamon Press, 1967).

Musgrave, P. W., 'Constant Facotrs in the Demand for Technical Education 1860–1960', in P. W. Musgrave (ed.), *Sociology, History and Education* (London: Methuen, 1970).

Musgrave, P. W. (ed.), *Sociology, History and Education* (London: Methuen, 1970).

Musgrove, F., *Patterns of Power and Authority in English Education* (London: Methuen and Co. Ltd., 1971).

Mwingira, A. C., 'Education for Self-Reliance: The Problems of Implementation', in R. Jolly (ed.), *Education in Africa: Research and Action* (Nairobi: East African Publishing House, 1969).

Myrdal, G., *The Asian Drama: An Inquiry into the Poverty of Nations* (London: Harmondsworth, 1968).

Myrdal, J. and Kessle, G., *China: The Revolution Continued* (London: Penguin, 1970).

Myrdal, G., 'The Effect of Education on Attitudes to Work', in R. Jolly, E. de Kadt, H. Singer and F. Wilson (eds.), *Third World Employment Problems and Strategy* (London: Penguin, 1973).

Nkrumah, K., *The Autobiography of Kwame Nkrumah* (London: Thomas Nelson, 1957).

Nove, A., *An Economic History of the U.S.S.R.* (London: Pelican, 1972).

Nyerere, J., *Socialism and Rural Development* (Dar es Salaam: Government Printing Office, 1967).

Nyerere, J., 'The Arusha Declaration', in J. Nyerere, *Freedom and Socialism: Uhuru Na Ujamaa* (London: Oxford University Press, 1968).

Nyerere, J., *Freedom and Socialism: Uhuru Na Ujamaa* (London: Oxford University Press, 1968).

Nyerere, J., 'Education for Self-Reliance' in I. Lister (ed.), *Deschooling* (London: Cambridge University Press, 1974).

Nyerere, J., *The Arusha Declaration Ten Years After* (Dar es Salaam: Government Printing Office, 1977).

O'Connor, J., 'On Cuban Political Economy', in H. Bernstein (ed.), *Underdevelopment and Development: The Third World Today* (London: Penguin, 1973).

Odia, S., 'Rural Education and Training in Tanzania', in *World Yearbook of Education* (1974).

OECD, (Organisation for Economic Co-operation and Development), *Study Group in the Economics of Education: The Residual Factor in Economic Growth* (Paris, 1964).

OECD, *Educational Policies for the Seventies* (Paris, 1970).

OECD, *Germany* (Paris, 1972).

OECD *Selection and Certification in Education and Employment* (Paris, 1977).

Palmer, M., Africa's Debt Problems, *New Society* (9 January 1975).

Parkin, F., *Class Inequality and Political Order: Social Stratification in Capitalist and Communist Societies* (London: MacGibbon and Kee Ltd., 1971).

Parkin, F. (ed.), *The Social Analysis of Class Structure.* (London: Tavistock Publications, 1974).

Parsons, T., *The System of Modern Societies* (Englewood Cliffs, NJ: Prentice Hall, 1971).

Paulston, R., 'Cultural Revitalization and Educational Change in Cuba', *Comparative Education Review*, 16 (1972).

Paulston, R., 'Cuban Rural Education: A Strategy for Revolutionary Development', in *World Yearbook of Education* (1974).

Payer, C., *The Debt Trap: The IMF and the Third World* (London: Penguin, 1974).

Pearse, A., 'Structural Problems of Education Systems in Latin America', in R. K. Brown (ed.), *Knowledge, Education and Cultural Change* (London: Tavistock, 1973).

Peisert, H., *Regionalanalyse Als Methode Für Der Bildungsforschung.* (Tubingen: Mimeo, 1965).

Pennar, J., Bakalo, I. I. and Bereday, G. Z. F., *Modernization and Diversity in Soviet Education: With Special Reference to Nationality Groups* (New York: Praeger, 1971).

Pick, G., *Die Deutsche Bildungskatastrophe: Analyse und Dokumentation* (Freiburg: Walter Verlag, 1964).

Porter, B., *The Lion's Share: A Short History of British Imperialism* (London: Longman, 1975).

Pollitt, B. H., 'Employment Plans, Performance and Future Prospects in Cuba', in R. Jolly, E. de Kadt, H. Singer and F. Wilson (eds.), *Third World Employment Problems and Strategy* (London: Penguin, 1973).

Pospielovsky, D., Education and Ideology in the USSR *Survey*, vol. 21, no. 1/2 (1976).

Prewitt, K. (ed.), *Education and Political Values: An East African Case Study* (Nairobi: East Africa Publishing House, 1971).

Price, R. F., *Education in Communist China* (London: Routledge and Kegan Paul, 1970).

Price, R., 'Politics and Culture in Contemporary Ghana: The Big-Man Small-Boy Syndrome', *Journal of African Studies*, vol I, no. 2 (1974).

Prybla, J. S., 'Notes on Chinese Higher Education', *The China Quarterly*, 62 (June 1975).

Rake, A., 'Country Weakened by Ambition', *The Times* (11 March 1977).

Rakowska-Harmstone, T. (ed.), *The Communist States in Disarray 1965–1971* (Minneapolis: University of Minnesota Press, 1972).

Ray, D., 'Mao and the Classless Society', *Survey*, vol. 74 (1970).

Reimer, E., *School is Dead: An Essay on Alternatives in Education* (London: Penguin, 1971).

Ringer, F., *The Decline of the German Mandarins: The Academic Community 1890–1933* (Cambridge Mass.: Harvard University Press, 1969).

Rinvolucri-Moore, M. J., *Education in East Germany* (London: David and Charles, 1973).

Roberts, P., 'The Village School Teacher in Ghana', in J. Goody (ed.), *Changing Social Structure in Ghana: Essays in the Comparative Sociology of a New State and an Old Tradition* (London: International African Institute, 1975).

Robertson, J., 'For Use Not For Profit', in D. Milton, N. Milton and F. Schurmann (eds.), *People's China* (London: Penguin, 1977).

Robinsohn, S. B., and Kuhlmann, J. C., 'Two Decades of Non-Reform in West German Education', *Comparative Education Review*, vol XI, no. 3 (1967).

Roca, S., 'Cuban Economic Policy in the 1970s: The Trodden Paths', *Studies in Comparative International Development*, vol XII (1977).

Rodney, W., *How Europe Underdeveloped Africa* (Dar es Salaam: Tanzania Publishing House, 1972).

Rostow, W. W., *The Stages of Economic Growth* (London: Cambridge University Press, 1960).

Rowlinson, W., 'German Education in a European Context', in T. G. Cook (ed.), *History of Education in Europe* (London: Methuen and Co. Ltd., 1974).

Sachse, E., 'Manpower Planning and Higher Education in the German Democratic Republic', *International Labour Review*, vol. 113, no. 3 (May–June 1976).

Samuel, R. H. and Thomas, R. H., *Education and Society in Modern Germany* (London: Routledge and Kegan Paul, 1948).

Scanlon, D. G., *Traditions of African Education* (New York: Columbia University Press, 1964).

Schaffer, H. G., 'A Critique of the Concept of Human Capital', in M. Blaug (ed.), *Economics of Education, I* (London: Penguin, 1968).

Schaffer, S. M., 'The Socialisation of Girls in the Secondary Schools of England and the Two Germanies', *International Review of Education*, XXII (1976).

Schmitt, K., 'Education and Politics in the German Democratic Republic', *Comparative Education Review*, vol. 19 (February 1975).

Schultz, T. W., 'Investment in Human Capital', in *American Economic Review* (March 1961).

Schurmann, F. and Schell, O. (eds.), *Republican China* (London: Penguin, 1968).

Schurmann, F., and Schell, O. (eds.), *Communist China* (London: Penguin, 1977).

Schurmann, F., Party and Government, in F. Schurmann and O. Schell (eds.), *Communist China* (London: Penguin, 1977).

Selden, M., *The Yenan Way in Revolutionary China* (Cambridge: Harvard University Press, 1971).

Shanin, T., *Peasants and Peasant Societies* (London: Penguin, 1971).

Shivji, J., *Class Struggles in Tanzania* (Dar es Salaam: Tanzania Publishing House, 1975).

Simon, B. and Bradley, I. (eds.), *The Victorian Public School: Studies in the Development of an Educational Institution* (London: Gill and MacMillan, 1975).

Slade Tien, J., 'A Lesson from China', *Harvard Education Review* (May 1975).

Smith, J. E., *Germany Beyond the Wall* (Boston: Little Brown and Co. Ltd., 1967).

Snow, E., 'Soviet Society', in F. Schurmann and O. Schell (eds.), *Republican China* (London: Penguin, 1968).

Snow, E., *China's Long Revolution* (London: Penguin, 1971).

Stavenhagen, R., 'Changing Functions of the Community in Underdeveloped Countries', in H. Bernstein (ed.), *Underdevelopment and Development: The Third World Today* (London: Penguin, 1973).

Stone, L., *Schooling and Society: Studies in the History of Education* (Baltimore: The Johns Hopkins University Press, 1977).

Taylor, W., *The Secondary Modern School* (London: Faber and Faber, 1963).

Tawney, R. H., *Equality* (London: Allen and Unwin, 1964).

Tomiak, J. J., 'Fifty-five Years of Soviet Education: The Grandeur of the Vision and the Might of Reality—United, Separated or Forever Divorced?', in T. G. Cook (ed.), *History of Education in Europe* (London: Methuen and Co. Ltd., 1974).

Toroka, S., 'Education for Self-Reliance: The Litowa Experiment', in L. Cliffe and J. Saul (eds.), *Socialism in Tanzania*, vols I and II (Nairobi: East Africa Publishing House, 1973).

Trevelyan, G. M., *English Social History* (London: The Reprint Society, 1944).

Trotsky, L., *The Revolution Betrayed* (New York: Pioneer Publishers, 1945).

Tudge, J., 'Education in the U.S.S.R. Russian or Soviet?', *Comparative Education*, vol II, no. 2 (1975).

Van De Laar, A. J. M., 'Toward a Manpower Development Strategy in Tanzania', in L. Cliffe and J. Saul (eds.), *Socialism in Tanzania*, vols I and II (Nairobi: East Africa Publishing House, 1973).

Van der Eyken, W., (ed.), *Education, the Child and Society A Documentary History 1900–1973* (London: Penguin, 1973).

Von der Muhll, G., 'Education, Citizenship and Social Revolution in Tanzania', in K. Prewitt (ed.), *Education and Political Values: An East African Case Study* (Nairobi: East Africa Publishing House, 1971).

Von Freyhold, M., 'Rural Development Through *Ujamaa Vijijini*: Questions of Economic and Technical Strategies', referred to in J. Shivji, *Class struggles in Tanzania* (Dar es Salaam: Tanzania Publishing House, 1975).

Von Freyhold, M., 'The Workers, the Nizers and the Peasants', quoted I. Shivji 1975.

Wallerstein, J., *Social Change, the Colonial Situation* (London: Wiley, 1966).

Ward, W. E. F., *A History of the Gold Coast* (London: Allen and Unwin, 1948).

Wardle, D., *English Popular Education 1780–1975* (London: Cambridge University Press, 1976).

Watson, A., *Living in China* (London: Batsford, 1975).

Weber, M., 'Class, Status and Party', in H. Gerth and C. Wright Mills (eds.), *From Max Weber: Essays in Sociology* (London: Routledge and Kegan Paul, 1948).

Weber, M., 'Bureaucracy', in H. Gerth and C. Wright Mills (eds.), *From Max Weber: Essays in Sociology* (London: Routledge and Kegan Paul, 1948).

Weber, M., 'Politics as a Vocation', in H. Gerth and C. Wright Mills (eds.), *From Max Weber: Essays in Sociology* (London: Routledge and Kegan Paul, 1948).

Weber, M., 'Capitalism and Rural Society in Germany', in H. Gerth and C. Wright Mills (eds.), *From Max Weber: Essays in Sociology* (London: Routledge and Kegan Paul, 1948).

Weber, M., *The Protestant Ethic and the Spirit of Capitalism* (London: Unwin University Books, 1970).

Weinstein, W. (ed.), *Chinese and Soviet Aid to Africa* (New York: Praeger, 1975).

Weisskopf, T., 'Capitalism and Underdevelopment in the Modern World', in R. C. Edwards, M. Reich and T. Weisskopf (eds.), *The Capitalist System: A Radical Analysis of American Society* (Cambridge, Mass.: Harvard University Press, 1972).

Westergaard, J. and Resler, H., *Class in a Capitalist Society* (London: Heinemann, 1975).

Whiteley, W. H. (ed.), *Language Use and Social Change* (London: Oxford University Press, 1971).

Williams, G., 'The Social Structure of a Neo-Colonial Economy', in C. Allen and R. W. Johnson (eds.), *African Perspectives* (London: Cambridge University press, 1970).

Williams, P., 'Lending for Learning? An Experiment in Ghana', *Minerva*, vol XII, no. 3 (1974).

Williams, R., *The Long Revolution* (London: Penguin, 1961).

Williamson, W., 'Continuities and Discontinuities in the Sociology of Education', in M. Flude and J. Ahier (eds.), *Educability, Schools and Ideology* (London: Croom Helm Ltd., 1974).

Williamson, W., 'Patterns of Education Inequality in West Germany', *Comparative Education*, vol. 13, no. 1 (March 1977).

World Bank Education Sector, *Education* (New York, 1974).

The World Year Book of Education (1974), *Education and Rural Development* (London: Evans Brothers Ltd., 1974).

Worsley, P., *Inside China* (London: Allen Lane, 1974).

Wraith, R. E., *Guggisberg* (London: Oxford University Press, 1967).

Yanowitch, M. and Dodge, N., 'Social Class and Education: Soviet Findings and Reactions', *Comparative Education Review*, vol. 12 (1968).

Young, M., *Knowledge and Control: New Directions for the Sociology of Education* (London: Collier Macmillan, 1971).

Young, M. and Whitty, G. (eds.), *Society, State and Schooling* (London: The Farmer Press, 1977).

Index

233